# Issues in Economic Development and Globalization

This is the second of two volumes in honour of Ajit Singh, the other one being *Issues in Finance and Industry*

*Also by Philip Arestis*

THE POLITICAL ECONOMY OF ECONOMIC POLICIES (*co-editor with Malcolm Sawyer*)

MONEY AND BANKING: Issues for the Twenty-First Century (*editor*)

MONEY, PRICING, DISTRIBUTION AND ECONOMIC INTEGRATION

RELEVANCE OF KEYNESIAN ECONOMIC POLICIES TODAY (*co-editor with Malcolm Sawyer*)

WHAT GLOBAL ECONOMIC CRISIS? (*co-editor with Michelle Baddeley and John McCombie*)

POST-BUBBLE US ECONOMY: Implications for Financial Markets and the Economy (*with Elias Karakitsos*)

FINANCIAL DEVELOPMENTS IN NATIONAL AND INTERNATIONAL MARKETS (*co-editor with Jesús Ferreiro and Felipe Serrano*)

ADVANCES IN MONETARY POLICY AND MACROECONOMICS (*co-editor with Gennaro Zezza*)

ASPECTS OF MODERN MONETARY AND MACROECONOMIC POLICIES (*co-editor with Eckhard Hein and Edwin Le Heron*)

ON MONEY, METHOD AND KEYNES: Selected Essays by Victoria Chick (co-editor with Sheila Dow)

IS THERE A NEW CONSENSUS IN MACROECONOMICS? (*editor*)

POLITICAL ECONOMY OF BRAZIL (*co-editor with Alfredo Saad-Filho*)

FINANCIAL LIBERALIZATION AND ECONOMIC PERFORMANCE IN EMERGING COUNTRIES (*co-editor with Luiz Fernando de Paula*)

*Also by John Eatwell*

AN INTRODUCTION TO MODERN ECONOMICS (*with Joan Robinson*)

WHATEVER HAPPENED TO BRITAIN?

KEYNES'S ECONOMICS AND THE THEORY OF VALUE AND DISTRIBUTION (*editor with Murray Milgate*)

THE NEW PALGRAVE: A Dictionary of Economics (*edited with Murray Milgate and Peter Newman*)

THE WORLD OF ECONOMICS (*edited with Murray Milgate and Peter Newman*)

THE NEW PALGRAVE DICTIONARY OF MONEY AND FINANCE (*edited with Murray Milgate and Peter Newman*)

GLOBAL UNEMPLOYMENT (*editor*)

UNDERSTANDING GLOBALISATION: The Nation-State, Democracy and Economic Policies in the New Epoch (*with Elizabeth Jelin, Anthony McGrew and James Rosenau*)

GLOBAL FINANCE AT RISK: The Case for International Regulation
(*with Lance Taylor*)

INTERNATIONAL CAPITAL MARKET: Systems in Transition (*edited with Lance Taylor*)

GLOBAL GOVERNANCE OF FINANCIAL SYSTEMS: The Legal and Economic Regulation of Systemic Risk (*with Kern Alexander and Rahul Dhumale*)

# Issues in Economic Development and Globalization

## Essays in Honour of Ajit Singh

Edited by

Philip Arestis

and

John Eatwell

First published 2008 by
PALGRAVE MACMILLAN

Palgrave Macmillan in the UK is an imprint of Macmillan Publishers Limited,
registered in England, company number 785998, of Houndmills, Basingstoke,
Hampshire RG21 6XS.

Palgrave Macmillan in the US is a division of St Martin's Press LLC,
175 Fifth Avenue, New York, NY 10010.

Palgrave Macmillan is the global academic imprint of the above companies
and has companies and representatives throughout the world.

Palgrave® and Macmillan® are registered trademarks in the United States,
the United Kingdom, Europe and other countries.

ISBN-13: 978–0–230–20358–7
ISBN-10: 0–230–20358–2

This book is printed on paper suitable for recycling and made from fully
managed and sustained forest sources. Logging, pulping and manufacturing
processes are expected to conform to the environmental regulations of the
country of origin.

A catalogue record for this book is available from the British Library.

Library of Congress Cataloging-in-Publication Data
Issues in economic development and globalization: essays in honour of
  Ajit Singh/edited by Philip Arestis and John Eatwell.
      p. cm.
  Includes bibliographical references and index.
  ISBN 978–0–230–20358–7 (alk. paper)
  1. Economic development.  2. Globalization—Economic aspects.
  I. Singh, Ajit, 1940–  II. Arestis, Philip, 1941–  III. Eatwell, John.
  HD82.187  2008
  338.9—dc22                                          2008022181

10  9  8  7  6  5  4  3  2  1
17  16  15  14  13  12  11  10  09  08

Printed and bound in Great Britain by
CPI Antony Rowe, Chippenham and Eastbourne

# Contents

# List of Tables

# List of Figures

# HARVARD UNIVERSITY
*Cambridge, Massachusetts 02138*

AMARTYA SEN
*Lamont University Professor and*
*Professor of Economics and Philosophy*

DEPARTMENT OF ECONOMICS
Littauer 205, North Yard
617.495.1871 (phone)
617.496.5942 (fax)

SUMMER ADDRESS
Centre for History and Economics
King's College, Cambridge, England
+ 44 1223 331197 (phone)
+ 44 1223 331198 (fax)

13 September 2007

Professor Ajit Singh
Queens' College
Cambridge CB3 9ET

Dear Ajit,

I am extremely sad to miss the meeting in your honour at the other Cambridge from where I have just returned to this Massachusetts variant of that old city of learning. The old city has not quite been the same since your arrival there in the sixties. I remember our first meeting, the excitement surrounding your research findings, your leadership role in the Faculty of Economics, your contributions to your College, and of course a hundred other things that enriched the lives and excitement around the Cam. It would have been so wonderful for me to be there and to join others in celebrating your achievements.

On a lighter note, I remember also your giving me a lift to the airport in London - this would have been in the late sixties when I had come to visit Cambridge. I remember also the animated discussion we got into during the journey. Since you were insistent that we finish the discussion and had to stop for coffee to do just that, I managed to miss the plane to Delhi. It is the only time, I think, I have missed a plane, and the cause of it was not a traffic jam, but an exciting intellectual argument about the nature of social justice!

I can't be there in person, but I hope you count me "in" when you all meet. If you can take me out of a plane to Delhi, you can certainly also put me into a meeting in Cambridge. That way we can celebrate together, again!

With my warmest regards,

Yours ever,

Amartya

*Note*: This letter from Professor Amartya Sen is reproduced with permission.

# Foreword

It is a great privilege to write the Foreword to this volume of papers presented at the retirement conference for Ajit Singh held in Queens' College, Cambridge, in 2007. I first met Ajit in 1963 when he came to Cambridge to work with Robin Marris on Robin's classic *Economic Theory of 'Managerial' Capitalism*. We quickly became friends (despite him trouncing me at table tennis) and I had a small part in Ajit's appointment to a teaching post in the faculty in 1965. I played squash every Sunday with Ken Berrill, then the chairman of the faculty board. Ken used me as the eyes and ears of the faculty. I mentioned to him that there was this very bright young Indian scholar who wished he had known, before applications had closed, about a faculty post whereby a person from the subcontinent was appointed to a teaching post for three years. Ken said, 'Tell the silly bugger to put in a late application.' Ajit did and though he was not appointed – our mutual friend Amiya Bagchi was – the appointments committee were so impressed by Ajit that he was asked to apply for the next teaching post that came up. He did so, was appointed and the rest, as they say, is history, wonderful positive history. Ajit's contributions to teaching, research and administrative reforms in the faculty over the next 40 years and more have been of immense value to Cambridge and to the profession generally.

The large range of topics and issues covered by the papers in this volume, to all of which Ajit has in his time made weighty often seminal contributions, attest to his influence in the profession. But even more than this was the atmosphere at the conference; it reflected the extraordinary affection and respect for Ajit and his work. I have never before experienced such an intense atmosphere of goodwill at a conference – and my possible numéraires include the gathering in Boston in 2005 to celebrate Paul Samuelson's 90th birthday. Partly, no doubt, it reflected the admiration for Ajit's battle with the cruel illness that has afflicted him for nearly two decades. His courage, perseverance and dogged refusal to allow it to stop him doing what he loves best – advancing knowledge by teaching and research and designing humane, practical, helpful policies – are awe-inspiring. Jo's devoted love and care are equally admired by their friends. As I said at the conference dinner, the day they celebrated their marriage was possibly the happiest day I and their other friends have had in Cambridge.

Ajit names as his mentors Dale Jorgenson, Harvey Leibenstein and Tibor Scitovsky (who were at Berkeley when he did his PhD there) and Nicky Kaldor and Brian Reddaway at Cambridge. It is true that his writings reflect their diverse influence – the later Kaldor writing on increasing returns and cumulative causation processes together with his critique of equilibrium economics, and Reddaway's down-to-earth, logical common-sense approach and criticisms, are especially evident. But Ajit is a most original and innovative political economist in his own right.

His work is characterized by incredibly detailed knowledge of the relevant facts, especially the sources and limitations of data, the application of state-of-the-art statistical methods when they are thought to be appropriate and necessary rather than just for their own sake, and well-thought-out theoretical frameworks and hypotheses. Such painstaking and careful scholarship, allied with flair and intuition and a deep seriousness of purpose arising from his political beliefs, his hatred of injustice and his warm humanity and basic kindness, have meant that he has made seminal contributions to our understanding of the growth of the firm; the role of stock markets in developing and developed economies, including revealing the fallacies associated with the conventional analysis of the nature and virtues of takeovers; the process of deindustrialization both now, taking in the rise and fall of rates of growth in post-war capitalism, and in India under British rule; and the optimal interrelated structure of institutions and policies, including tariffs, in the processes of development. Ajit is one of the outstanding and respected voices that must be heard when alternatives to the conventional wisdom on both developing and developed economics are discussed.

His output of papers, books and reports over the years is remarkable. All, read clearly, reflect the thorough research and preparation that have gone into them, and they persuade by the careful analysis of empirical evidence and logical theoretical structures. Ajit's criticisms of mainstream theory never consist of setting up strawpeople, the better to knock them down. Rather, he draws out the testable inferences of the theories and, when they are not supported by careful empirical investigation, he devises well-thought-out, logical, alternative explanations, which have inferences that are consistent with empirical findings.

Ajit has managed while doing all this to be a devoted, much loved teacher of undergraduates and supervisor of PhD students, an astute and determined faculty politician and tripos reformer, a person of principle prepared to fight fairly but hard for what he believes in, regardless of the consequences for his professional advance in the faculty. In the process he has, of course, made enemies, some of whom in retrospect have acknowledged the correctness of his views and the wrong-headedness of their own. But much more important are the myriads of friends – former students and colleagues here and overseas – that he has made over the years.

In conclusion I wish to pay a personal tribute to his kindness, support and consideration over the many years of our friendship. Ajit has never been a narrow-focused economist; he has always been well informed on and involved in the major political issues of the day (with which he combines an encyclopaedic knowledge of what is happening in world cricket). When I returned to Australia in early 1967, I was meticulously briefed by Ajit (and Martin Bernal) on the history and then present position of the Vietnam War, which stood me in good stead when I became one of the leaders of the anti-Vietnam War movement in South Australia.

The present volume, which contain fine relevant papers on important topics by internationally respected authors, suitably witness to the achievements of the splendid scholar and admirable human being we know Ajit to be.

G. C. HARCOURT
*Jesus College, Cambridge*

# Notes on the Contributors

**Alice Amsden** is Barton L. Weller Professor of Political Economy at the Department of Urban Studies and Planning, Massachusetts Institute of Technology, USA.

**Philip Arestis** is University Director of Research, Cambridge Centre for Economics and Public Policy, Department of Land Economy, University of Cambridge, UK.

**Ha-Joon Chang** is Reader in the Political Economy of Development at the Faculty of Economics, University of Cambridge, UK.

**John Eatwell** is President of Queens' College, Cambridge, and Professor of Financial Policy and Director of the Centre for Financial Analysis and Policy at Judge Business School, University of Cambridge, UK.

**James K. Galbraith** is Lloyd M. Bentsen Jr Chair in Government/Business Relations and Professor of Government at the Lyndon B. Johnson School of Public Affairs, The University of Texas at Austin, USA.

**G.C. (Geoff) Harcourt** is Emeritus Reader in the History of Economic Theory at the University of Cambridge, Emeritus Fellow at Jesus College, University of Cambridge, UK, and Professor Emeritus of Economics at the University of Adelaide, Australia.

**Arnim Langer** is Research Officer in Economics and Politics (West Africa) at the Centre for Research on Inequality, Human Security and Ethnicity (CRISE), Queen Elizabeth House, University of Oxford, UK.

**Deepak Nayyar** is Professor of Economics at Jawaharlal Nehru University, New Delhi, India.

**Peter Nolan** is Sinyi Professor of Chinese Management and Chair of the University of Cambridge's Development Studies Committee at the Judge Business School, University of Cambridge, UK.

**Codrina Rada von Arnim** is Assistant Professor at the Department of Economics, University of Utah, USA.

**Robert Rowthorn** is Emeritus Professor and Fellow of King's College, University of Cambridge, UK.

**Ashwani Saith** is Professor of Rural Economics, Department of Rural Development, Environment and Population Studies, Institute of Social Studies, The Netherlands.

**Frances Stewart** is Director at the Centre for Research on Inequality, Human Security and Ethnicity (CRISE), University of Oxford, UK.

**Lance Taylor** is Arnhold Professor of International Cooperation and Development at the New School for Social Research, New York, USA.

**John Toye** is Senior Research Associate, Department of International Development, University of Oxford, UK.

**Adrian Wood** is Professor of International Development at the Department of International Development, Queen Elizabeth House, University of Oxford, UK.

# 1
# Introduction: Ajit Singh

*Philip Arestis and John Eatwell*

Ajit Singh studied, initially as an undergraduate, at Government College, Chandigarh, Punjab University. He read Sanskrit (for nationalist reasons) and Mathematics as his subjects. In order to understand how India could become a modern, prosperous country, he also studied Economics. In 1958, Ajit went to the US to study Economics. An important motivation for going to America was that the educational system there permitted one to work one's way through university, whereas in the UK, the usual destination of students from India at the time, studying could only have been at his parents' expense.

In the US, Ajit studied for a Master's degree in Economics at Howard University. Not only was Howard very cheap, even for foreign students in those days, but the graduate school also functioned in the evenings. That enabled Ajit to work during the day at the India Supply Mission and thus to pay his way. After completing his Master's degree at Howard, Ajit went to Berkeley in September 1960 to begin a PhD. In 1961–2, the Economics Department awarded him the much-coveted Alice J. Rosenberg Research Fellowship at Berkeley, on the basis of his academic performance in his first year.

At the invitation of Robin Marris, Ajit went to Cambridge (UK) for the calendar year 1963. This led to a post at the Department of Applied Economics and subsequently, in 1965, to an Assistant Lectureship in the Faculty of Economics, and to an official Fellowship at Queens' College at the same time. In 1968, Ajit was appointed to posts as a Lecturer in the Faculty of Economics and Politics and as Director of Studies in Economics at Queens' College. He was given tenure in 1971 by the University of Cambridge. In 1991, he was appointed to an *ad hominem* University Readership and promoted to a personal Chair in Economics by Cambridge University in October 1995. Ajit Singh also held, between 1987 and 1994, the Dr. William M. Scholl Visiting Chair in the Department of Economics at the University of Notre Dame in the US. He was a senior economic adviser to the governments of Mexico and Tanzania and a consultant to various UN developmental organizations, including the World Bank, the ILO, UNCTAD and UNIDO. He was appointed to a Fellowship at the Cambridge MIT for 2002–3, and in 2004 was elected as an Academician of the British Academy of Social Sciences.

As many developing countries – particularly the NICs – have achieved a significant degree of industrialization since the 1960s, work on the corporate economy, takeovers and the stock market has acquired a far wider field of application. In the 1990s, Ajit examined the question of the desirability of establishing a stock market in a centrally planned economy. Although that work was undertaken with special reference to China, its argument is more general and applicable to many Third-World countries as well. (That work was the subject of an Economic Focus in *The Economist* magazine, 2 September 1989, p. 69.) At the same time, Ajit and collaborators provided the first systematic study of corporate financial structures in the NICs. The purpose of that research programme was to analyse the relationship between corporate organization, corporate finance, and economic and industrial development. More generally, it was to discover what kinds of financial systems and property rights were most conducive to industrialization in developing countries, as well as promoting international competitiveness in advanced economies. With the recent change in the political balance of power between the North and the South, and the East and the West, and the onslaught of international financial institutions – with their recipes for liberalization, privatization and deregulation for rich and poor countries alike – that work had also had significant and timely policy implications at the microeconomic and structural levels. These latter aspects have been further developed and applied in the case of East and South-East Asian and Latin-American countries.

By the mid-1990s, Ajit had established an international reputation in the following three areas, and presumably in recognition of this he was promoted to an *ad hominem* professorship in the Economics Faculty in 1995.

### Modern business enterprise and the theory of the firm:

Corporate organization; corporate finance and governance in advanced countries and emerging markets; takeovers, mergers and the stock market; the financial system and its efficiency in promoting economic growth and development in both advanced and emerging countries.

**Deindustrialization and long-term structural changes in the UK and other advanced economies:**

North–South competition; employment and unemployment in the North and the South; liberalization and globalization of financial, labour and product markets.

**Industrialization of the Third World:**

Economic development and economic policy in developing countries since 1950.

All these areas of Ajit's expertise continue to be very important in the real world and have significant implications both for economic theory and for policy, and Ajit remains active in all of them.

The focus of Ajit's previous research under the first two areas was advanced countries. Thus, his well-known work on corporate growth, mergers and takeovers in the stock market was based on corporate data from the UK and the US. Similarly, his pioneering studies of de-industrialization were based on the experiences of advanced countries. However, since the mid-1990s, Ajit's work has concentrated increasingly on emerging countries. The subjects he was exploring in the first of the three areas have acquired a new stature on the international agenda. It has been argued by the Bretton Woods institutions and by leading US government officials, including Alan Greenspan and Larry Summers, that the fundamental causes of the Asian crisis of 1997–99 lay in the 'Asian way of doing business'. More specifically, crony capitalism in the sense of close relationships between governments, business and finance, and deficits in corporate governance and competition were blamed for the crisis. In his research, Ajit takes serious issue with these claims and suggests that the reform strategy advocated by the international financial institutions is increasingly being questioned as to whether it is a step in the right direction. Ajit's research also shows that capital account liberalization advocated by the IMF with greater or less vigour for developing countries is not helpful for development.

Not only does Ajit's research on aspects of corporate behaviour in emerging markets have direct policy implications, it is also significant for economic theory. His three IFC technical papers on corporate finance indicated that, contrary to *a priori* reasoning, developing-country corporations finance their growth much more from external than from internal sources (that is, retained profits). In relation to external sources, they have surprisingly large recourse to stock markets, indeed much more so than advanced country corporations.

This anomalous finding, which has been referred to as the 'Singh paradox', is generating further research. Similarly, Ajit and his associates have found that, contrary to theoretical speculation and anecdotal evidence, emerging markets display greater intensity of product market competition than do advanced country markets. Using the methodology of persistency of profitability studies, widely employed in assessing the intensity of competition in advanced countries, Ajit and his collaborators suggest that emerging market firms display a lower persistence of profitability than advanced countries, in both the short and the long run.

Nicholas Kaldor's influence on Ajit's work is most evident in the book of essays, *Competitiveness Matters: Industry and Economic Performance in the US*, co-edited with Candace Howes, on industry and economics performance in the US economy. The book includes contributions by leading American economists working in this area, as well as a substantial introductory chapter by Ajit and Howes. The latter reviews and advances further the debate on the concept of competitiveness and its application to the US economy. This chapter also interprets, *inter alia*, US deindustrialization issues in terms of the analyses and concepts of Cambridge economists. In addition, Ajit contributes an essay analysing the relationship between the Anglo-Saxon financial system, the market for corporate control and international competitiveness.

Kaldor's influence is also manifest in Ajit's recent work on the Indian economy. The relevant papers on this topic suggest that the faster growth of services compared with manufacturing – characteristic of the Indian economy in recent decades – does not necessarily indicate a structural imbalance with harmful consequences for the country's long-term economic growth. The IT sector, which has been the mainspring of the rapid growth of service provision, meets all the Kaldorian criteria by which manufacturing is regarded as an engine of growth. The Indian IT sector meets these criteria particularly well and should therefore be regarded as an additional engine of economic growth for the economy. These papers, alongside others, also consider issues of premature deindustrialization, and of a growth in unemployment in the formal sector, which many emerging countries are experiencing.

In recent years, Ajit has been participating in a new research field concerning law, finance and development. The main research in this area since the later 1990s has been carried out by economists from Harvard University – Professor A. Shleifer and his associates, R. La Porta, F. Lopez-de-Silanes and R. W. Vishny, collectively known in the literature as LLSV). On the basis of a large number of studies published in leading international journals, LLSV have suggested that a country's 'legal origin' (crudely basic legal philosophy) determines its corporate law, which in turn determines the level and terms of finance advanced to corporations, and ultimately determines the rate of economic growth. LLSV's findings, based mainly on a cross-section of fifty countries during a single year in the mid-1990s, are controversial. Ajit, the economist, in collaboration with two lawyers (Professor Simon Deakin of Cambridge, and Professor John Armour of Oxford) are the principal investigators in an interdisciplinary, ESRC-funded research project. Their research has collected, for the first time, time-series information for thirty-five years (1970–2005) for four 'mother' countries in relation to legal origin (that is,the UK, the US, Germany and France). Their results indicate that, contrary to the legal origin theory, time-series evidence suggests that common law countries manifest no greater degree of shareholder protection than civil law countries, and that there was no relationship – again, contrary to the legal origin analysis – between shareholder protection and stock market development. These results call into question the advocacy of the Anglo-Saxon model of corporate governance as a universal standard because of the assumed greater legal protection afforded to shareholders.

To sum up, as an economic researcher, Ajit Singh has been guided by the W. B. Reddaway dictum (paraphrased here) *that it is better to be technically crude and relevant than to be technically sophisticated and irrelevant.* This has meant that Ajit has often taken up big questions where knowledge is quite incomplete and yet requires an urgent policy response. Thus, his current research on ongoing industrial revolutions in India and China and their impact on the West has an immediacy and cannot wait several years for the relevant data to be assembled and processed in order to provide policy guidance. Further experiences suggest that big questions such as these require institutional and historical analyses as well as economic theory and appropriate econometric methodology. Ajit Singh's main conclusions are as follows:

(i) it is a social imperative for India and China to continue with their respective industrial revolutions;
(ii) the faster growth of services over manufacturing manifested in India's recent growth experience is not a structural imbalance with

harmful consequences for long-term growth, as some economists would argue: IT-related services are as much an engine of growth as manufacturing;

(iii) although India and China provide competition for advanced countries in manufactures (comprising as they do about 20 per cent of world output), they also continue to provide a stable and growing source of demand;

(iv) those who argue that the recent doubling of the world labour force as a consequence of liberalization and globalization is harmful for workers in the advanced countries, fail to take into account the demand-side potential in India and China, as above, as well as the long-term dynamism of the US economy, based on oligopolistic competition between their large corporations providing an institutionalized mechanism for technical progress in new product development; and

(v) it is, however, argued that current global financial imbalances require an international cooperative approach to rebalancing, rather than imposing adjustment on large new entrants to the global market.

Throughout his academic career at Cambridge, Ajit Singh has taken a very active part in policy work related to economic development in poorer countries. He has also been much concerned with North–South economic interactions and how these can be improved to the mutual benefit of both rich and poor countries. At a practical level, this work has involved advocacy, policy advice and interactions with ministers, officials and civil society in developing countries, and senior civil servants in international organizations. In this context, Ajit's 2005 paper, 'Special and Differential Treatment: The Multilateral Trading System and Economic Development in the Twenty-first Century', in Kevin P. Gallagher (ed.) *Putting Development First*, Zed Books, London, 2005, pp. 233–63, is significant. He argues that the concept of special and differential treatment (S&DT) for developing countries (DCs) represented an important advance in international economic law in the second half of the twentieth century – for its recognition of the notion of non-reciprocity in international economic relations. It is essentially the principle of affirmative action in the sphere of international economic relationships. This principle was reaffirmed unequivocally at the Doha Ministerial Meeting of the World Trade Organization (WTO) in 2001. It is widely acknowledged that S&DT lies at the heart of the Doha development agenda. However, since that time there has been a deep gulf between rich and poor countries on the interpretation and implementation of S&DT. This paper aims to reduce this difference between the North and the South by clarifying the analytical issues involved, including the question of the anti-development bias of the current multilateral trading arrangements, as well as issues of graduation and differentiation. The paper concludes that the strong endorsement of S&DT at Doha gives the international community a fresh chance to change course, and to put economic development at the heart of the agenda for the current and future evolution of the multilateral trading system. However, it is also argued that taking development goals seriously would require a new definition and a new conceptualization of S&DT than the narrow meaning given to it under the Uruguay Round and WTO agreements.

We are extremely grateful to Palgrave Macmillan for their encouragement to put together this volume in honour of Ajit Singh, and to the relevant staff there for making this project possible. We are, of course, equally grateful to the authors for their contributions to this volume. Queens' College, Cambridge, very generously hosted a conference to celebrate Ajit Singh's numerous contributions, not merely to this College but also to the University of Cambridge and to the discipline of economics. We thank them all for their input to this book and for the relevant celebrations.

# 2
# The Third World Industrial Revolution in Historical Perspective

*Ha-Joon Chang*

## Introduction

In most mainstream discourse on globalization and economic development, the experience of so-called import-substitution industrialization (ISI) during the 1960s and the 1970s is typically portrayed as a period of economic inefficiency and stagnation (typical accounts include Bhagwati, 1985, 1998; Sachs and Warner, 1995). It is argued that the developing countries pursued disastrous policies of protection and regulation during the ISI period, driven by their xenophobic reactions to colonialism and misguided by 'wrong' economic theories such as Marxism, Latin American structuralism and the 'infant industry' argument. They are said to have embraced neo-liberal models since the 1980s because they came to realize how bad their performance was compared to that of those countries that did not use the ISI strategy, such as the East Asian 'miracle' economies.

However, the 1960s and the 1970s were actually a period of impressive economic progress in the developing countries, as we shall discuss later. Recently, an increasing number of studies have pointed out that the ISI period generated much better growth performance than that which the neo-liberal policies have managed during the last two decades or so (Weisbrot *et al.*, 2000, 2006; Ocampo, 2001; Chang, 2002, ch. 4). At the individual country level, it is also shown that virtually all successful developing countries of the last half century – starting from Japan in the 1950s through to Korea, Taiwan and Singapore in the 1960s and the 1970s, down to today's China, India and Vietnam – have used 'heterodox' policies, including protectionism, regulation of foreign investment, extensive state ownership, etc. (Chang, 2007). Ocampo (2001) puts it thus: 'the longest-lasting episodes of rapid growth (e.g., the East Asian or, more recently, the Chinese and Indian "miracles" or, in the past, the periods of rapid growth in Brazil and Mexico) do not coincide with phases of extensive liberalization' (p. 13).

The first person who saw the true significance of the ISI experience is, however, Ajit Singh. In his 1984 paper, 'The Interrupted Industrial Revolution of the Third World: Prospects and Policies for Resumption', Ajit called the 1960s and the 1970s the period of 'industrial revolution' in the Third World. In this paper, Ajit emphasized the enormity of the economic and social transformation that had occurred in the Third World during the so-called ISI period and argued against neo-liberal policies that were preventing the resumption of the Industrial Revolution. This was a truly remarkable stance to take at the time, when both the right (on the ground that it was a misguided attempt to go against market forces) and the left (on the ground that it was at worst 'underdevelopment' and at best 'dependent development') were busy denouncing the ISI experience. Ajit continued to advance the point (e.g. Singh, 1990), but it is only recently that people have come to realize the full significance of the 1960s and the 1970s.

## 'Bad old days' or the Third World Industrial Revolution?

During the 'bad old days' of the 1960s and the 1970s, the developing countries grew at 3 per cent a year in per capita terms (see Table 2.1). Latin America, where the ISI is supposed to have spectacularly failed, grew at 3.1 per cent during this period, while sub-Saharan African countries grew at 1.6 per cent (not shown in Table 2.1 but calculated from World Bank and UNDP datasets). How do you judge that performance?

The growth in the ISI period was led by the manufacturing industry, warranting the description of the period as the Third World Industrial Revolution. As we can see from Table 2.2, manufacturing growth in developing countries was faster than in the developed countries (the First World) but slower than in the socialist countries (the Second World) in the 1960s, and faster than in both the First and the Second Worlds in the 1970s. Of course, population growth was more rapid in developing countries (by 1 to 1.5 percentage points) during this period, so the gap in growth rate in per capita terms is smaller that what is suggested by aggregate figures. However, even considering that, we can still say that the developing countries' manufacturing growth rate in per capita terms was comparable to that of the rich countries in the 1960s and much higher than the latter in the 1970s for the developing world.

*Table 2.1*   Per capita GNP growth performance of the developing countries, 1960–80

|  | 1960–70 (%) | 1970–80 (%) | 1960–80 (%) |
|---|---|---|---|
| Low-income countries | 1.8 | 1.7 | 1.8 |
|   Sub-Saharan Africa | 1.7 | 0.2 | 1.0 |
|   Asia | 1.8 | 2.0 | 1.9 |
| Middle-income countries | 3.5 | 3.1 | 3.3 |
|   East Asia and Pacific | 4.9 | 5.7 | 5.3 |
|   Latin America and the Caribbean | 2.9 | 3.2 | 3.1 |
|   Middle East and North Africa | 1.1 | 3.8 | 2.5 |
|   Sub-Saharan Africa | 2.3 | 1.6 | 2.0 |
|   Southern Europe | 5.6 | 3.2 | 4.4 |
| All developing countries | 3.1 | 2.8 | 3.0 |
| Industrialized countries | 3.9 | 2.4 | 3.2 |

*Note*: The 1979 and 1980 figures used are not final, but World Bank estimates. Given that the estimates were supposed to be on the optimistic side, the actual growth figures for 1970–80 and 1960–80 would have been slightly lower than those which are reported in this table.
*Source*: World Bank (1980), Appendix Table to Part I.

*Table 2.2*   Average annual growth of manufacturing, 1960–80

|  | 1960–70 (%) | 1970–80 (%) |
|---|---|---|
| Developing countries | 7.6 | 8.0 |
| Developed market economies | 5.9 | 3.7 |
| Centrally planned economies | 9.0 | 7.3 |
| World | 6.6 | 4.9 |

*Source*: Singh (1984), p. 52, Table 3.

Moreover, the growth record of the developing countries during the Third World Industrial Revolution compares favourably with what today's rich countries (or now-developed countries) achieved during their own Industrial Revolution. Table 2.3 shows that annual per capita income growth rate among the 11 now-developed countries (NDCs) for which data are available during 1820–75 ranged from 0.6 per cent (Italy) to 2 per cent (Australia), with the unweighted average and the median values both at 1.1 per cent. The table also shows that between 1875 and 1913, per capita income growth rates ranged from 0.6 per cent (Australia) to 2.4 per cent (Canada), with the unweighted average at 1.7 per cent

*Table 2.3* Per capita growth performance among the NDCs in earlier times

|  | 1820–1875 (%) | 1875–1913 (%) |
|---|---|---|
| Australia | 2.0 | 0.6 |
| Austria | 0.8 | 1.5 |
| Belgium | 1.4 | 1.0 |
| Canada | 1.2 | 2.4 |
| Denmark | 0.9 | 1.6 |
| Finland | 0.8 | 1.5 |
| France | 1.1 | 1.2 |
| Germany | 1.2 | 1.5 |
| Italy | 0.6 | 1.3 |
| Netherlands | 1.1 | 0.9 |
| Norway | 0.7 | 1.2 |
| Sweden | 0.8 | 1.4 |
| UK | 1.3 | 1.0 |
| USA | 1.3 | 1.9 |
| Unweighted average | 1.1 | 1.7 |
| Median | 1.1 | 1.4 |

*Source*: Calculated from Maddison (1995).

and the median at 1.4 per cent. Therefore, the growth rates during the Third World Industrial Revolution, at 3 per cent, were a good two to three times higher than the growth rates seen in the Industrial Revolution in the NDCs (depending on the period we are looking at).

## The 'brave new world'

I have shown that the growth performance of the developing countries during the 'bad old days' of ISI in the 1960s and the 1970s was far from disastrous, contrary to the neo-liberal mythology. On the contrary, the growth rate was much higher than those recorded in the latter countries during their Industrial Revolution. Moreover, it was comparable to (somewhat lower in the 1960s and somewhat higher in the 1970s than) what the developed countries recorded during the same period, which for the latter countries was the so-called 'Golden Age of Capitalism'. More importantly, the growth rates of the developing countries since the 1980s, when they abandoned the supposedly disastrous ISI policy and entered the 'brave new world' of neo-liberalism, have been much lower than that during the 'bad old days' of ISI.

*Table 2.4*   Per capita GDP growth rates of the developing countries, 1980–2000

|  | 1980–90 (%) | 1990–2000 (%) | 1980–2000 (%) |
|---|---|---|---|
| Developing countries | 1.4 | 2.0 | 1.7 |
| East Asia and Pacific | 6.4 | 6.0 | 6.2 |
| Europe and Central Asia | 1.5 | −1.8 | −0.2 |
| Latin America and the Caribbean | −0.3 | 1.7 | 0.7 |
| Middle East and North Africa | −1.1 | 1.2 | −0.1 |
| South Asia | 3.5 | 3.7 | 3.6 |
| Sub-Saharan Africa | −1.2 | −0.2 | −0.7 |
| Developed countries | 2.5 | 1.7 | 2.1 |

*Notes*: The figures are only approximate, as they were constructed by subtracting the population growth rates from GDP growth rates. This had to be done because the World Bank stopped publishing decade-wise per capita GDP growth rates from its 1998 *World Development Report*. For country classification, see the table on p. 334 of World Bank (2000/1).
*Source*: World Bank (2002), p. 233, Table 1 for the population growth figures and p. 237, Table 3 for the GDP growth figures.

It may not be surprising that neo-liberal policies implemented since the 1980s have increased income inequality and poverty in many developing countries. However, if those policies have not even generated improved economic growth, then they have a serious problem. For they were supposed to usher in a period of accelerated growth, even at the cost of some 'soft' things like inequality and poverty. The neo-liberal mantra has been that 'you first have to create wealth before you can redistribute it'.

As we can see from Table 2.4, the exact opposite of this neo-liberal prediction has happened. During the 1980s and the 1990s, the developing world experienced a fall in economic growth rate. During the period, per capita income in the developing countries was growing at around half the rate that used to prevail in those countries in the 1960s and the 1970s (3 per cent vs 1.7 per cent).

In particular, Latin America, the most enthusiastic convert to neo-liberalism since the 1980s, used to grow at 3.1 per cent in per capita terms in the 'bad old days' of ISI. But over the next 20 years (1980–2000), it grew at only a quarter of this speed, at 0.7 per cent. Even if we disregard the 1980s as the decade of adjustment, the growth record of the 1990s (1.7 per cent) is much poorer compared to those of the 1960s and the 1970s. Even more worryingly, in the new century Latin America has not even kept up the growth rate of the 1990s. Between 2000 and 2005, the continent's economies virtually stood still, heralding another

*Table 2.5* Per capita GDP growth rates in developing countries: 'bad old days' vs 'brave new world'

|  | 'Bad old days' 1960–80 (%) | 'Brave new world' 1980–2004 (%) |
| --- | --- | --- |
| All developing countries | 3.0 | 2.2 |
| Latin America and the Caribbean | 3.1 | 0.5 |
| Sub-Saharan Africa | 1.6 | −0.3 |

*Sources*: World Bank; United Nations.

'lost decade'. During this five-year period, per capita income in Latin America grew only by 3 per cent (Weisbrot *et al.*, 2005, p. 8) – or at an annual growth rate of 0.6 per cent.

Per capita income actually shrunk in the sub-Saharan African countries in the 1980s (−1.2 per cent per annum) and the 1990s (−0.2 per cent per annum). Between 2000 and 2003, growth has returned to the region, but at a very low rate of around 0.5 per cent (Mkandawire, 2005, p. 9, Figure 1). This means that, even if the region continues to grow at that rate for another 15 years, its per capita income in 2020 will be still lower than it was in 1980. Given that the Bretton Woods institutions have practically run the economy in most sub-Saharan African countries over the last two decades or so, this is a damning record for neo-liberalism.

Table 2.5 extends the data for the 'brave new world' from 1980–2000 to 1980–2004, to reflect more recent trends. While this raises the average growth rate of the developing countries (from 1.7 per cent to 2.2 per cent), this is not because neo-liberal policies have finally become effective. It is in large part because of the rapid growth of China and India, two giants (which now collectively account for about 30 per cent of developing-country output) that have liberalized their economies during this period but flatly refused to wholly embrace the neo-liberal agenda. The huge absorption of African natural resources by China is behind a slight lift in the sub-Saharan African growth rate, or more accurately in this case a fall in the rate of economic contraction (from −0.7 per cent to −0.3 per cent). However, extending the time period to 2004 makes the Latin American performance worse, as I noted above (a fall from 0.7 per cent to 0.5 per cent). The falling growth rate in Latin America is particularly embarrassing for the neo-liberal orthodoxy, as the best-performing economies in the region are the ones that defy the orthodoxy

(Venezuela and Argentina), while the faithful pupils fail to reap the benefits of reform, which presumably should become bigger as time passes by.

## The Age of Imperialism

To complete our historical picture, let us look at the record of developing countries before the 'bad old days', that is, during the Age of Imperialism – say, a century and a half before the 'bad old days' (1820–1960). During this period, many countries were colonies, often for centuries, without any freedom to control even what went on inside their borders, not to speak of cross-border flows of resources, including international trade. To ensure that colonies did not become economic competitors to the imperialist countries, a number of actions were taken (for further details, see Chang, 2002, pp. 51–4).

High value-added manufacturing activities were outlawed, exports from the colonies that competed with the colonizer's products were banned (e.g. the 18th century ban by the British on cotton textile imports from India, or 'calicoes', and the 1699 British ban on the export of woollen cloth from its colonies, such as Ireland and America) and policies were deployed to encourage primary production in the colonies (e.g. export subsidies for raw materials). Most importantly, the use of tariffs by colonial authorities was banned. If they were considered necessary for revenue reasons, then they would be countered in a number of ways. When in 1859 the British colonial government in India imposed small import duties on textile goods (3–10 per cent) for purely fiscal reasons, the local producers were taxed to the same magnitude in order to provide a 'level playing field' (Bairoch, 1993, p. 89). Even with this 'compensation', the British cotton manufacturers put constant pressure on the government for the repeal of the duties, which they finally got in 1882. In the 1890s, when the colonial government in India once again tried to impose tariffs on cotton products – this time in order to protect the Indian cotton industry, rather than for revenue reasons – the cotton textile pressure groups thwarted the attempt. Until 1917, there was no tariff on cotton goods imports into India.

The weaker countries that were somewhat more fortunate and escaped the fate of colonial occupation were forced into 'unequal treaties' that deprived them of policy autonomy, especially over tariffs. They were not allowed to impose more than a nominal, flat-rate tariff, typically 3–5 per cent, for purely revenue purposes. It is extremely disconcerting to note that binding tariffs at a low, uniform rate (although not necessarily below

*Table 2.6* Historical rates of economic growth by major regions during and after the Age of Imperialism (1820–1950) (annual per capita GDP growth rate, %)

| Regions | 1820–70 | 1870–1913 | 1913–50 | 1950–73 |
|---|---|---|---|---|
| Western Europe | 0.95 | 1.32 | 0.76 | 4.08 |
| Western offshoots* | 1.42 | 1.81 | 1.55 | 2.44 |
| Japan | 0.19 | 1.48 | 0.89 | 8.05 |
| Asia excluding Japan | −0.11 | 0.38 | −0.02 | 2.92 |
| Latin America | 0.10 | 1.81 | 1.42 | 2.52 |
| Eastern Europe and former USSR | 0.64 | 1.15 | 1.50 | 3.49 |
| Africa | 0.12 | 0.64 | 1.02 | 2.07 |
| World | 0.53 | 1.30 | 0.91 | 2.93 |

*Note*: *Australia, Canada, New Zealand and the USA.
*Source*: Maddison (2003), p. 126, Table 3–1a.

5 per cent) is exactly what modern day free-trade economists recommend to developing countries.

Britain first used unequal treaties in Latin America, starting with Brazil in 1810, as the countries in the South American continent acquired political independence. Starting with the Nanking Treaty (1842), which followed the Opium War (1839–42), China was forced to sign a series of unequal treaties over the next couple of decades. These eventually resulted in a complete loss of tariff autonomy, and, very symbolically, a Briton being the head of customs for 45 years – from 1863 to 1908. From 1824 onwards, Thailand (then Siam) signed various unequal treaties, the most comprehensive being in 1855. Persia signed unequal treaties in 1836 and 1857, and the Ottoman Empire in 1838 and 1861.[1]

Even Japan lost its tariff autonomy following the unequal treaties signed after its opening-up in 1853. It was only able to end the unequal treaties in 1911 (Johnson, 1982, p. 25). In this context, it is also interesting to note that when Japan forcefully opened up Korea in 1876, it exactly imitated the Western countries and forced Korea to sign an unequal treaty that deprived the latter of its tariff autonomy – despite the fact that it still did not have tariff autonomy itself.

During the Age of Imperialism, growth performance in developing countries was really poor. As shown in Table 2.6, per capita GDP growth in Latin America was 0.1 per cent during 1820–70, when they were subject to unequal treaties. It rose to 1.8 per cent during 1870–1913. Interestingly, this was when most countries in the region abandoned free trade, as they acquired tariff autonomy with the expiry of the unequal treaties, and maintained some of the highest tariffs in the world.

*Table 2.7*   Growth rates of per capita GDP in selected Asian countries during the Age of Imperialism

|               | 1913–50 (%) | 1950–99 (%) | Growth acceleration (percentage points) |
|---------------|-------------|-------------|-----------------------------------------|
| Bangladesh    | −0.2        | 0.9         | 1.1                                     |
| Burma         | −1.5        | 2.0         | 3.5                                     |
| China         | −0.6        | 4.2         | 4.8                                     |
| Hong Kong     | n.a.        | 4.6         | n.a.                                    |
| India         | −0.2        | 2.2         | 2.4                                     |
| Indonesia     | −0.2        | 2.7         | 2.9                                     |
| Korea (South) | −0.4        | 6.0         | 6.4                                     |
| Malaysia      | 1.5         | 3.2         | 1.7                                     |
| Nepal         | n.a.        | 1.4         | n.a.                                    |
| Pakistan      | −0.2        | 2.3         | 2.5                                     |
| Philippines   | 0.0         | 1.6         | 1.6                                     |
| Singapore     | 1.5         | 4.9         | 3.4                                     |
| Sri Lanka     | 0.3         | 2.6         | 2.9                                     |
| Taiwan        | 0.6         | 5.9         | 6.5                                     |
| Thailand      | −0.1        | 4.3         | 4.4                                     |

*Note*: n.a. Not available.
*Source*: Maddison (2003), p. 143, Table 3–14.

It is even more interesting to note that another high-growth economy at the time, namely the USA, which also grew at 1.8 per cent during this period, had even higher average industrial tariff rates (in fact the highest in the world during most of the period between the 1830s and the 1940s).[2] In Africa, per capita GDP growth accelerated from around 0.5 per cent during 1820–1950 to 2.1 per cent during 1950–73, when most of the countries in the continent became independent. In Asia, excluding Japan, economic performance vastly improved from virtually no growth (or even slight decline) in per capita income during the Age of Imperialism to 2.9 per cent in 1950–73, when most of the region's countries gained independence.

As Table 2.7 shows, in the 1913–50 period, during which most were colonies or subject to unequal treaties, the growth rates of the Asian countries, even in those countries that have later become known as 'miracle economies', were very poor. During the 1913–50 period, only four out of 13 Asian countries for which data are available recorded positive growth in per capita income (Taiwan, Sri Lanka, Malaysia and Singapore, which then together formed British Malaya). Only in Malaysia and Singapore (1.5 per cent) was the growth rate substantial – those for

Taiwan and Sri Lanka were 0.6 per cent and 0.3 per cent, respectively. In the remaining nine countries, which accounted for the vast bulk of the region's population, per capita income actually declined during this period.

In contrast, during the post-imperialist period, all 15 countries in the table recorded positive growth. Even the slowest-growing economy, Bangladesh, recorded a 0.9 per cent growth in per capita income, which would have been the second highest in Asia (after British Malaya), had it occurred in the imperialist period. More importantly, in the post-imperialist period, growth rates rose in all 13 countries for which the data were available, with Taiwan (6.5 percentage points) and Korea (6.4 percentage points) showing particularly rapid accelerations.

Of course, nothing definite can be 'proven' by continent-wide average statistics spanning one and a half centuries, because a lot of things are going on at the individual country level. However, the pattern is striking. In *all* parts of the developing world, economic growth accelerated dramatically after the end of colonialism and unequal treaties.

## The shrinking policy space

Thus, the picture seems rather clear. The developing countries did better when they had more policy autonomy. When they were colonies or subject to unequal treaties, their growth performance was abysmal. When they gained policy autonomy after independence or the expiry of unequal treaties, their performance improved markedly – leading to the Third-World Industrial Revolution. When their policy autonomy was reduced following the spread of neo-liberalism after the 1980s, their growth slowed down.

Unfortunately, totally ignoring such evidence, the rich countries have worked hard to reduce the policy autonomy, or policy space if we use the currently popular expression, of the developing countries. Since the 1980s, the World Bank and the IMF massively expanded their 'programme' (as opposed to 'project') loans in the form of the Structural Adjustment Programmes (SAPs) – and many of its subsequent reincarnations, which are too numerous to list – and broadened the scope and enhanced the strength of the conditionalities attached to their loans.

Aid policies of the developed countries have also contributed to the shrinking of policy space. In the old days, the main conditions attached to aid by the donor countries was that the recipients bought (at least a certain portion of) the goods and services that were needed for the aid-funded projects from the national companies of the donor countries.

However, since the 1980s, the conditions have stretched to include policy recommendations similar to what the Bank and the Fund demand on their loans. This is not surprising, when we recall that after all the Bank and the Fund are controlled by the countries that are main providers of foreign aid to developing countries. Rich countries also frequently threaten to cut their aid to countries that do not follow their instructions, for example in the WTO negotiations or in various bilateral and regional Free Trade Agreement negotiations.

The shrinkage in policy space has been particularly striking in the area of trade and industrial policies. First of all, since the 1980s, the Bank and the Fund have made trade liberalization – involving tariff cuts, tariffication of quantitative restrictions and the reduction in non-tariff barriers (NTBs) – a key condition attached to their loans. The conclusion of the Uruguay Round of the GATT talks in 1994 and the subsequent launch of the WTO in 1995 have brought hitherto unthinkable issues into the arena of multilateral trade politics – patents (through TRIPs), regulation of foreign investment (through TRIMs), trade in services (through GATS) – and have also shrunk the space for many of the more 'traditional' areas like tariffs.

While it is important to recognize that there is still considerable policy space in the WTO (Akyuz *et al.*, 1998; Amsden, 2005), it should not be forgotten that there is a constant attempt by the developed countries to reduce the remaining space. For example, in the run-up to the Cancún ministerial meeting of the WTO in September 2003, the developed countries tried very hard – and failed in the end – to put the multilateral investment agreement (MIA), which aims to make virtually all restrictions on foreign direct investment (and possibly those on portfolio investment) 'illegal', on the WTO negotiation agenda. (For a critique of the MIA proposal, see Chang and Green, 2003; for an analysis of the result of the Cancún meeting, see Chang, 2003.) Currently, the rich countries are trying to vastly reduce industrial tariffs in developing countries through the so-called NAMA (non-agricultural market access) negotiations (see Khor and Goh, 2004; Akyuz, 2005; Chang, 2005). Even though the 'zero-tariff' proposal made by the USA in December 2002 is considered to be a deliberately radical opening gambit, the core US proposal is to bring average industrial tariffs in developing countries down to 5–7 per cent by 2010, the lowest level since the days of colonialism and unequal treaties when the weaker countries were deprived of policy autonomy, especially the right to set tariffs.[3] With very few exceptions, they will be also lower than the rates that prevailed in today's developed countries until the early 1970s.[4]

And it is not just the WTO that restricts developing countries' policy space in trade and industrial policies. The developed countries, especially the USA, have used bilateral and regional FTAs and bilateral investment agreements (BITs) to impose on developing countries restrictions that they cannot get accepted in the WTO. The US has pursued a number of bilateral and more importantly regional FTAs (NAFTA in 1995; Central American Free Trade Agreement, being ratified by member countries – or not; and Free Trade Area of the Americas has been on the agenda for a while). The European Union is currently pushing for the misleadingly named Economic Partnership Agreement (EPA), which is essentially a WTO-plus FTA (including areas excluded from the WTO like government procurement and agreements that are enhanced versions of WTO agreements, such as the intellectual property rights proposal).

In addition to these (aid and loan) conditionalities and new international trading rules, the (real and imagined) threat of capital flight in the environment of open capital markets further limits policy autonomy of developing countries. Fearing 'punishment' by the 'foreign investor' (as if all foreign investors share the same interests and want the same things), developing country governments adopt policies that they think (or that they are told) will please the foreign investor – especially in terms of macroeconomic policy, corporate taxation, labour law and environmental regulation. And there are the international media, the credit rating agencies, consulting firms and various international organizations who regularly publish materials that praise countries doing the 'right' thing and rubbish those who don't, although they will do a U-turn when it suits them.[5]

At this point, it is important to note that policy space is also constrained by domestic interest groups in the developing countries themselves. There are those citizens of developing countries whose interests lie in restricting their own government's policy space. Financiers may want their government to be locked into 'prudent' macroeconomic policies through institutions like central bank independence, currency board, autonomous revenue agency, deficit rules and inflation targeting. Some of them may want their government's freedom to control cross-border capital movements curtailed or even totally taken away, so that they can take the money out of the country if and when necessary.[6] Exporters of agricultural products may want to keep their government on the 'straight and narrow path' of free trade through the WTO, bilateral and regional FTAs, and the restraints of the World Bank and other international organizations. And there are also those who want their own government's policy space to be restricted for ideological reasons. These days many economists in developing countries are ideologically committed to the free market and want the policy space of their governments to be restricted lest their policies deviate from (what they think are) what the 'science' of economics says.[7]

## Is policy space necessary?

When developing countries protest against the constant shrinking of the policy space available to them, the rich countries deploy a series of counter-arguments, supposedly showing why the shrinkage in policy space for developing countries is only fair for the rest of the world and good for the developing countries themselves. Let us examine these arguments one by one and see whether they make sense.

### 'Extra policy space for developing countries is unfair.'

In their push for the reduction in policy space for developing countries, the rich countries often deploy the rhetoric of the 'level playing field'. We should 'level the playing field', it is argued by rich countries, by removing the 'unfair' advantages that developing countries are currently enjoying in their competition with the developed countries, such as higher tariffs, weaker protection of intellectual property rights and more stringent restrictions on foreign investment.

The level playing field is the right principle to adopt when the players are equal. However, when the players are unequal, it is the wrong principle to apply. For example, if a team of 13-year-old children are playing football against the Brazilian national team, it is only fair that the playing field is not level and that children are allowed to attack from up the hill. Indeed, in most sports, unequal players are not even allowed to compete against each other. In boxing, wrestling and many other sports, they have weight classes. In many sports there are age classes. In sports like golf, we even have an explicit system of 'handicaps' that allows weaker players to compete with advantages in (inverse) proportion to their playing skills. And so on.

What looks like levelling the playing field often structurally advantages the rich countries. Take the case of tariffs. The Uruguay Round resulted in all countries except for the poorest ones reducing tariffs quite a lot in proportional terms. But the developing countries ended up reducing their tariffs a lot more in absolute terms, for the simple reason that they started off with higher tariffs. For example, before the WTO agreement, India had an average tariff rate of 71 per cent. This was cut to 32 per cent.

The US average tariff rate fell from 7 per cent to 3 per cent. Both are similar in proportional terms (each representing around a 55 per cent cut), but the absolute impact is very different. In the Indian case, an imported good that formerly cost $171 would now cost only $132 – a significant fall in what the consumer pays (about 23 per cent) that would dramatically alter consumer behaviour. In the American case, the price the consumer pays would have fallen from $107 to $103 – a price difference that most consumers will hardly notice (about 4 per cent). In other words, the impact of tariff cuts of the same proportion is disproportionately larger for the country whose tariff rate is higher.

Another example is intellectual property rights. The TRIPS (Trade Related Intellectual Property Rights) agreement in the WTO has strengthened the protection of patents and other intellectual property rights. Unlike trade in goods and services, where everyone has something to sell, this is an area where developed countries are almost always sellers, and developing countries are almost always buyers. Therefore, increasing the protection for intellectual property rights means that the cost is mainly borne by the developing nations. The same problem applies to the TRIMS (Trade Related Investment Measures) agreement, which restricts the WTO member countries' ability to regulate foreign investors. Once again, most poor countries only receive, and do not make, foreign investment. So while their ability to regulate foreign companies is reduced, they do not get 'compensated' by any reduction in the regulations that their national firms operating abroad are subject to, as they simply do not have such firms. Basic (as opposed to commercial) R&D subsidies is another example. This is one of the few subsidies allowed by the WTO. But this is not a subsidy that developing nations can use, even if they are allowed to – they simply do not do much basic R&D, so there is little for them to subsidize.

## 'There is ample extra policy space for developing countries anyway.'

It is true that the developing countries have extra policy space. This is constitutionally guaranteed by 'special and differential treatments' (SDT) in the WTO. The rich countries also argue that developing countries get extra policy space by being allowed the 'flexibility' to keep more sectors off the liberalization agenda. So GATS is said to be flexible because it allows countries to keep some sectors off their market-opening commitments. The same notion of flexibility was bandied about in the (now-dormant) negotiation for the MIA in the run up to the Cancún ministerial meeting in 2003. In NAMA, it is said that there is some flexibility because developing countries can reserve some sectors from their tariff-binding and tariff-cutting commitments, although the scope for these is supposed to be highly limited. In its EPA negotiations, the EU also argues that it gives extra space to developing countries by allowing them to reserve 20 per cent of their products from liberalization commitment, while it will liberalize all trade.

The problem with SDT is the word 'special'. To call something 'special treatment' is to say that the person getting the treatment is getting an unfair advantage. However, in the same way we wouldn't call stairlifts for wheelchair users or Braille writings for the blind 'special treatments', we should not call the higher tariffs and other means of protection more extensively (but not exclusively) used by the developing countries 'special treatments' – they are just differential treatments for countries with differential capabilities and goals.

SDT has been vastly reduced in scope, when compared to the pre-WTO regime. Often, the special treatment amounts to no more than delaying the implementation of a universal scheme by several years. For example, in the case of TRIPS, the fact that countries at different stages of development may need different IPR regimes is totally ignored, with the same regime being imposed on all countries. The only concession that developing countries got was to have some extra time for adopting the regime – ten (recently extended to 18) years for the least developed countries and five years for all other developing countries.

The 'flexibility' argument is also highly problematic. First, while developing countries may 'reserve' some of the existing sectors, they are not allowed to add any new sectors to this list. Therefore, it is impossible for them to put new infant industries on the reservation list. This is a very anti-developmental outlook as it implies a very strong bias towards the maintenance of the current economic structure. Second, even for sectors that are reserved now, the flexibility is only one-way. For, once a sector is liberalized, there is no going back. For example, the whole idea of tariff binding in the WTO is based on this notion. The exercise is based on the belief that there is a tariff rate in a sector over which the tariff should *never* rise.

**'Developing countries do not even fully use the policy space they have – so they don't really need more.'**

When hearing worries about the lack of policy space, rich countries often point out that most developing countries are not even fully using the policy space they have, which proves that they really don't need more policy space. For example, they point out that few countries keep their tariff rates at the maximum rates bound in the Uruguay Round. This, they argue, is proof that these countries actually don't need higher tariffs.

However, this is a disingenuous argument. Formal rules (for example as defined by the WTO) do not fully determine an agent's options. For example, a country may not fully use the policy space allowed in international agreements like the WTO because their loan and aid conditionalities may dictate otherwise. Many rich countries routinely threaten (of course, informally) disobedient developing countries with cuts in aid or a reduction in market access. On their part, developing countries are scared to push the boundaries of the policy space, because they do not want to be blackballed in the international financial market by adopting heterodox policies. Especially under the condition of open capital market, any action that is not acceptable will be condemned by the financial sector and the international financial media and may lead to an outflow of capital. Fearing the possibility, many governments refrain from taking such action.

Saying that the less-than-full use of policy space proves that developing countries do not need more policy space is like saying that people living in a dictatorship love the political regime because most of them are not in open revolt against the regime.

### 'We only want to prevent the developing countries from harming themselves.'

Many free-trade economists like to present themselves as defenders of the interests of the developing countries. The World Bank, for example, in its famous *East Asian Miracle* report, warned that other developing countries should not try to emulate the interventionist trade and industrial policies of East Asia, because they do not have the administrative capabilities to make these complex policies work (World Bank, 1993, e.g. p. 26). In doing so, the Bank wants to be seen as protecting the developing countries from harming themselves by employing policies that have little chance of success. Interestingly, Adam Smith was doing the same for the Americans in his *Wealth of Nations*, when he was advising them not to protect manufacturing.[8]

Some would go even further. They would quite explicitly pitch themselves against the ignorant and often corrupt developing-country governments beholden to interest groups, in defence of the 'common man', who would benefit from free trade. For example, right after the collapse of the Cancún ministerial talks of the WTO in September 2003, Willem Buiter, the then chief economist of the EBRD (European Bank for Reconstruction and Development), lamented that 'although the leaders of the developing nations rule countries that are, on average, poor or very poor, it does not follow that these leaders necessarily speak on behalf of the poor and poorest in their countries. Some do; others represent corrupt and repressive elites that feed off the rents created by imposing barriers to trade and other distortions, at the expense of their poorest and most defenceless citizens'.[9]

Thus seen, whichever variant of the free-trade view one takes, the shrinking of policy space for developing-country governments in the area of trade and industrial policies is a good thing, as it prevents the developing countries from making costly policy mistakes, whether out of misguided belief in interventionism (the World Bank version) or due to interest group politics (the Buiter version).

One obvious difficulty with this view is, of course, that throughout history shrinkage in policy space has produced poor economic outcome. On the whole, the developing countries have been very good at 'responsibly' using the policy autonomy and space that they have. What is curious, however, is that that the free-trade economists who display such paternalistic attitude to the developing-country policy choice are usually people who would vehemently denounce most government regulations for their underlying paternalism and argue for individual 'freedom to choose'. They would say that governments should not try to restrict people's freedom of choice out of fear that they may make 'wrong' choices, because, after all, the ability to make mistakes and learn from them is the genuine sign of autonomy and free choice.

There is something deeply troubling about this. A consistent free-trade economist who values autonomy and choice for individuals should be willing to do the same for developing countries as independent entities – that is, unless they adopt the libertarian view and deny the legitimacy of any collective decision. However, if they did that, they would also have to deny the legitimacy of any multilateral decision (the WTO, the IMF, the World Bank) or indeed any governmental decision (aid conditionalities imposed by foreign governments), which they are not doing. If so, they cannot avoid the accusation of employing a double standard. They passionately advocate the individual's 'right to be wrong', on the ground of individual autonomy, but they are not willing to respect national autonomy of the developing countries, thus denying them the same 'right to be wrong'.

## Summary and conclusions

In this chapter, I have examined the growth records of the developing countries over the last two centuries – the Age of Imperialism, the 'bad old days' of ISI and the 'brave new world' of neo-liberalism. When they were colonies or subject to unequal treaties, the developing countries experienced extremely slow economic growth (and we are not even taking into account the issues of political legitimacy, cultural/racial domination and the social inequity associated with colonialism and imperialism). When they were allowed quite large policy space between the 1950s and the 1970s, their growth accelerated beyond expectation. Once the policy space started shrinking after the 1980s, their average growth rate fell to half of what it was in the 'bad old days' of import substitution in the previous period.

It turns out that the 'bad old days' was in fact the time of the Third World Industrial Revolution, as Ajit Singh pointed out before anyone else. Based on the contrast between that experience and the periods before and after, I have argued that policy autonomy, or policy space, is very important in determining developing countries' economic performance. I have critically examined the arguments deployed by rich countries in defence of their attempts to further reduce the policy space available for developing countries. All the arguments are found wanting, both theoretically and empirically.

Policy space is a matter of vital importance. Long-range historical records suggest that it has an enormous influence on a country's ability to achieve economic development. If the Third World Industrial Revolution is to be resumed, especially in Latin America and sub-Saharan Africa, developing countries need to be given sufficient policy autonomy and space to determine for themselves which policies are suitable for them.

## Notes

1. The 1838 Convention of Balta Liman with Turkey (then the Ottoman Empire) bound Turkish import duties at 3 per cent (Fielden, 1969, p. 91).
2. Average tariffs in Latin America were between 17 per cent (Mexico, 1870–99) and 47 per cent (Colombia, 1900–13). See Table 4 in Clemens and Williamson (2002). Between 1820 and 1870, when they were subject to unequal treaties, per capita income stood still in Latin America (growth rate of −0.03 per cent per year). Annual per capita income growth in Latin America rose to 1.8 per cent during 1870–1913, when most countries in the region acquired tariff autonomy, but even that was no match for the 3.1 per cent growth rate in per capita income that the continent achieved during the 1960s and the

1970s. The Latin American income growth figures are from Maddison (2003), Table 8(b).

3. The EC proposal will bring average industrial tariffs down to 5–15 per cent. The Korean and Indian proposals will bring them down to 10–25 per cent and to 10–50 per cent, respectively.

4. The exceptions are Britain and the Netherlands between the late nineteenth and the early twentieth centuries; Germany briefly in the late nineteenth century; and Denmark after the Second World War. See Tables 3 and 5 in Chang (2005).

5. For example, the credit rating agencies started downgrading the Asian countries *after* the outbreak of the 1997 crisis. As another example, the IMF started criticizing Argentina *after* the policy it used to recommend to the country led to the economic collapse.

6. The former undersecretary of the US Treasury, John Taylor, is reported to have said that free transfer of capital in and out of a country without delay is a 'fundamental right' (testimony on 1 April 2003, before the Subcommittee on Domestic and International Monetary Policy, Trade, and Technology of the Committee on Financial Services at the US House of Representatives, as cited in Wade, 2005, p. 92).

7. And this ideological commitment makes them believe that anything other than strict free-market policies are irrational, short-sighted and giving in to populism. For example, several months before the 2002 Argentinian financial crisis, Domingo Cavallo, the famous free-market finance minister of the country, wrote an article in the *Financial Times* (date unknown) in which he argued that the monetary inflexibility accorded by the country's currency board was necessary because of his compatriots' inability to control their spending.

8. In his *Wealth of Nations*, Adam Smith wrote: 'Were the Americans, either by combination or by any other sort of violence, to stop the importation of European manufactures, and, by thus giving a monopoly to such of their own countrymen as could manufacture the like goods, divert any considerable part of their capital into this employment, they would retard instead of accelerating the further increase in the value of their annual produce, and would obstruct instead of promoting the progress of their country towards real wealth and greatness' (Smith, 1973 [1776], pp. 347–8).

9. Letter to the editor, *Financial Times*, 16 September 2003.

## References

Akyuz, Y. (2005) 'The WTO Negotiations on Industrial Tariffs: What is at Stake for Developing Countries?', mimeo, Third World Network, Geneva Office.

Akyuz, Y., H.-J. Chang and R. Kozul-Wright (1998) 'New Perspectives on East Asian Development', *Journal of Development Studies* 34 (6).

Amsden, A. (2005) 'Promoting Industry under WTO Law', in K. Gallagher (ed.), *Putting Development First: The Importance of Policy Space in the WTO and IFIs*, London: Zed Press.

Bhagwati, J. (1985) *Protectionism*, Cambridge, MA: MIT Press.

Bhagwati, J. (1998) 'The Global Age: From Skeptical South to a Fearful North', in his *A Stream of Windows: Unsettling Reflections on Trade, Immigration, and Democracy*, Cambridge, MA: MIT Press.

Chang, H.-J. (2002) *Kicking Away the Ladder: Development Strategy in Historical Perspective*, London: Anthem Press.

Chang, H.-J. (2003) 'Future for Trade', *Challenge* 46 (6).

Chang, H.-J. (2005) *Why Developing Countries Need Tariffs: How WTO NAMA Negotiations Could Deny Developing Countries' Right to a Future*, Geneva: South Centre.

Chang, H.-J. (2007) *Bad Samaritans: Rich Nations, Poor Policies, and the Threat to the Developing World*, London: Random House.

Chang, H.-J. and D. Green (2003) *The Northern WTO Agenda on Investment: Do as We Say, Not as We Did*, Geneva: South Centre.

Clemens, M. and J. Williamson (2002) 'Closed Jaguar, Open Dragon: Comparing Tariffs in Latin America and Asia before World War II', NBER working paper 9401, Cambridge, MA, National Bureau of Economic Research.

Fielden, K. (1969) 'The Rise and Fall of Free Trade', in C. Bartlett (ed.), *Britain Pre-eminent: Studies in British World Influence in the Nineteenth Century*, London: Macmillan.

Khor, M. and C. Y. Goh (2004) 'The WTO Negotiations on Non-Agricultural Market Access: A Development Perspective', paper presented at the Asia–Pacific Conference on Trade: Contributing to Growth, Poverty Reduction and Human Development, Penang, Malaysia, 22–24 November 2004.

Maddison, A. (1995) *Monitoring the World Economy*, Paris: OECD.

Maddison, A. (2003) *The World Economy: Historical Statistics*, Paris: OECD.

Ocampo, J. (2001) 'Rethinking the Development Agenda', paper presented at the American Economic Association annual meeting, 5–7 January 2001, New Orleans, USA.

Sachs, J. and A. Warner (1995) 'Economic Reform and the Process of Global Integration', *Brookings Papers on Economic Activity*, 1.

Singh, A. (1984) 'The Interrupted Industrial Revolution of the Third World: Prospects and Policies for Resumption', *Industry and Development* 12.

Singh, A. (1990) 'The State of Industry in the Third World in the 1980s: Analytical and Policy Issues', working paper 137, Kellogg Institute for International Studies, Notre Dame University.

Smith, A. (1973 [1776]) *An Inquiry into the Nature and Causes of the Wealth of Nations*, ed. Edwin Cannan, New York: Random House.

Wade, R. (2005) 'What Strategies are Viable for Developing Countries Today?: The World Trade Organization and the Shrinking of "Development Space"', in K. Gallagher (ed.), *Putting Development First: The Importance of Policy Space in the WTO and IFIs*, London: Zed Press.

Weisbrot, M., D. Baker and S. Rosnick (2006) 'The Score Card on Development: 25 Years of Diminished Progress', UN DESA working paper 31.

Weisbrot, M., R. Naiman and J. Kim (2000) 'The Emperor Has No Growth: Declining Economic Growth Rates in the Era of Globalisation', briefing paper, September, Center for Economic and Policy Research, Washington, DC.

World Bank (1980) *World Development Report, 1980*, New York: Oxford University Press.

World Bank (1993) *The East Asian Miracle*, New York: Oxford University Press.

World Bank (2000/1) *World Development Report, 2000/1: Attacking Poverty*, New York: Oxford University Press.

World Bank (2002) *World Development Report, 2002: Building Institutions for Markets*, New York: Oxford University Press.

# 3
# Explaining Differential Performance: The Institutional Factor in Indian and Chinese Development

*Ashwani Saith*

## At the races

Ever since the achievement of independence in India in 1947, and of liberation in China in 1949, there has been intense interest in the comparative economic performance of the two Asian giants. China showcased revolutionary socialism; India aspired to a 'socialistic pattern of society' and boasted a parliamentary democracy. Who would win? In the charged post-colonial era of the cold war, on the eve of the release from the century of colonialism, the eyes of the many nations were on this race. The two great powers were also in the stands, with more than just a gambling stake or voyeuristic interest in the outcome – it was no ordinary day at the races.

Nehru, writing in 1954, is very forthright 'the most exciting countries for me today are India and China. We differ, of course, in our political and economic structures, yet the problems we face are essentially the same. The future will show which country and which structure of government yields greater results in every way'.[1] Fifty-two years later, in 2006, Prime Minister Nehru's question of the future is given an answer by India's current Prime Minister, Dr Manmohan Singh: 'It is almost sixty years since Independence ... Look at where China was and where it is today. Look at where the countries of South-east Asia were and where are they today? When I see them, I wonder whether we are living up to our full potential or not' (Singh, 2006).

Both countries wanted to modernize their systems and achieve rapid long-term growth with equity. However, perhaps in their own perceptions, the two horses were running different, independent, races. India mostly compared its performance with its own past, demonstrating the achievements of the new proud independent nation with the stagnation and mass deprivation of the colonial era. Against a stationary, stagnant object, this was not a particularly difficult race to win. A second yardstick was again the internal comparison with its own adopted plan targets – had they been achieved? Usually of course they had not. China, on the other hand, never seriously compared its own performance with its Himalayan neighbour. Doing better than India was not the issue: the challenge was to catch up with the West. In 1958, the Chinese Communist Party launched the campaign to 'Catch up with Great Britain in Fifteen Years'. China had set itself targets on a truly Himalayan scale.

Starting together in terms of similar initial conditions and levels of development, the two economies grow apart with China pulling ahead across the entire broad front of development indicators. In the very recent past, say since 2002, there has been an acceleration in the macroeconomic performance of the Indian economy, generating much triumphalism amongst the Indian elite, inducing speculation as to whether India is catching up with China, if the two economies are converging, with the seriously optimistic in India daring to ask if India might soon overtake China.

## Matched competitors?

Was the outcome of the race biased by the initial inequality between the competitors at the starting line? Were the two fairly matched? The comparison cannot be limited to a single economic axis, and account has to be taken of other initial conditions, colonial legacies and systemic features. Both systems inherit semi-feudal, semi-colonial economies characterized by mass rural poverty. Tawney (1932), Mallory (1926) and Buck (1938) testify to the structural vulnerabilities of the Chinese peasantry, just as Dutt (1902, 1904), Naoroji (1901), Digby (1901) and others attest to the state of rural destitution in late colonial India. Both societies display acute, entrenched forms of patriarchy with its flagrant manifestations of gender violence and oppressions. But alongside this, there is evidence that both systems had maturing non-agricultural economies involving comparatively developed systems of technology. Mark Elvin (1972, 1973) advances the notion of the high-level equilibrium trap for explaining Chinese economic stagnation in pre-liberation China; variously, many historians, including Tapan Raychaudhuri (1969), Amiya Bagchi (1976) and Bipin Chandra (1969) have argued that deindustrialization under colonialism interrupted an embryonic, potentially viable process of capitalist economic development. By the time of independence, both countries had distressed agricultural systems and high inequalities with a not insignificant rate of potential economic surplus, but without any institutional framework or economic mechanisms for utilizing this productively for modern economic growth.

Similarities notwithstanding, there are also some profound differences. One prime contrast lies in the realm of society and culture. China is characterized by the overwhelming dominance of the Han ethnic group; numerically it constitutes roughly 90 per cent of the population. There is just one dominant language which functions effectively as the lingua franca across the entire nation. Such cultural homogeneity provided a vital, actively enabling environment for the specific needs of Chinese development. It created the platform for a broad acceptance and legitimation of state authority structures; for a commonality of sociocultural orientations and 'national' interests; and contributed crucially to the viability of what I call the mass mobilization mode of transformation. The contrast with India could not be wider, with its mosaic of languages and cultures; its frictional cellular structures and finely tuned grammar of social exclusion in terms of caste, class, ethnic and religious identities. It is this homogeneity that enabled China to transform so radically its institutions and economy in such a short frame of time, just as it is the complexity and anti-polarity of Indian society that rendered rapid Indian change more contested and difficult.

The vital difference remains in the constitution of initial state power in the two systems, and that is itself a product of the political forces and processes that achieved independence from colonialism. While both post-independent governments inherited a stagnating agriculture, with most of the surplus squeezed out by a non-investing class of landlords, there was one telling difference. This landlord class lost out in the socialist revolution in China; but landed interests, albeit in a modified form, remained powerful in India as an integral part of the winning coalition of classes that gained independence, protected by, and well ensconced in, the ruling political party, and able to thwart any further redistributive or collectivist agrarian reforms.

In China, power emerges in the hands of a revolutionary socialist party based on peasants and workers; the poor controlled the commanding heights. The mass acceptance of this revolutionary power, alongside the high degree of cultural homogeneity, lays the basis for the mass mobilization mode of production certainly in the period up to, and partially beyond, the reforms of 1978. Oppressive and exclusionary power structures are swept away in the revolutionary struggles involving military action against colonials and indigenous class oppositions.

In contrast, in India, the control of the independence movement remains fundamentally in the hands of the middle and upper classes, and thus the structures that emerge with independence, including the state, while being nationalist in language and some substance, remain primarily the instruments of the broad class interests of the propertied sections that form the backbone of the Indian National Congress party at the time. Gandhian non-violence, while intrinsically laudable, was also opportunistically used at key conjunctures to prevent the leadership and control of rising potential mass movements to slip away from the indigenous elite. The direct violence of Japanese colonialism further radicalized and hastened the Chinese revolution, whereas the sophisticated cunning of the British rulers was mindful that post-independence power should remain in the hands of the Indian elite with which it could continue, in due course, to do business.

Despite all the specificities, in 1950, India and China had remarkably similar economic structures. Thomas Weisskopf estimates a per capita GDP (in US$ at 1960 prices) of 65 for China, and 62 for India. In the labour force, the share of agriculture was 77 per cent in China and 72 per cent in India; industry: 7 per cent in China and 11 per cent in India; and other sectors: 16 per cent in China and 17 per cent in India. In China, in 1952, the share of agriculture in total output was 48 per cent; in India, in 1950, it was 51 per cent. Large-scale manufacturing and utilities generated 9 per cent of the total output in China and 6 per cent in India; small-scale manufacturing and construction accounted for 9 per cent in China and 10 per cent in India (Weisskopf, 1980, pp. 81–2). The competitors were clearly well matched at the starting line.

## Who is ahead?

### The bottom line[2]

What has happened thus far? There can really be little argument that China has performed emphatically better than India. Starting from a virtually identical position in 1950, China's per capita income stands at twice the level of India in 2003; it has a much lower incidence of headcount poverty regardless of the specific methodologies used; its life expectancy at 71 is 6 years more than that of the average Indian; its adult literacy rate is 91 per cent compared to 65 per cent for India; it has more than twice as many physicians per head of population than India; only 8 per cent of its under-fives are moderately underweight and none are severely so, whereas for India as many as 47 per cent are moderately or severely underweight; only 14 per cent of these children suffer from moderate or severe stunting in China, but as many as 46 per cent do in India.

At the outset, while China had less arable land per capita, this was cultivated more intensively and with higher physical yields, so that per capita agricultural output was not much different from the Indian level. By 1978, clearly discernible differences in the conditions of the agricultural sector had emerged and distances in social indicators had magnified dramatically in favour of superior Chinese performance, and, by the turn of the millennium, the gaps in productivity indicators had become chasms. In terms of agricultural yields (in kilograms per hectare) for the 2003–05 period, wheat stood at 2,688 in India against 4,155 in China; rape/mustard was 909 in India and nearly twice that level, at 1,778, in China; and rice in India was 3,034 and more than twice as much, at 6,233, in China. The annual growth rates for yields during the 1990–2005 period for rape/mustard were 0.6 per cent in India and 3 per cent in China; and those for rice, 1.0 per cent in India and 2.1 per cent in China. Not only are the levels higher, but they are also diverging for some of the main crops.

On other comparisons, Chinese electricity consumption per capita, a crucial indicator, is 893 kWh in China, compared with just 379 in India; cement production is 650 m tons per year in China and 109 in India; steel production is 163 m tons in China and 29 m tons in India. In China, as much as 53 per cent of GDP comes from industry; in India, only 26 per cent. Of course, in comparison, India obtains 52 per cent of its GDP from services, while the percentage for China is only 32 – though it is questionable if this comparison fully reflects a mature, or a partially residual, services sector. Regardless of this, the Chinese growth rates in agriculture, industry and services are all above the Indian ones.

And for those who might point to India's sterling IT sector performance, it is worth noting that the fixed line and mobile phone subscribers per 1,000 people in China were 424 in 2003, as against just 71 in India; that Internet users per 1,000 people in China were 63, as against 17 in India; and that personal computers per 1,000 persons were 28 in China (in 2002) compared with 7 in India. Yet others might wish to dwell on the merchandise bilateral trade surplus in India's favour, as trade burgeons between them; but they would do well to scrutinize the pattern of trade and reflect on the sobering finding that more than 50 per cent of India's exports to China were made up of iron ore, while the largest imports from China into India were machinery.

### Already a gap at the midway point

Even while noting the debate over the dating of the Indian neo-liberal reforms, variably between 1980 and 1990, the crucial fact is that the differential performance was already observable in good measure by 1978. By 1980, the share of GDP from industry had exploded to 48.5 per cent in China, but was only 21.9 per cent in India; for 2003, the figures were 53 per cent and 26 per cent, respectively. A massive gap had opened up, significantly, by 1980, and has persisted since then. On the other hand, the share of agriculture in GDP had, by 1980, dropped in China to 30.1 per cent (compared to 42.8 per cent for India); and it fell further to just 15 per cent by 2003 (23 per cent for India). India showed a much higher share for services throughout, being 35.3 per cent in 1980 (21.4 per cent for China) and 52 per cent in 2003 (32 per cent for China) (Weisskopf, 1980). It is this sort of comparison that has prompted many to regard China as the world's factory, and India as the world's office.

Thus, from the same starting point around 1950, China had outpaced India dramatically in the first three decades of planned development and pulled away further on most material and human development indicators in the second, market-led phase. Significantly, this was notable also in the rural sector: between 1961–70, the average annual growth rate of agricultural production was −0.4 per cent in India and 3.7 per cent in China; for the following decade 1971–80, the rates were 0.4 per cent and 1.5 per cent, respectively (Saith, 1995b, Table 5).

The answer to the question as to who won the race is therefore not much in doubt. Indeed the margin of the victory, after the first 50 years, is quite astonishing, and one that might have alarmed Nehru should he have seen it, and one that could well explain the touch of ruefulness in Manmohan Singh's implicit acknowledgement of economic defeat.

### A winning ingredient: rural collectives

If a wide gap was already apparent halfway in the race, explanations must also be sought in factors active prior to the reforms. There are close similarities between the early Indian and Chinese development strategies, at least at the level of idea and intent, if not in terms of ground realities of implementation and of outcomes. In both economies, the state-led, public-sector-based industrialization process was the key driver. In the context of the seminal Indian Second Five Year Plan (1956–61), Prasanta Chandra Mahalanobis had argued the case for a land reform, for a land army that would provide universal employment to the rural landless for the purposes of constructing rural infrastructure, and had conceptualized the need for a rural or traditional small scale industrial sector that would be given some protection and which would balance the anticipated deficit of the employment equation for the modern industrial sector. This has considerable resonance with key elements of the Maoist development strategy in rural China. The parallel goes further. In both, the central government did not invest heavily in rural development. And while the Indian process wound up protecting or subsidizing the rural elite, the Chinese actually siphoned a surplus from agriculture and the peasantry in favour of modern industrialization. Yet, the rural sector and the peasantry did remarkably better in China than in India. Why? How?

### The institutional factor: enabling or constraining change?

The real contrast was in the foundation: in the nature of the state and in the institutional realities of economy, society and polity within which the ideas and plans were to be realized. The overwhelmingly significant difference was in the institutional configuration of the rural sector.

The term institutional is interpreted here in its broadest form. Usually, these institutional dimensions, which underpin and stabilize socioeconomic and political transactions and societal arrangements, are the cement that bind units, provide the parameters of dynamic evolutions usually with a high degree of path dependent, clay-clay stickiness, and add a degree of inertial ballast to the system as a whole. Continuity is thus written into the script, not discontinuous change; evolutionary trends, rather than revolutionary breaks. No doubt old India and China could have been similarly thus regarded. But the Chinese revolution broke the inherited feudal mould; Indian independence merely tinkered marginally with the basic institutional frame. While the institutional framework served as a contextual rigidity and as an 'inherited' development constraint in India, in contrast the Chinese socialist development state was able to address the institutional framework as a prime policy target variable, to be refashioned instrumentally as deemed functionally optimal with respect to accelerating the growth process. This dimension provides an underlying unifying leitmotif over the entire period since 1949 in China. Kojima Reiitsu, the astute analyst of China, described this as the perennial Chinese search for institutions that seek out, release and exploit new potential sources of accumulation and growth, irrespective of the ideological lexicon adopted at the time. This resonates with Deng Xiaoping's celebrated aphorism: 'I do not care about the colour of the cat so long as it catches the mice'. Continuity across seemingly conflicting regime types is provided by the underlying foundation of implicit societal consensus prioritizing sustained material advancement and national strength.

## Handling the Ricardian constraint: a comparison of the land reform processes

As early as the Second Five Year Plan, various economists, including Michal Kalecki (1964) and Maurice Dobb (1951), had pointed to the need to break the Ricardian constraint, a euphemism for the power of the landed classes, that would otherwise hold back Indian growth. The need for meaningful land reforms, which catered both to equity and efficiency considerations, was paramount. But no such resolution took place. Indian agrarian reforms have a long history of leading eventually to not much. This process culminated in North India, in the post-Independence Zamindari Abolition Act that provided firm ownership rights only to a class of superior tenants who formed the first land-operating layer under the erstwhile land owning *zamindars* and *taluqdars*. These beneficiaries were strongly represented in the Congress Party, and this has much to do with the subsequent loss of all momentum for further redistributive or radical land reforms in the direction of cooperatives. In the absence of a labour market pull factor, the agrarian structure has shown acute signs of disaggregation through the progressive subdivision of owned holdings under conditions of a turgid and blocked land market. The result is that there is massive (near-)landlessness, a dominance of uneconomic marginal, fragmented holdings, with the vast majority of holdings being below a scale which can even guarantee a reasonable level of living. This trend has been secular and relentless. In such scenarios, the small islands of commercial agriculture do not have any compensatory capacity of employment generation, and general production-orientated strategies structurally fail to reach the poor sections of the rural population. The role of cooperative and collective rural institutional arrangements has been widely emphasized, including for instance by Joan Robinson: 'Some kind of cooperative or collective property in land and in means of production is necessary to provide a frame in which modernization can go on without polarization between wealth and misery which it is bringing about all over the Third World today' (Robinson, 1979, p. 135). It is worth recording that each of the successful East Asian cases has incorporated such a powerful egalitarian land reform virtually as an initial precondition.

China effectively overcame the Ricardian barrier through the replacement of the feudal agrarian structure by egalitarian and simultaneously dynamic, growth-orientated people's communes. The initial land reforms of 1949–52 left substantial residual asset inequalities which were addressed through the subsequent creation of elementary and then advanced producer cooperatives, culminating in the formation of the first, problematic type of large people's communes covering 98 per cent of the countryside by September 1958. The final stages of the transition had taken just three years. The remodelled, smaller, three-tier commune then held sway from 1962 till the launch of the reforms.

The second reform of 1979–83, when the rural collectives were essentially dismantled and land redistributed back to the peasant households, was as dramatically precipitous. In a country as vast as China, the revolutionary collectivist reforms had been virtually reversed to peasant holdings in the breathless space of just two years.

This abolition of the people's communes, while providing each household with the universal land endowment which served as a cushion and insurance against the vicissitudes of the new strategy, had itself also created the need for such insurance by cutting off the direct access that peasants had earlier to the jobs and economic surpluses generated by the dynamic commune and brigade run enterprises. The balance sheet of the second land reform is complex. But what it demonstrates again is the ability of the system to reshape its basic institutions and organizational framework to make them functional to the perceived needs of any reorientations in the development strategy. The contrast with the Indian scenario could not be more extreme.

### Chinese collective labour accumulation versus Indian rural public works

It is instructive to look inside the rural people's communes in China's period of high collectivism, 1962–78.[3] With characteristic ideological ingenuity, Mao introduced a notion of labour accumulation, in contradistinction to capital accumulation. Essentially, he argued that in a populous poor agrarian economy, there was an opportunity to create rural land-related infrastructure through an investment of this peasant labour into accumulation projects, hence labour accumulation (LA). Such labour was dramatically mobilized across China, and formed one of twin engines of rural development – all this in a period when it is acknowledged that the pattern of intersectoral resource flows was tilted against the rural sector by State policy. Such LA had a major impact on agricultural productivity in large parts of rural China, and provided both the demand and supply side impulses that triggered off a dynamic growth process within the communes. The other engine was rural industrialization within the commune. This also used surplus labour from within the collective and generated high financial surpluses, which went into four major uses: further diversification of the unit's non-farm portfolio of activities; significantly, into projects of agricultural development; into providing a social consumption floor to all the members of the unit; and into further strengthening the capacity of local government. Peasants contributed high productivity labour in rural non-farm activities and hard manual labour in LA projects, but they were paid in work points at an implicit wage rate that was linked to the average consumption level of the peasant households of the unit concerned. As a result, financial surpluses earned by the rural non-farm units accumulated almost automatically and were recycled with their dynamic multipliers generating locally egalitarian growth. LA has been criticized, naïvely, by many as an example of corvée, or coerced, unpaid labour. This is patently incorrect, since the labour investment of households in any one year on a productive project earned its returns once the project's benefits came online after completion, and these benefits accrued to all members of the collectively owned unit – hence its label, labour accumulation. While there were surely some white elephants, no serious scholar or observer of rural China of the period could fail to register the remarkable impact of such a massive, countrywide, bootstraps type of operation. It launched and catalysed the rural development process. From the point of view of rural households, this was additional work for additional income, not just from the LA project, but also from the indirect returns that came from the rural industrialization that it enabled. This process, which I call the mass mobilization mode of transformation, was essentially fired by ideological zeal and commitment interfaced with well-thought–out, cooperative, payment systems with a robust economic logic for that stage of development. The process was locally self-financing, and hence both sustainable for an extended period, as well as capable of nationwide replication.

It would be unthinkable that this scale of rural investment and transformation could have been initiated by free market signals within an inegalitarian agrarian structure, as indeed the dismal experience of rural South Asia confirms. The current discussions over the alleged financial constraint to the implementation of any universal employment guarantee scheme in India provides a good example. The schemes have to be prefinanced. There has never really been a hard enough look taken at their productivity. And even when the infrastructure created by the scheme is productive, the government is unable to include the incremental benefits in its resource mobilization net. This enormously limits their scope and coverage. There are some fundamental blindspots in the manner in which such interventions are designed, implemented, evaluated and legitimized: their methodology hides the reality that the primary beneficiaries of these public investments made in the name of the rural poor turn out to be the free-riding rural rich.[4]

## The productivity versus employment trade-off: mechanization

Two examples demonstrate how this vexatious trade-off was resolved by the institutional rules of the rural collective. First, the power of the collective institutional arrangements with regard to land ownership is again demonstrated by the case of labour-displacing but productivity-enhancing technological change. This could take the form of the mechanization of various otherwise labour-intensive operations, extending from land preparation to planting, irrigation, harvesting, threshing, etc. In the Indian case, this leads to labour displacement and the loss of wages for the laid-off workers; in the Chinese case, the productivity gains are shared by all workers, who now acquire some time for other productive activities. Thus, while both India and China had acute problems of surplus labour, China adopted extensive rural mechanization even while stressing labour accumulation projects in parallel. The gap between private and social profitability of mechanization was not relevant in the Chinese collective, but was wide in the Indian case, taking the form of the loss of incomes of displaced agricultural workers.

Another pertinent example of efficacious institutional change in China, is provided by the case of rural industrial enterprises. At the time of the formation of the people's communes, the scattered traditional low productivity and low technology rural crafts and manufacturing activities were centralized within the cooperative structure, and then rationalized and modernized as cooperative ventures. There was no danger of the familiar story of the destitution of the uncompetitive rural handicrafts sector, since here the displaced persons could be absorbed in the agricultural sector if necessary. The growth of rural demand, in any event, limited the need for such relocations. Also, these enterprises were located within the commune and were thus owned by the peasants, not by rich landlords. Thus, the process and product upgrading and modernization using mechanized labour-displacing methods in these rural handicraft enterprises could be managed without creating the classic flow of impoverished expelled rural artisans. The conflict, so characteristic of capitalist systems, between higher productivity through labour displacement on the one hand, and employment generation and distributional outcomes on the other, was pre-empted, with institutional change converting the nature of the game.

In contrast, in India, rural artisans and handicrafts have suffered steady erosion through unsustainable competition with modern manufactures. Over the decades, the outcome has been the virtual disappearance of the traditional manufacturing sector from village India, with only non-tradeable goods and services surviving in pockets. The share of incomes of villagers that is earned from activities located in the village have steadily declined, being replaced by various forms of labour and poverty-propelled participation in unskilled self-employment activities. Even when there are profitable rural enterprises, their surpluses do not get rechannelled into rural development, poverty reduction, infrastructure or further accumulation within the rural sector. The owners tend to invest in urban trade and property, leading to a further atrophying of the rural sector, thus intensifying the pressure to migrate.[5]

### The mass mobilization mode (MMM) of transformation

In 1955, an Indian delegation visited China (and Japan) to study the role of agrarian cooperatives in development and carry back transferable lessons applicable in the Indian rural landscape. The ensuing report bears testimony to the explosion of collective energy in rural China:

> The phenomenal success achieved by the Chinese in the formation of agrarian cooperatives has astonished all, both inside China and outside it. To a visiting team from India, such as ours, who are used to individual cultivation, the Chinese success appeared no less than a miracle. Naturally, the first question that strikes anybody is, how was all this achieved in such a short period? (GOI, 1956, p. 86)

In Mao-speak, the answer lay 'in releasing the enthusiasm of the masses'. Anti-socialists tend to query, if not dismiss altogether, any claims of voluntarism in such transformations; it is interesting then to read the reaction of a contemporary visiting Indian team of bureaucrats and politicians in 1956 on this issue:

> Coercion is the negation of enthusiasm. The enthusiastic outburst of energy which we saw, could not be expected from a people who had been coerced into cooperatives. We noticed among them a great patriotic fervour which reminded us of the great patriotic zeal which had seized our own people in their fight for freedom in the thirties and forties of the century. To the peasants in China, increased income and better living was only one aspect of the producers' cooperatives.

We were repeatedly told that in joining cooperatives, they were working for the development of the country and towards a Socialist transformation of Society. (GOI, 1956, p. 95)

One key instrumental mechanism in the MMM was the campaign responding to a slogan launched by the Party. The campaign could involve a political action against perceived enemies of the revolution, or be an intervention to modify group behaviour whether in the cultural or economic domains, or be an action to catalyse particular forms of investment, development or environmental change. Often, there would be a successful role model held up for emulation, as for instance in the case of the development of the Dazhai brigade where sheer peasant labour was pitted against extreme natural odds to demonstrate the socialist capacity to mould and wrest its own future even in the face of highly adverse circumstances. Other powerful campaigns involved the development of the five small rural industries within the collective framework; yet another was the Four Pests campaign of the 1950s against mosquitoes, flies, rats and sparrows. Vast amounts of labour were enthusiastically mobilized and expended. When these were successes, they were phenomenal; when they were failures, the scale of replication was also massive. The latter was demonstrated in the case of the elimination of sparrows in the countryside, and the subsequent discovery that they had been crucial for protecting the crops from various insects; another failure was the case of rural small-scale chemical and fertilizer plants that wound up severely polluting local water bodies. However, these problems, which remained the exception rather than the rule, were acknowledged and addressed, as far as possible, as they became apparent.

Several latent and active factors combined to form the preconditions for the successful exploitation of the MMM. First, the existence of cultural homogeneity on a near-national scale; second, a powerful sense of ownership of the state by the masses and a strong sense of identification with it; third, the mass appeal of many major rural policy interventions made by the state, e.g. land reforms, rural industries, rural socioeconomic security policies; fourth, an efficient organizational framework for enabling two-way flows of information; fifth, a powerful, unified command structure; sixth, the use of instruments for the ideological motivation of the rural masses; finally, success itself was the lubricant for sustaining the process – the benefits of economic achievements were widely shared and there for most to experience, and this made the hard work seem right and worthwhile.

## Structural outcomes

Most economic observers of India are so mesmerized by the so-called convergence in the overall growth rates that they tend to ignore the plight of the rural sector. Virtually in every respect it has fallen steadily further behind the levels attained in China, whether in terms of indicators of positive structural change, employment generation, output growth, input use and productivity, exports and investment. Rural capital investment fell in real terms. Rural employment suffered. Rural income poverty rates fell, officially, though no plausible pathology could be demonstrated for this outcome to be credible, other than a faulty poverty-line methodology. Again, there are signs of enclaves of commercialization and capitalization in agriculture, with the entry of corporates, MNCs and financial companies into rural markets. But these are tiny, even if growing, islands of capitalist intervention. Rural poverty is being exported increasingly into the urban sector for lack of options. Close observers of Indian agriculture refer to a state of agrarian crisis, manifest in the suicide of over 100,000 farmers over the past decade in a number of states, including Maharashtra and Punjab, two of the richest in India. It is clear that the rural sector lacks the capacity to serve as a 'sink' or reservoir for holding the massive 'residual' un- and under-employment for the rural population. But worryingly, there are few signs that the high growth rates of the non-agricultural economy are translating into a significantly increased capacity for labour absorption. The high growth rates here have created few jobs in manufacturing. While services have generated jobs, it is unclear what proportion of these are poverty-driven, survival-orientated activities of the poor obstinately scratching out a living, as against dynamic high-productivity jobs. The Lewisian process of transfer of labour has stalled. And the inexorable process of subdivision of owned holdings in agriculture now shows that only a miniscule fraction of rural households own enough land to make a poverty-line income from agriculture alone. The rural sector in India has seriously underperformed in terms of averages for the sector; when the process of rural polarization is factored into this, it becomes plain that the conditions of the majority are even worse than those implied by the averages.

China provides a contrast. Despite the rural population falling continuously further behind the urban beneficiaries of China's explosive growth, there is some credible speculation at present that China might well be approaching the Lewisian turning point in labour markets. After a period of widening intrarural income inequalities, some recent survey findings reported by A. R. Khan (2005) suggest a reduction in rural inequalities, primarily sourced in a reduced gap in wage incomes, in the receipt of transfer incomes (mainly migrants' remittances) and in progressive fiscal transfers (implying some role for state policy). Rural China does need the Chinese government to act effectively and quickly in some important areas of economic and social policy; but, this notwithstanding, the overall story is one of outstanding success with little resemblance to the experience of the overwhelming majority of the rural population in India.

## Is India catching up?

There is much talk in India of catching up with China. Is this just premature triumphalism, voicing the good times of the emerging new elites? There is a simplistic answer to this in terms of growth rates, but the comparison has other relevant dimensions.

### Persisting divergence

Important gaps persist: India significantly lags behind in agricultural performance, employment generation and poverty reduction. The pace of Chinese infrastructure development is in a different league from India's. The demographic patterns of the two also continue to diverge, with China's one-child policy and improving longevity now manifesting in a prematurely ageing population structure with a high dependency load on a slow-growing workforce, while India's population pyramid remains much broader at the base. Optimistically, this has been identified as the source of a demographic premium in favour of India, but its realization would clearly be contingent on meeting several preconditions, and that calls for additional doses of optimism. Hunger has become a faded memory in China, though it remains a daily reality for very many in India. China's lack of liberal political democracy survives intact; so does the rich man's version of Indian parliamentary democracy that keeps coming up trumps for the middle and upper classes. Chinese socialism has not yielded liberal political rights; and neither India's socialistic, nor its neo-liberal, paths have delivered adequate material and human development benefits to the masses. No osmotic convergence is in evidence in either system in this regard. So, many trends display divergence.

### Some convergence

Are there indications of positive convergence, of catching up on some of each other's positive features? In the past decade, the Indian economy has posted high growth rates but the level has remained consistently higher for China, implying that in terms of *absolute* levels of achievement, there is little likelihood of India catching up or overtaking China. There will eventually be convergence in literacy and education, as India expands its coverage in the future from universal primary to secondary schooling. But even here, indicators focusing on quality or on resources per student fail to converge. Likewise, the absolute gap in longevity might decrease as diminishing returns set in and make each additional life-year more difficult and expensive to achieve; but the quality of health care might well continue to show diverging trends alongside this. But there are also signs that some traditional Indian advantages might have begun to wear out. The Chinese educational system is placing a high emphasis on languages, especially English, and the historical advantage still enjoyed by India might soon erode.

## Much 'pervergence'

By 'pervergence' I mean a convergence, where the two systems catch up on each other's negative features. There is indeed a steady flow of evidence suggesting that the two systems are perverging, arising from China's rapidly beginning to display some of the negative socioeconomic and political governance features of the Indian system. It is difficult to say if the loss of the values of socialist community has been greater and more devastating than the loss of democratic and 'socialistic' norms and ways of being, if ever these prevailed in India. In both systems, the public good has been thoroughly privatized.

China's achievements with regard to poverty reduction have been undermined by the recent dramatic rise in the socioeconomic vulnerability of the rural population, predominantly on account of their inability to access increasingly expensive health and education systems. It is arguable that post-reform education policies are creating significant educational and social exclusion, and leading to the serious emergence of child labour, thus laying the foundations for the creation of a new underclass of underprivileged, undereducated people in China. Health outcomes are similarly regressive. While the levels of Chinese health-related indicators remain well ahead of the Indian ones, there are distressing signs of shrinkage of access to health services for a significant proportion of the population. From a near universal coverage system, albeit with varying quality levels, the last two decades display a trend of atrophy (Chen and Shiva Kumar, 2007, p. 164).

While the overall sex ratios are similarly low, in the range of 930 to 945 females per 1000 males, what is alarming is the recent trend in sex ratios at birth. Both countries show despicable outcomes, confirmation that patriarchical biases in India are alive and well even if many a girl child is not; and that in China a generation of revolutionary gains in the domain of gender appear to have been casually reversed in half that time, with a reversion to the traditional attitudes of patriarchal dominance within families, with strong son preference, and an exalted role for the male head of the household. Pervergence here is dramatic and occurring in double-quick time.

Governance issues are becoming increasingly important, with high levels of corruption. Transparency International's Corruption Perception Index sees China and India dropping down the table, and while India has always been bad, China, as a new entrant, has fast caught up with India. For India, political parties, the judiciary, the police and parliament and legislature get the worst scores on the corruption index. This says something about the quality of democracy, beyond simply the issue of its formal existence. There is an inexorable, attritional deterioration in the quality of public life in the country, with flagrant corruption, criminality and communalism in the body politic. For China, the entry of big business into the upper echelons of the Communist Party and leadership at all levels of government perhaps obviates the need for businessmen to try to influence politicians with bribes; this tendency of the cosying up of the Party and business provides a new dimension to the notion of the 'embedded state'. The mind travels to *Animal Farm*, where the post-revolution subjects 'looked from man to pig, and from pig to man, and could not tell which was which'.

The state of the environment provides another distressing example of China's race to the bottom with India. Indian and Chinese cities are equally murky, their rivers as polluted; and if the last tiger is consumed in China, it will most likely be an Indian poacher who will have delivered it to the traditional pharmacist or niche restaurant. Finally, in both systems, inequality at the upper end has skyrocketed, taking extreme and vulgar forms, to levels that cannot remotely be justified in terms of any hypothesized functionality with respect to incentives for investment and growth.

There is, then, evidence of some positive convergence, but also of much 'pervergence'. Arguably, China is clearly catching up faster with India's negative traits than India is with China's positive features. This raises the question whether too much attention has been focused on the wrong race.

## Socialism: pioneer of capitalism?

Of course, a comparative reflection on the development experience of these two great civilizations cannot really be reduced to a multiple-choice balance sheet, or be treated as laboratory evidence for the 'superiority' of capitalism vis-à-vis socialism. In focusing exclusively on the numerics of the economic race, one loses sight of the complex evolutionary processes of societal dynamics, and the historical significance of Indian democracy and Chinese socialism as catalysts of such transformations.

After lengthy eras of feudal and colonial experience, both countries broke away at the same historical moment. They also detached, to different degrees, from the world system and began to rely on autonomous, though not autarkic, planned development in an attempt at rapid and egalitarian development to overcome the inertia and deficits generated by colonial domination. This break can be described in Toynbee's terminology of challenge and response, or in terms of Gerschenkron's analysis of the role of the state as an agent of transformation overcoming relative historical backwardness, or in Marxian categories and dynamics in terms of modes of production. While each approach highlights the discontinuous nature of this change, none can satisfactorily explain its timing, nor predict its subsequent course, its permanence or its dissipation. The early development paths of both China and India represented oppositional projects to market-based capitalist change, though with profound differences of substance partially disguised by the radical vocabulary of Indian planning. The Chinese path was a full-blooded socialist one, whereas the Indian one was described as being 'socialistic' rather than socialist. Oskar Lange described it as an example of a 'national revolutionary pattern' of change. The Indian state, regardless of its propertied-class base, spoke of controlling the commanding heights of the Indian economy, of redirecting a state-led development process towards achieving social objectives. Underlying it implicitly was an imagined community and nation reflecting the aspirations set down in the constitution. It is interesting to note that in both countries this initial transformative project, based on such a reality (in China) or a notion (in India) of shared community values, lasts only three decades up to the new era of reforms ushering in capitalist growth, albeit with its variations, in both countries. In this current phase, while both emphasize economic modernization, there is an atrophying of the initial socialist or socialistic aspirations that epitomized the first independent governments. Now, both countries have re-entered the global capitalist order, but on dramatically revised terms – not as basket cases but as dynamos of global growth. The oppositional project has

yielded to its antithesis. This raises the question of the historical significance of the state-led non-capitalist or socialist interventions in each
country. These could be understood as historical systemic corrections
to the evolutionary accumulation of inefficiencies in economic institutions, and the extreme inequalities in material consumption, status and
political power. Viewed thus, China has clearly emerged with a massively
successful correction in terms of economic and human development; an
agenda of political democratization dominates the future. For India, the
corrections are far less dramatic, and the emergent economy and nation
retains the extreme inequalities and exclusions that it set out to overcome. Its politically democratic system has on the whole failed to deliver
inclusive economically democratic outcomes thus far. With its superior
fiscal strength, and its much more culturally cohesive sociocultural fabric
and strong central state, China would appear to be rather better placed
to enact further socially progressive corrections than might be extracted
in the Indian case, where the new elite dominates state and society
and successfully resists any serious attempts at any significant forms of
redistribution other than the periodic handouts induced by fear and the
need to manage to win elections every few years. In the long sweep of
historical change, socialism in China and planned development in India
have served as far more effective pioneers of capitalism in the two countries than imperialism or colonialism ever did. Just as the other India
is made to wait on its political democracy to deliver sustainable growth
that is inclusive and egalitarian, the other China waits to add meaningful political rights to its considerable economic gains. The clock ticks
impatiently on how long either people will be held back.

## Notes

1. Quoted in Frankel (1984, p. 120); cited by Ghosh (2002).
2. The data in this section are assembled from a variety of official Chinese, Indian
   and international sources.
3. For detailed analysis of the Chinese experience before and after the Reforms,
   see Saith (1987, 1993, 1995a, 2001, pp. 90–4) and Griffin and Saith (1981).
4. For an elaboration, see Saith (2005).
5. I have analysed this process in general in Saith (1992), and with specific
   reference to the Indian case in Saith (2001).

## References

Bagchi, A. K. (1976) 'De-industrialisation in India in the Nineteenth Century:
Some Theoretical Implications', *Journal of Development Studies* 12 (2).

Buck, J. Lossing (1938) *Land Utilization in China*, Chicago: University of Chicago Press.

Chandra, Bipin (1969) Contribution in M. D. Morris (ed.) (1969) *The Indian Economy in the Nineteenth Century: A Symposium*, Delhi: IESHR.

Chen, Lincoln C. and A. K. Shiva Kumar (2007) 'Turnaround in China's Health Policies?', *Indian Journal of Human Development* 1 (1): 161–8.

Dernberger, Robert F. (ed.) (1980) *China's Development Experience in Comparative Perspective*, Cambridge, MA: Harvard University Press.

Digby, William (1901) *'Prosperous' British India: A Revelation from Official Records*, London: T. Fisher Unwin.

Dobb, M. H. (1951) *Some Aspects of Economic Development: Three Lectures*, Occasional Paper, Delhi School of Economics: University of Delhi.

Dutt, Romesh (1902, 1904) *The Economic History of India*, 2 vols, London: Routledge & Kegan Paul (1902); Kegan Paul, Trench Trubner (1904).

Elvin, Mark (1972) 'The High-level Equilibrium Trap: The Causes of the Decline of Invention in Traditional Chinese Textile Industries', in W. E. Willmott (ed.) *Economic Organization in Chinese Society*, Stanford: Stanford University Press.

Elvin, Mark (1973) *The Pattern of the Chinese Past*, Stanford: Stanford University Press.

Frankel, Francine R. (1978) *India's Political Economy 1947–1977: The Gradual Revolution*, Princeton, NJ: Princeton University Press.

Ghosh, Suniti Kumar (2002) *The Himalayan Adventure: India-China War of 1962 Causes and Consequences*, Bombay: Rajani X. Desai.

Government of India (GOI) (1956) *Agrarian Cooperatives in China and Japan: Report of an Indian Visiting Delegation*, New Delhi: Planning Commission.

Griffin, K. B. and Ashwani Saith (1981) *Growth and Equality in Rural China*, Singapore: Maruzen.

Kalecki, M. (1964) 'Financial Problems of the Third Plan: Some Observations', *Economic Strategy and the Third Plan*, Indian Statistical Institute Series 21, New York: Asia Publishing House.

Khan, A. R. (2005) 'Inequality and Poverty in China in the Post-Reform Period: An Overview', *http://www.azizkhan.net/ChinaBagchiFest.pdf*

Mallory, Walter H. (1926) *China: Land of Famine*, New York: American Geographical Society.

Naoroji, Dadahai (1901) *Poverty and Un-British Rule in India*, London: Swan Sonnenschein.

Raychaudhuri, T. (1969) Contribution in M. D. Morris (ed.) (1969) *The Indian Economy in the Nineteenth Century: A Symposium*, Delhi: IESHR.

Robinson, Joan (1979) *Aspects of Development and Underdevelopment*, Cambridge: Cambridge University Press.

Saith, Ashwani (1978) 'Agrarian Structure, Technology and Marketed Surplus in the Indian Economy', PhD dissertation, University of Cambridge, UK.

Saith, Ashwani (1987) 'Contrasting Experiences of Rural Industrialisation: Are the East Asian Successes Transferable?', in R. Islam (ed.), *Rural Industrialisation and Employment in Asia*, New Delhi: ILO/ARTEP.

Saith, Ashwani (1992) *The Rural Non-Farm Economy: Processes and Policies*, Geneva: ILO.

Saith, Ashwani (1993) 'Chinese Rural Industrialisation: Some Lessons for Reforming and Developing Economies', ARTEP-ILO working paper, ILO, New Delhi, December.

Saith, Ashwani (1995a) 'From Collectives to Markets: Restructured Agriculture-Industry Linkages in Rural China: Some Micro-level Evidence', *Journal of Peasant Studies*, 22 (2): 201–60.

Saith, Ashwani (1995b) 'Reflections on South Asian Prospects in East Asian Perspective', Issues in Development discussion paper, ILO, Geneva.

Saith, Ashwani (2001) 'From Village Artisans to Industrial Clusters: Agendas and Policy Gaps in Indian Rural Industrialisation', *Journal of Agrarian Change*, 1 (1): 81–123.

Saith, Ashwani (2005) 'Poverty and Anti-Poverty: Troubling Tendencies and Quarrelsome Questions', Joan Robinson Memorial Lecture, Centre for Development Studies, Thiruvanthapuram, Kerala.

Singh, Manmohan (2006) 'Independence Day Address to the Nation', 15 August.

State Statistical Bureau (SSB) People's Republic of China. *Statistical Yearbook of China*, and *National Statistical Yearbook*, Beijing, various issues.

Tawney, R. H. (1932) *Land and Labour in China*, London: George Allen & Unwin Ltd.

Weisskopf, Thomas (1980) 'Patterns of Economic Development in India, Pakistan and Indonesia', in R. Dernberger (ed.), *China's Development Experience in Comparative Perspective*, Cambridge, MA: Harvard University Press, ch. 2.

# 4
# The Renaissance of China and India: Implications for the Advanced Economies*

*Robert Rowthorn*

## Introduction

China and India were once the richest areas in the world. They were first overtaken by Western Europe, then by European offshoots, such as the USA, and finally by some of the East Asian economies (Figure 4.1). Both China and India are now catching up rapidly. Barring some catastrophe, within a few decades China and India will once again be the largest economies in the world and their per capita incomes will be much higher than today. This chapter is concerned with the implications of this development for the existing advanced economies.

## China and India compared

Both India and China have undergone economic reforms designed to promote capitalist development, in each case with notable success, although the process is more advanced in China.

China had a lower per capita income than India in 1980. Since then Chinese growth has been so fast that per capita income is now more than twice that of India. However, Indian growth is accelerating and the country is apparently moving onto a Chinese-style growth path.

Measured at purchasing power parity, per capita income in China is still less than one sixth of the US level, but is growing extremely fast. Since 2000 per capita income has risen at 8.4 per cent a year as compared to 1.8 per cent in the USA. With these growth rates it would take China only 30 years to catch up with US per capita income. Until recently India's growth rate was well below that of China and since 2000 its per

*This chapter is an updated version of Rowthorn (2006).

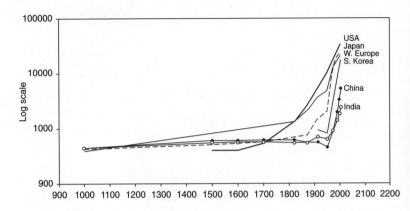

*Source*: Maddison (2001) updated using World Bank data.
*Figure 4.1*    GDP per capita, 1000–2004 (1990 international $ at PPP)

capita income has grown at an average rate of 4.6 per cent a year. At this rate it would take 95 years for India to catch up with the USA.

The above projections are unrealistic for two reasons. Chinese growth is likely to slow down in the medium term and Indian growth has been accelerating. I have therefore produced some more realistic projections of my own. I assume that both China and India will grow rapidly in the near future and that both will gradually slow down as their per capita incomes get closer to the US level. The slowing down process is modelled using a standard convergence equation (see Appendix 1).

Figure 4.2 shows projected values of GDP per capita, population and total GDP in China and India in 2050. GDP per capita is measured at purchasing power parity (PPP), which is the standard method for comparing living standards. Total GDP is measured in two ways – at purchasing power parity and at market exchange rates. All quantities are shown relative to the USA. Taking the USA = 100, it is projected that per capita GDP in China and India will be equal to 63 and 45, respectively, by 2050. Both countries will have much larger populations than the USA and, despite their lower per capita incomes, both countries will rival or surpass the USA in terms of total production by the end of the period. The exact relationship depends on how GDP is measured. Using the PPP measure of total output, both China and India comfortably overtake the USA by 2050. Such a comparison can be misleading as a guide to the global power of these countries, because it gives too much weight to the output of non-traded services, such as health and retail distribution. Although valuable to the local residents, these items are of secondary importance

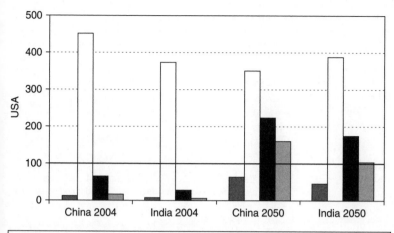

*Source*: UN and author's own projections based on World Bank data.
*Figure 4.2* Projected development of China and India, 2004–50 (per cent of USA)

in international affairs. The alternative is to use market exchange rates which give more weight to internationally traded items such as manufactured goods. Even with this measure, total production in China is 60 per cent larger than in the USA by 2050, whilst India and the USA are about equal. These projections should not be taken literally, but they do indicate the orders of magnitude involved.

It is often said that India has a different growth path from China, with a greater role for modern services, a smaller role for manufacturing and a much lower investment rate (Das, 2006; Dasgupta and Singh, 2005). There is some truth in these claims but they should not be exaggerated. The lower investment rate in India is associated with slower economic growth than in China, and as growth accelerates in India the investment rate is rising. India also has significant exports in IT-related areas such as software and call centres, whereas Chinese exports in these areas are still small. India's strength in services is indicated by the relatively high productivity in this sector, which employs 22 per cent of the workforce but accounts for more than 50 per cent of value added (Table 4.1). However, the manufacturing sector is now growing rapidly and the latest Five Year Plan has a target of 12 per cent a year growth in manufacturing output (Table 4.2). Indian manufactured exports are also growing fast.

India's strength in information technology is indicated by the fact that software exports have more than doubled in the past three years.

*Table 4.1*   India, China and South Korea compared

|  | India 2004 | China 1996 | China 2004 | Korea 1972 | Korea 1982 |
|---|---|---|---|---|---|
| GDP per capita (PPP at 2000 international $) | 2885 | 2971 | 5419 | 3014 | 5387 |
| Exports as % GDP | 19.1 | 20.1 | 34.1 | 19.4 | 33.2 |
| % of employment: |  |  |  |  |  |
| Agriculture | 60.4* | 47.7 | 44.1** | 50.5 | 32.1 |
| Industry | 16.9* | 25.5 | 21.2** | 17.9 | 27.9 |
| Services | 22.7* | 26.8+ | 34.7***+ | 31.7 | 40.1 |
| % of Value added: |  |  |  |  |  |
| Agriculture | 21.1 | 19.5 | 13.1 | 28.7 | 16.0 |
| Industry | 27.1 | 47.5 | 46.2 | 26.2 | 37.0 |
| Services | 51.7 | 33.0 | 40.7 | 45.1 | 47.0 |
| % urban | 28.5 | 32.2 | 39.6 | 43.6 | 60.1 |

*Note*: *1999/2000 (agriculture includes extraction); **2002; +includes activities not adequately defined.
*Sources*: Employment: China: ILO Labour Statistics Database (http://laborsta.ilo.org) plus Banister (2005a, Table 4), services include activities not adequately defined;
India: Dasgupta and Singh (2005, Table 3) adapted from Joshi (2004), agriculture includes mining; Korea: Korean Statistical Information Service (http://www.kosis.kr).
Other Data: World Bank, *World Development Indicators* (Korean 1972 by extrapolation using Maddison (2001)).

In 2005–06 India had a trade surplus of more than $22 billion on such items, which is equivalent to one sixth of total exports. A study by NASSCOM–McKinsey in 2005 estimated that India now accounts for 65 per cent of the global market in offshore IT and 46 per cent of the global business process offshoring segment (BPO). It also estimated that the 'total addressable market for global offshoring is approximately $300 billion, of which $110 billion will be offshored by 2010. India has the potential to capture more than 50 per cent of this opportunity and generate $60 billion by growing at 25 per cent year-on-year till 2010'.[1] India's strength in IT can also be very useful in the manufacturing sector, helping them to raise productivity and develop new, high, value-added products in this sector.

So far, at least, IT-related services are less important for China where the manufacturing sector plays a much larger role. Manufacturing production has grown strongly in recent years, and industry as a whole, including construction, now accounts for 46 per cent of value added.

*Table 4.2* Macroeconomic indicators for Indian Five Year Plans

|  | 8th Plan 1992–1997 (actual) | 9th Plan 1997–2002 (actual) | 10th Plan 2002–2007 (actual) | 11th Plan 2007–2012 (target) |
|---|---|---|---|---|
| Growth rate of GDP (% p.a.); *of which* | 6.7 | 5.5 | 7.2 | 9 |
| Agriculture | 4.7 | 2 | 1.7 | 4.1 |
| Industry; *of which* |  | 4.6 | 8.3 | 10.5 |
| Manufacturing | 7.6 | 4.5 | 8 | 12 |
| Services | 7.5 | 8.1 | 9 | 9.9 |
| Investment rate (% of GDP) | 24.8 | 23.8 | 27.8 | 35.1 |

*Note*: The numbers shown here are reproduced in the form they were given in the original planning documents. This explains why some are whole numbers and why there is an observation missing.
*Source*: Government of India Planning Commission (2002, 2006).

This is achieved with only 21 per cent of the workforce, reflecting the relatively high productivity of Chinese manufacturing.[2] Despite the rapid growth of manufacturing output, the total number of people employed in this sector has actually fallen over the past decade. Massive labour shedding by old government enterprises has outweighed the creation of new jobs in the rest of the manufacturing sector. As incomes have risen and the country has urbanized, Chinese service employment has grown rapidly. Part of this reflects rising demand for services and part of it is because the service sector is acting like a sponge to absorb surplus from the countryside and the old state enterprises.

## Implications for the future

It seems likely that within a few decades China and India will once again become the largest economies in the world and their per capita incomes will rise dramatically. This will have many diverse implications. Both countries are likely to become great military powers and have the economic muscle to threaten the present global dominance of the United States. There are also environmental issues to consider. The growth of China and India has been accompanied by a strong growth in $CO_2$ emissions which looks set to continue. Their per capita emissions may never reach the present US level but, with their huge populations, they are likely to become the world's greatest polluters. Another example is oil.

The consumption of oil by China has been increasing rapidly and it appears that it will soon overtake the USA as a user of this fuel. The Indian demand for oil is much lower, but the country's consumption of this fuel is also increasing.

## Economic impacts

As China and India develop, their trade will increase in volume and its composition will alter. Manufactured exports will continue to predominate in the case of China and they will become increasingly important for India. The Nasscom 2005 report mentioned above implies that India's IT-related service exports could eventually exceed $150 billion. India is also likely to become a major exporter of sophisticated manufactures.

What is the potential for overall growth in Chinese and Indian trade? In 2004, Chinese exports were 34 per cent of GDP and for India the figure was 19 per cent (Table 4.1). As the two countries develop, these ratios may rise for a time but in the long run, the trade ratios of China and India should eventually converge to a level that is more commensurate with their future status as economic giants. Both countries will eventually have huge domestic markets and will produce for themselves most of the sophisticated goods and services they require. Foreign trade will still be important, but it is unlikely that their trade to GDP ratios will greatly exceed those of other large economies, such as the USA, the EU and Japan. Excluding intra-EU trade, in all of these economies total exports of goods and service are around 10–14 per cent of GDP. It is unlikely that China and India will be much different. However, given the future size of their economies, and the future sophistication of their domestic production and exports, the development of these countries will have profound implications for the existing advanced economies.

The following outlines some of the main ways in which the advanced economies may be affected by the rise of China and India.

### Lead eroded

The technological lead of today's rich countries will decline as other countries, such as China and India, begin to catch up with them. They will also be overtaken in terms of total production. This in turn will erode their military and political power, for, as Paul Kennedy (1988) argued, power in international affairs depends on relative, not absolute, economic strength. A dominant country, such as the USA, may continue to grow economically and its citizens may enjoy an ever rising standard of living, but its power will be undermined if its share in world production is greatly reduced. This is what happened to Britain in the twentieth century, and the same will happen to the USA in this century.

## Scarce resources

The growth of China and India will cause a large increase in the demand for natural resources (UNCTAD, 2005a, ch. 2). If the result is a steep rise in resource prices, the advanced economies will experience a loss of real income as their imports become more expensive, and they may experience dislocation as they seek to adjust to new scarcities. Some idea of the potential loss can be obtained from existing trade statistics. The amount spent by the main advanced economies on imported fuels and mining products ranges from 2.1 per cent of GDP for the EU-25 to 2.7 per cent for Japan. This is the proportion by which real income in these countries would be reduced if prices were to double and if there were no change in consumption patterns or methods of production.

## Global knowledge pool

As countries such as China and India develop, the global resources devoted to science and technology will increase several fold. Some of the extra knowledge will be retained in the originating countries, but much of it will diffuse into the rest of the world. Just as China and India are importing technology from us today, we shall be able to import technology on a large scale from them in the future. In this way, the economic development of poorer countries may ultimately contribute to faster growth in the present rich countries. By increasing the global resources devoted to research and development it may also promote the discovery of technologies that are more environmentally friendly and able to avoid the otherwise harmful effects of economic growth. As China emerges as a great centre of science and technology, it will be taking up a role which it played centuries ago as a leading industrial innovator (Needham, 1954). India was never so important in this respect, although at one time it was also a leader in certain fields such as textiles.

## Comparative advantage

As China and India become richer their comparative advantage will alter. Productivity will rise across the board, but it will probably increase fastest in 'knowledge-intensive' goods and services, and least in 'labour-intensive' items. There may also be shifts in the pattern of earnings. Chinese and Indian universities are educating huge numbers of graduates and their current surplus of uneducated workers will eventually be depleted, sooner in China perhaps than India. As a result, the relative pay of uneducated workers is likely to increase in the future as compared to that of more educated workers. Thus, labour-intensive activities may experience both lower than average productivity growth and higher than average wage growth. If this happens, the relative cost of labour-intensive products and their prices will rise as compared to those of knowledge-intensive products. According to the theory of comparative advantage, such a shift in the internal structure of unit costs should be accompanied by a shift in the terms and pattern of international trade. As labour-intensive products become relatively more expensive, the importing countries may have to pay more of their own output to purchase them and thereby suffer a loss of real income. Alternatively, the importing countries may reduce their imports of labour-intensive products and seek more costly domestic substitutes instead. Either way, the rich countries will lose. This issue has been investigated theoretically by Paul Samuelson (2004). Appendix 2 extends his analysis using a simple model and numerical example.

The above shift in comparative advantage will occur gradually. As China and India move into more sophisticated exports, this will create an opportunity for other developing countries to expand their labour-intensive exports. This will help to slow down a shift in terms of trade against the rich countries. Eventually, when the whole world is highly developed, labour-intensive activities may return to the present rich countries, but this will be a long time in the future. In the meantime, the rich countries will continue to import labour-intensive products on a large scale, but their sources of supply will shift around the globe in-line with shifting comparative advantage. This will help to keep down the cost of such products for the importing countries. Another factor to consider is that as China and India grow their demand for sophisticated products from the existing advanced economies will also grow. They will be powerful competitors, but they will also provide large and expanding markets for the goods and services that we produce.

The Flying Geese Theory of Akamatsu (Ozawa, 2005) predicts that, as China gets richer, it will gradually phase out it exports of clothing and other labour-intensive goods whose production will be relocated to other countries. It will follow the precedent of such countries as South Korea, which 15 years ago was a large exporter of clothes, but is now on the verge of becoming a net importer of these items. The progression will be somewhat different in the case of India. Despite its low per capita income, India is not at present a large exporter of labour-intensive manufactures, and the Flying Geese Theory implies that such exports should grow rapidly in the near future as India's mass of cheap rural labour is mobilized (Mayer and Wood, 2001). The picture is complicated by the fact that India is already a significant exporter of IT-related services and advanced manufactures, and such exports are booming. Exports of labour-intensive manufactures will never enjoy the same importance for India as they have for China or Korea.

If the growth of China and India causes the terms of trade to shift against the advanced economies, how large might the resulting loss be? In 2004, clothing imports into the advanced economies were in the region of 0.5–0.6 per cent of GDP. If clothing imports were to double in price over a period of years the impact on real incomes would be negligible. Of course, there are many other labour-intensive imports in addition to clothing, and some high-tech imports have a significant labour-intensive component. There are no precise statistics available, but suppose that the average advanced economy spends 2.5 per cent of GDP on imported labour-intensive items from developing countries. Allowing another 2.5 per cent for fuels and minerals yields a total figure equal to 5 per cent of GDP. This indicates the direct loss that would occur if all such items were to double in price because of Chinese and Indian growth. Such a loss would be quite severe if it came all at once, but spread over many years it would have only a marginal impact. For example, suppose that the USA were to experience a loss equal to 5.0 per cent of GDP spread over a period of 25 years. Then, instead of growing at its normal annual rate of 1.8 per cent, per capital income would grow at 1.6 per cent. Instead of rising by 56 per cent over a 25-year period, per capita income would rise by 49 per cent. The effect would be similar in other advanced economies. These economies could absorb a gradual loss of this magnitude without much difficulty. Besides, they are now rich and have reached the point where further increases in per capita income make a comparatively small difference to human happiness (Ingelhardt and Klingemann, 2002).

Another factor to consider is that as China and India grow their demand for sophisticated products from the existing advanced economies will also grow. They will be powerful competitors, but they will also provide large and expanding markets for the goods and services that we produce.

The main worry is not that the growth of China and India will impose a huge trade loss on the advanced economies. Of more concern is the possibility that the entry of these two giants onto the world stage may provoke structural changes which are very harmful to particular subgroups of people in the advanced economies, even though their aggregate effect on national income is quite small.

## Absolute advantage

In the course of development, there is often a widespread increase in productivity embracing virtually the whole economy. If wages lag systematically behind productivity growth the result will be a universal reduction in real unit costs. The effect of this on exports depends on what happens to the exchange rate. If the real exchange rate is rigid then a universal reduction in unit costs will make all products from the developing country more competitive in international markets. This will cause exports of all kinds to increase and will constrain the growth of imports, resulting in a huge trade surplus – even greater than we have recently observed in China. Such a situation is not sustainable in the long run and the real-exchange rate must eventually appreciate. When this occurs, the initial trade advantage of low unit costs will be eliminated. Unit costs may remain low in local prices, but the high exchange rate will increase these costs in terms of foreign currency.

By definition, a uniform reduction in unit costs in the developing country has no effect on relative costs of production and hence its effect on relative prices will normally be of second order. Indeed, there may be no change at all in relative prices. This is the case in the simple two country model of international trade that is presented in Appendix 2. In this model, one of the trading partners is a developed country (the North) and the other is a developing country (the South). The mark-up of prices over unit costs in the South is the same in all sectors of the economy, which ensures that relative prices are unaffected by uniform changes in local unit costs. Moreover, the exchange rate adjusts so as to preserve equality between imports and exports, and there is no change in the volume or composition of international trade. Each country sells just as much of each product as it did before the change in unit costs and hence their terms of trade are unaffected.

In the above example, a uniform reduction in unit costs in the South has no immediate impact on its Northern trading partner. However, this is only part of the story. As unit costs in the South fall (compared to prices), the result is an increase in the local rate of profit. Higher profits make the South more desirable as a location for production and may attract investment from the North. Alternatively, firms in the North may use the threat of relocation to the South as a bargaining counter to persuade their own workers to accept lower wages. Thus, firms that might have invested in, for example, the United States may decide that China is now more profitable and therefore cut back on their American activities. Or they may use the threat of moving to China as a means to reduce the pay of their American employees. Such issues have been explored by Richard Freeman (2005a, 2005b). His thesis is that the opening up of China and India has effectively doubled the global labour supply that is available to capitalist firms, thereby strengthening the hand of capital against labour.

The potential for investment in China and India is enormous. A recent UNCTAD survey of business and expert opinion indicates that these are amongst the most attractive countries in the world in which to invest (Table 4.3). It is conceivable that rising investment in these countries could lead to a global shortage of savings, causing world interest rates to rise and choking off investment in the advanced economies. This is a theoretical possibility, but it has not happened yet. At the present time, the combined economies of China and India have a current account surplus and they are a net provider of savings to the rest of the world.

To what extent does the possibility of investing in China and India influence the bargaining power of employers in the advanced economies? If a firm can obtain much higher profits in China and India than in the advanced economies, it may either move to one of these countries or use the threat of relocation to extract wage and other concessions from its current workforce at home. So much is obvious. The practical question is whether it is really true that firms can make much higher profits in China and India than in the existing advanced economies. Some individual firms certainly can, but there must also be many firms that still find it profitable to invest in the

*Table 4.3*   Most attractive global business locations: responses of experts and transnational corporations*

| Responses from experts | Responses from corporations |
|---|---|
| 1. China (85%) | 1. China (87%) |
| 2. United States (55%) | 2. India (51%) |
| 3. India (42%) | 3. United States (51%) |
| 4. Brazil (24%) | 4. Russian Federation (33%) |
| 5. Russian Federation (21%) | 5. Brazil (20%) |
| 6. United Kingdom (21%) | 6. Mexico (16%) |
| 7. Germany (12%) | 7. Germany (13%) |
| 8. Poland (9%) | 8. United Kingdom (13%) |
| 9. Singapore (9%) | 9. Thailand (11%) |
| 10. Ukraine (9%) | 10. Canada (7%) |

*Note*: *Countries are ranked according to the number of responses that rated each as the most attractive location.
*Source*: UNCTAD (2005b).

advanced economies, for otherwise how do we explain existing investment behaviour? The advanced economies still attract far more direct investment than goes to China and India. The *World Investment Report* estimates that over the period 2002–04, these economies attracted nearly 70 per cent of global direct investment flows and more than six times as much as China, including Hong Kong, and India combined (UNCTAD, 2005b, Annex Table B1). Moreover, the Chinese figure is somewhat inflated by 'round-tripping', whereby funds originating in mainland China are sent abroad and then, disguised as foreign capital, are reinvested in China where they are classified as FDI. The flow statistics suggest that the share of China in new direct investment has been rising, but this is not reflected in the stock statistics which show that the share of China in the world stock of inward direct investment has fallen from 11.2 per cent in 2000 to 7.9 per cent in 2004 (UNCTAD, 2005b, Annex Table B2). This fall was mainly accounted for by Hong Kong, but there has been some decline in the rest of China. During the period 2002–04, the share of India in world FDI was less than 1 per cent.

Any firm that is thinking of investing in China or India must be concerned about the profitability of its operations. If an investment project has a long time horizon the firm must also take some view about the future evolution of costs and revenues. Measured in US dollars at the current market exchange rate, wages in China and India are extremely low, and even in urban Shanghai manufacturing workers earn less than 9 per cent of the US hourly wage (Table 4.4). If there were no international differences in productivity, such a huge gap in wage rates would imply that profit rates in China and India were truly gigantic and it would be a mystery why so much investment still occurs in the advanced economies.

*Table 4.4*  International wage comparison (measured in $US at current exchange rates)

| | |
|---|---|
| USA 2004 | 100 |
| India 2004 | 6.1 |
| China 2004 | 7.1 |
| China average urban 2002 | 4.4 |
| China average TVE 2002* | 3.4 |
| Shanghai municipality urban 2002 | 8.7 |

*Note:* *TVE = town and village enterprises.
*Sources:* The 2004 figures are based on Mercer Consulting (2005); the 2002 figures are for hourly compensation in manufacturing and are based on Banister (2005b, Table 4) and BLS data.

In reality, productivity is often much lower in China and India, and the advantage of low wages are largely offset by the fact that output per worker is also low.

There are two reasons why Chinese wages are so low when measured in current dollars. Real wage rates in China are much lower than in the advanced countries, and the cost of living, measured in dollars, is also very low. Prices within China are on average around a quarter of the US level, whereas real wages are less than one-sixth. Neither of these conditions will last. Real wages have been increasing rapidly and this growth should continue in the future (Figure 4.3). Moreover, because of domestic price inflation and future currency revaluation the Chinese cost of living, measured in dollars, should also increase. This is what always happens when poor countries develop. Like China, they begin with a very low cost of living, measured in dollars, but as they get richer the dollar cost of living increases until eventually it approximates to

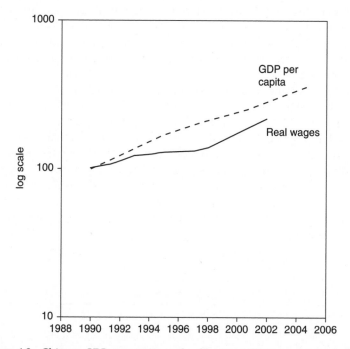

*Figure 4.3* Chinese GDP per capita and urban manufacturing wages indices (1990 = 100)

Note: The wage series refers to wages and does not include other forms of labour compensation.
*Sources*: IMF *World Economies Outlook 2006*, Banister (2005a, Table).

the level observed in the advanced economies. Such convergence is a manifestation of Baumol's 'cost disease' (Baumol, 1967) and is caused by the failure of lagging sectors, such as construction and local services, to match the rapid productivity growth observed in dynamic export sectors such as manufacturing. Higher wages in the dynamic sectors spill over into the lagging sectors and are partly passed on to consumers in the form of higher prices. The operation of this mechanism in China has been confirmed in a recent study by Qin (2006) who finds that economic growth is leading to serious inflationary pressures in labour-intensive service industries. The Chinese government has also announced plans to strengthen the legal rights of workers which may add further to cost pressures (Buckley, 2006).

Table 4.5 provides a hypothetical example to illustrate how these various factors might combine. In this example, consumer prices measured in dollars increase 3.5 per cent a year faster in China than America, and real wages rise 5 per cent a year faster. For this to happen, dollar wage rates in China must grow about 8.5 per cent a year more than American wages.

Sustained over a couple of decades, such growth rates would have a dramatic effect on relative wages. Measured in dollars, the hourly compensation of the average urban manufacturing worker in China in 2002 was only 4.4 per cent of the US average (Table 4.4). With the assumed growth rates, this compensation of such a worker in 2025 would be 29 per cent of the American level. For a Shanghai worker the figure might be somewhat higher. This example puts a question mark over the argument that productivity in China will outstrip wages and that profit rates will continue to increase. On the contrary, it is more likely that in certain regions of China rising wages will begin to squeeze profits.

On the available information it is difficult to judge whether there is a latent profit squeeze in China. Some weak evidence is provided by the fact that real wages, in manufacturing at least, have been rising much faster than GDP per capita in recent years (Figure 4.3). However,

*Table 4.5*  Real wages and dollar wages: a numerical example (percentage annual growth rates)

|  | China | USA | China–USA |
|---|---|---|---|
| (1) Cost of living in dollars | 5.5 | 2.0 | 3.5 |
| (2) Real wage rate | 6.5 | 1.5 | 5.0 |
| (3) Wage rate in dollars [ = (1) + (2) ] | 12.0 | 3.5 | 8.5 |

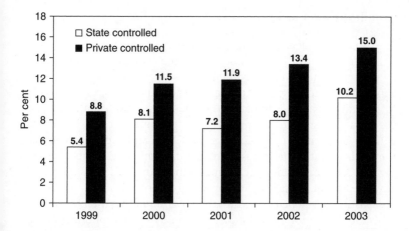

*Source*: OECD (2005).
*Figure 4.4*   Financial performance of Chinese industrial companies, rates of return on physical assets

a recent OECD survey of Chinese business found that profit rates in the private sector have been rising strongly and are now apparently very high by international standards (Figure 4.4). In 2003, the average rate of return on physical capital in private industrial companies in China was 15 per cent whereas the equivalent rate of return for non-financial corporations in most OECD countries is in the range 6–12 per cent (Glyn, 2006, ch. 6). Such comparisons must be treated with caution. The rates of return in question may not refer to exactly the same thing, measurement conventions may be different, the Chinese business environment may be riskier, present Chinese profit rates may be a poor guide to the future since wages are increasing so rapidly, and average profit rates may not be a good indication of the return that is available on marginal projects. Despite these qualifications, it does seem to be the case that investment in China is at present highly profitable and that rates of return have been increasing. The question is how long will this continue? Ultimately the answer will depend on what happens to wages and productivity. If dollar wages increase fast enough, then despite continued productivity growth Chinese profit margins will fall, albeit from a high level. In the above numerical example, dollar wages were assumed to grow at 8 per cent a year faster than in the United States. It is hard to believe that, over a prolonged period of time, productivity growth could be sufficient to offset relative wage increases of this magnitude.

## Concluding remarks

The renaissance of China and India will have economic costs and benefits for today's advanced economies. There may be a terms of trade loss as fuels, minerals and labour-intensive goods and services become more expensive. Although potentially large in absolute terms, this loss is likely to be quite small in comparison to the total output of the advanced economies. If spread over a long period of time, it could be absorbed without much difficulty. Moreover, as China and India become richer they will invest more in research and development, thereby promoting the discovery of new technologies that can be used by the existing advanced economies. They will provide huge markets for the exports of the existing developed countries, thereby stimulating international specialization and promoting both static and dynamic economies of scale. Such benefits could outweigh the terms of trade loss caused by the higher cost of natural resources and labour-intensive imports.

Another potential loss is in the realm of investment. If there are financial or managerial constraints on the overall scale of global investment, it is possible that firms will prefer to invest in China and India rather than in the existing advanced economies. Even if there is not much actual diversion of investment to China and India, the threat of relocation may become a powerful bargaining tool that employers can use against their workers. In aggregate terms, it is unlikely that the growth of China and India will seriously damage the existing advanced economies. However, it may provoke structural changes that are harmful to particular subgroups of people. Economists tend to regard such effects as temporary adjustment costs, but it is clear from the modern experience of deindustrialization that the effects of structural change may last for generations and be very painful to the communities involved. Dealing with structural change in a humane fashion may be the greatest economic challenge posed by the renaissance of China and India.

## Appendix 1: projected Chinese and Indian growth

This appendix describes how the projections shown in Figure 4.2 were derived. Table 4.6 shows relative per capita incomes in 2004 and the growth rates of per capita GDP over the period 1990–2004.

Projections are based on equations of the following type:

$$\frac{dy}{dt} = -\beta y$$

*Table 4.6* Catching up with the USA: GDP per capita

|  | USA | China | India |
|---|---|---|---|
| Per capita GDP in 2004 as % of USA (measured at PPP) | 100 | 14.9 | 7.9 |
| Annual growth rate 2000–04 | 1.8% | 8.4% | 4.6% |
| Time needed to catch up with USA (with above growth rates) |  | 30 years | 95 years |

*Source*: *World Development Indicators 2005*, World Bank, Washington.

where $y = \log(\frac{Y}{Y_{USA}})$ and $Y = $ GDP per capita (at PPP). For the period 2000–04 the following coefficients were estimated: China, $\beta = 0.031$; India, $\beta = 0.010$. The future growth of GDP per capita is projected using the following coefficients: China, $\beta = 0.031$; India, $\beta = 0.025$. The coefficient for China is the same as the historical one; the coefficient for India is much higher than the historical one, reflecting the assumption that India is moving towards a Chinese-style trajectory. Future population growth is projected using the UN Population Division (2002 revision) medium variant.

**Market exchange rates**

GDP at the market exchange rate is derived as follows. Let

$\overline{Y} = $ GDP per capita in current US dollars (at the market exchange rate)

$R = \dfrac{\text{market exchange rate}}{\text{PPP exchange rate}}$

$\overline{y} = \log\left(\dfrac{\overline{Y}}{\overline{Y}_{USA}}\right)$

$r = \log(R)$

The following relationship holds identically:

$$\frac{\overline{Y}}{\overline{Y}_{USA}} = R\left(\frac{Y}{Y_{USA}}\right)$$

which in logarithmic form can be expressed as $\overline{y} = r + y$. We assume that $r = \alpha y$ for some constant $\alpha$. This ensures that $r = 0$ when $y = 0$. Hence

$R = 1$ when $Y = Y_{USA}$. The value of $\alpha$ is estimated using the following equation:

$$\alpha = \frac{r_{2004}}{y_{2004}}$$

## Appendix 2: a simple model and numerical example

This section presents a simple model designed to illustrate how changes in wage rates and technology in developing countries (the South) may affect their trading partners in the advanced economies (the North). The model embodies within a single framework the insights of Samuelson (2004) and Freeman (2005a, 2005b).

There are two countries 'North' and 'South', labelled N and S, respectively, and two goods labelled '1' and '2'. Good 1 is skill-intensive and good 2 is labour-intensive. Following Wood (1994), we assume that the North has entirely abandoned the production of good 2 because it is no longer profitable and now produces only good 1, whereas the South produces both goods. The North exports some of its output of good 1 in return for imports of good 2 from the South. The exchange rate adjusts so as to ensure that exports and imports are equal in total value. Transport costs are zero and there are no trade barriers. Prices in each country are therefore the same, measured in a common currency. Let $p_1$ and $p_2$ be the prices of goods 1 and 2.

Real incomes are derived by deflating monetary incomes as follows. All individuals, wherever they are located, have the following utility function:

$$U = 2\sqrt{C_1 C_2} \tag{1}$$

where $C_1$ and $C_2$ are the amounts of good 1 and good 2 consumed. For an individual with monetary income of $M$, utility is maximized when:

$$C_1 = \frac{M}{2p_1}$$

$$C_2 = \frac{M}{2p_2}$$

Utility is given by:

$$U = \frac{M}{\sqrt{p_1 p_2}} \tag{2}$$

The quantity $U$ is a measure of real income.

All individuals divide their expenditure equally between the two goods. This implies that half of the North's monetary income is spent on the home produced good 1 and the other half on imports of good 2. Let $Y_{N,1}$ be the total amount of good 1 produced in the North. Since this country produces nothing else, the monetary income of the North is equal to $p_1 Y_{N,1}$. Thus, Northern consumption of each good is given by

$$C_{N,1} = \frac{p_1 Y_{N,1}}{2p_1} = \frac{Y_{N,1}}{2}$$

$$C_{N,2} = \frac{p_1 Y_{N,1}}{2p_2} = \frac{Y_{N,1}}{2} \left( \frac{p_1}{p_2} \right)$$

Hence

$$\text{value of exports} = p_1 \left( Y_{N,1} - C_{N,1} \right) = \frac{p_1 Y_{N,1}}{2}$$

$$\text{value of imports} = p_2 C_{N,2} = \frac{p_1 Y_{N,1}}{2}$$

The terms of trade are given by:

$$\frac{\text{volume of imports}}{\text{volume of exports}} = \frac{C_{N,2}}{Y_{N,1} - C_{N,1}} = \frac{p_1}{p_2}$$

Aggregate real income (utility) in the North is derived by deflating monetary income as follows:

$$\overline{Y}_N = \frac{p_1 Y_{N,1}}{\sqrt{p_1 p_2}}$$

Thus,

$$\overline{Y}_N = Y_{N,1} \sqrt{\frac{p_1}{p_2}} \tag{3}$$

This formula indicates that any increase in $p_2/p_1$ (the relative price of labour-intensive good 2) will harm the North.

The terms of trade are determined by conditions of production in the South. Assume that production takes place under constant returns to scale and that labour is the only input. Let $\ell_{S,1}$ and $\ell_{S,2}$ be the amounts of labour required in the South to produce a single unit of goods 1 and 2, respectively. Let $w_{S,1}$ and $w_{S,2}$ be the money wage rates in sectors 1 and 2. Real wage rates are given by

$$\overline{w}_{S,1} = \frac{w_{S,1}}{\sqrt{p_1 p_2}}$$

$$\overline{w}_{S,2} = \frac{w_{S,2}}{\sqrt{p_1 p_2}}$$

Suppose that production takes one period and that wages are advanced to workers at the beginning of the period. Since labour is the only input, the wages advanced to workers are the only form of financial investment that a firm makes. The rate of profit is therefore equal to profits divided by wages. Assume that capital mobility equalizes profits rates across sectors in the South and let $\pi_S$ be the resulting uniform profit rate. This implies that

$$p_1 = (1 + \pi_S) w_{S,1} \ell_{S,1}$$

$$p_2 = (1 + \pi_S) w_{S,2} \ell_{S,2}$$

Hence,

$$\frac{p_1}{p_2} = \frac{w_{S,1} \ell_{S,1}}{w_{S,2} \ell_{S,2}} \tag{4}$$

From (3) it follows that

$$\overline{Y}_N = Y_{N,1} \sqrt{\frac{w_{S,1} \ell_{S,1}}{w_{S,2} \ell_{S,2}}} \tag{5}$$

Let $\ell_{N,1}$ and $\ell_{N,2}$ be the amounts of labour required in the North to produce a single unit of goods 1 and 2, respectively, and let $w_{N,1}$ and $w_{N,2}$ be the corresponding money wage rates. Since good 2 is not actually produced in the North, $w_{N,2}$ must be interpreted as the wage that employers would have to pay if production of this good did take place. It is assumed that $p_2 < w_{N,2} \ell_{N,2}$. This ensures the cost of producing good 2 is greater than its selling price, which is consistent with the fact that the North does not produce this good. The rate of profit in sector 1 in the North satisfies the equation

$$p_1 = (1 + \pi_N) w_{N,1} \ell_{N,1}$$

This completes the model.

In the above model, the impact of trade on the North comes entirely through relative prices, which in turn reflect relative costs of production within the South. The absolute level of costs is irrelevant. A uniform proportionate increase or reduction in Southern costs will have no effect on relative prices and hence no effect on the terms of trade. However, it will affect the rate of profit in the South and this may have an indirect effect on the economy of the North. For example, suppose that productivity in the South increases faster than wages. This will raise the rate of profit in the South and may attract capital that would otherwise be invested in the North. Alternatively, firms within the North may use the threat of relocation to the South to reduce wages in the North and increase their own profits.

## A numerical example

To explore these issues further we shall consider a simple numerical example based on the above model. This is laid out in Table 4.7. The first column of the table shows the amounts of labour initially required per unit of output in each sector in each country, together with prices, nominal wages, real wages and profit rates. The remaining columns show the effect of progressive modifications to some of the parameters. Modifications are denoted by an asterisk. The profit rate in the South is always the same in both sectors. Prices are measured in a common currency and are uniform across countries. The table also shows output in each sector in country N. Output is zero in sector 2. With the assumed prices, wage rates and productivity, the profit rate in the North in sector 2 is negative. This justifies the assumption that production in this sector is equal to zero. The last row shows aggregate real income in the North.

In the shift from column (1) to column (2) labour input per unit of output is reduced by one-fifth in each sector in the South. Labour productivity in the North remains the same, and there is no change in money wage rates or prices in either country. Real wage rates in North and South are therefore unaltered. Aggregate real income in the North is also unaffected. The profit rate in the North remains at 20 per cent but the profit rate in the South increases to 50 per cent. This illustrates how a uniform reduction in Southern costs has no effect on relative prices and leaves real income and profits in the North unaffected. However, it does increase the rate of profit in the South. The appearance of this profit differential increases the bargaining power of employers in the North vis-à-vis their workers, since they can threaten to relocate their production in the South unless workers accept lower wages. Column (3) shows what happens if workers in the North accept lower wages. It is assumed that wages in the North are reduced by enough to equalize profit rates in the two countries. This does not affect the aggregate real income of the North, but it does lead to a redistribution of income from labour to capital. These comparisons illustrate how uniform changes in costs within a country leave the

*Table 4.7*   Comparative and absolute advantage: a numerical example

|  | (1) | (2) | (3) | (4) | (5) |
|---|---|---|---|---|---|
| $\ell_{S,1}$ | 5.0 | 4.0* | 4.0 | 4.0 | 3.5* |
| $\ell_{S,2}$ | 10.0 | 8.0* | 8.0 | 8.0 | 8.0 |
| $\ell_{N,1}$ | 1.0 | 1.0 | 1.0 | 1.0 | 1.0 |
| $\ell_{N,2}$ | 3.0 | 3.0 | 3.0 | 3.0 | 3.0 |
| $w_{S,1}$ | 2.0 | 2.0 | 2.0 | 2.0 | 2.0 |
| $w_{S,2}$ | 1.0 | 1.0 | 1.0 | 1.2* | 1.2 |
| $w_{N,1}$ | 10.0 | 10.0 | 8.0* | 8.0 | 7.0* |
| $w_{N,2}$ | 8.0 | 8.0 | 6.4* | 6.4 | 5.6* |
| $p_1$ | 12.0 | 12.0 | 12.0 | 12.0 | 10.5* |
| $p_2$ | 12.0 | 12.0 | 12.0 | 14.4* | 14.4 |
| $\overline{w}_{S,1}$ | 0.17 | 0.17 | 0.17 | 0.15* | 0.16* |
| $\overline{w}_{S,2}$ | 0.08 | 0.08 | 0.08 | 0.09* | 0.10* |
| $\overline{w}_{N,1}$ | 0.83 | 0.83 | 0.67* | 0.61* | 0.57* |
| $\overline{w}_{N,2}$ | 0.67 | 0.67 | 0.53* | 0.49* | 0.46* |
| $\pi_S$ | 20% | 50%* | 50% | 50% | 50% |
| $\pi_N$ | 0% | 20% | 50%* | 50% | 50% |
| $Y_{N,1}$ | $10^9$ | $10^9$ | $10^9$ | $10^9$ | $10^9$ |
| $Y_{N,2}$ | 0 | 0 | 0 | 0 | 0 |
| $\overline{Y}_N$ | $10^9 \times 1.00$ | $10^9 \times 1.00$ | $10^9 \times 1.00$ | $10^9 \times 0.91$* | $10^9 \times 0.85$* |

terms of international trade unaffected. However, they may affect other countries indirectly through their impact influence on profit rates and thereby investment. This illustrates the principle of absolute advantage.

The shift from column (3) to column (4) shows how the North as a whole may be affected by a non-uniform change in production costs in the South. This shift involves an increase in money wages in the labour-intensive sector 2, whereas money wages remain unchanged in sector 1. The result is an increase in the relative price of labour-intensive goods causing an unfavourable shift in the terms of trade for the North, causing the aggregate real income of the North to fall. This example assumes that real wages fall sufficiently to preserve the old rate of profit in the North. This is not the only possible assumption. One could alternatively assume that the terms of trade loss is born entirely by the employers, in which case profits will be severely squeezed.

The shift from column (4) to column (5) illustrates what may happen if productivity growth in the South is uneven. There is a reduction in the amount of labour required per unit of output in sector 1, but there is no change in the other sector. Wage rates and the profit rate in the South do not alter. As before, relative price of good 1 falls and the terms of trade shift against the North. Aggregate real income in the North is thereby reduced. It is assumed that wages in the North fall sufficiently to preserve the old rate of profit. This illustrates how the North may be harmed by technological advances within the skill-intensive sector of the South.

The above example highlights how important it is to distinguish between absolute and relative cost changes. In this example, a uniform reduction in costs in the South did not directly harm the North, although it did provoke a redistribution of income from labour to capital in the North. In contrast, a shift in relative production costs within the South did harm the North, causing the terms of trade to shift and thereby reducing the aggregate real income of the North. In a more complex model, one could show how shifts in relative costs in the South may provoke structural change in the North and benefit some types of worker at the expense of others.

## Notes

1. Noshir, Partner, McKinsey & Company, www.nasscom.in/Nasscom/templates/NormalPage.aspx?id=2599.
2. Official figures used by the ILO understate employment in manufacturing. The figure given here includes an adjustment due to Banister (2005a).

## References

Banister, J. (2005a) 'Manufacturing Employment in China', *Monthly Labor Review* July: 11–29.

Banister, J. (2005b) 'Manufacturing Earnings and Compensation in China', *Monthly Labor Review* August: 22–40.

Baumol, W. J. (1967) 'Macroeconomics of Unbalanced Growth: The Anatomy of Urban Crisis', *American Economic Review* 57: 415–26.

Buckley, C. (2006) 'Foreign Investors may Quit if China Tightens up Labour Law', *Times*, June 19.

Das, G. (2006) 'The India Model', *Foreign Affairs* http://www.foreignaffairs.org/20060701faessay85401/gurcharan-das/the-india-model.html.

Dasgupta, S. and A. Singh (2005) 'Will Services be the New Engine of Indian Economic Growth', *Development and Change* 36 (6): 1035–57.

Freeman, R. (2005a) 'Does Globalization of the Scientific/Engineering Workforce Threaten U.S. Economic Leadership', NBER working paper 11457.

Freeman, R. (2005b) 'China, India and the Doubling of the Global Labor Force', available at: http://www.zmag.org/ znet/viewArticle/5523.

Glyn, A. (2006) *Capitalism Unleashed*, Oxford: Oxford University Press.

Government of India Planning Commission (2002) *Tenth Five Year Plan*, vol. 1, New Delhi: ch. 2.

Government of India Planning Commission (2006) *Towards Faster and More Inclusive Growth*, New Delhi.

Inglehart, R. and H. D. Klingemann (2002) 'Genes, Culture, Democracy and Happiness', http://www.worldvaluessurvey.org/library/set_search.html.

Joshi, S. (2004) 'Tertiary Sector- Driven Growth in India: Impact on Employment and Poverty', *Economic and Political Weekly* 39 (37): 4175–8.

Kennedy, P. (1988) *The Rise and Fall of the Great Powers: Economic Change and Military Conflict from 1500 to 2000*, London: Unwin Hyman.

Maddison, A. (2001) *The World Economy: A Millennial Perspective*, Paris: OECD.

Mayer, J and A. Wood (2001) 'South Asia's Export Structure in a Comparative Perspective', *Oxford Development Studies* 29 (1): 5–29.

Mercer Consulting (2005) *European Survey of Employment Costs*, Mercer Human Resource Consulting, April.

Needham, J. (1954) *Science and Civilisation in China*, vol. 1, Cambridge: Cambridge University Press.

OECD (2005) *Economic Survey of China*, Paris: OECD.

Ozawa, T. (2005) *Institutions, Industrial Upgrading, and Economic Performance in Japan – The 'Flying Geese' Paradigm of Catch-up Growth*, Northampton, MA: Edward Elgar.

Qin, D. (2006) 'Is China's Growing Service Sector Leading to Cost Disease?', *Structural Change and Economic Dynamics* 17 (3): 267–87.

Rowthorn, R. E. (2006) 'The Renaissance of China and India: The Implications for the Advanced Economics', UNCTAD discussion paper, Geneva: United Nations.

Samuelson, P. A. (2004) 'Where Ricardo and Mill Rebut and Confirm Arguments of Mainstream Economists Supporting Globalization', *Journal of Economic Perspectives* 18 (3): 135–46.

UNCTAD (2005a) *Trade and Development Report 2005*, Geneva: United Nations.

UNCTAD (2005b) *World Investment Report 2005*, Geneva: United Nations.

Wood, A. (1994) *North-South Trade, Employment and Inequality: Changing Fortunes in a Skill-Driven World*, Oxford: Clarendon Press.

# 5
# The Rise of China and India: Implications for Developing Countries

*Deepak Nayyar*

## Introduction

The last two decades of the twentieth century, beginning circa 1980, witnessed rapid economic growth in China and India. In the first decade of the twenty-first century, the rapid growth has been sustained in China and has accelerated in India. This remarkable growth performance provides a sharp contrast with the world economy over the same period and with the preceding hundred years in these two Asian giants. Indeed, except for Japan and the East Asian-4, economic history provides few parallels of such rapid and sustained growth. The past quarter of a century has thus witnessed the return of the forgotten dragon and the vanishing tiger to the world economy. So much so, that it is no longer possible to consider prospects for the world economy in 2025 or 2050 without placing China and India centre stage.

The object of this chapter is to analyse the economic implications of the rise of China and India for developing countries, situated in the wider context of the world economy. I will sketch a profile of China and India, in the world economy, by outlining the broad contours of their significance in the past, present and future, before considering the main forms of engagement and channels of interaction for these countries with the world economy and, in particular, with developing countries. The focus will be on international trade, international investment, international finance and international migration. Later I will examine the implications of rapid economic growth in China and India for the developing world. In doing so, I ask whether these two Asian giants could be the new engines of growth, touching upon the underlying economic causation and exploring their possible impact on developing countries.

## China and India in the world economy

The significance of China and India in the global context has changed over time. The discussion in this section provides a historical perspective of the past, a snapshot picture of the present and an extrapolated scenario of the future.

### The past

The emerging significance of China and India in the world economy must be situated in historical perspective. Table 5.1, which is based on estimates made by Angus Maddison (2003), presents the evidence on the shares of China and India in world population and in world income for selected years during the period from AD 1 to AD 2001. It shows that, 2000 years ago, China and India accounted for almost 60 per cent of world population and world income. At the time, China's share in world population and world income was a little more than one quarter, whereas India's share was almost one-third. The picture was similar over the period from 1000 to 1700. During these seven centuries, China and India, taken together, accounted for 50 per cent of world population and

*Table 5.1*    China and India in the world economy (percentage share in population and income)

| Year | Share of world population | | | Share of world GDP | | |
|------|-------|-------|-------|-------|-------|-------|
|      | China | India | Total | China | India | Total |
| 0001 | 25.8  | 32.5  | 58.3  | 26.1  | 32.9  | 59.0  |
| 1000 | 22.1  | 28.0  | 50.1  | 22.7  | 28.9  | 51.6  |
| 1500 | 23.5  | 25.1  | 48.6  | 24.9  | 24.4  | 49.3  |
| 1600 | 28.8  | 24.3  | 53.1  | 29.0  | 22.4  | 51.4  |
| 1700 | 22.9  | 27.3  | 50.2  | 22.3  | 24.4  | 46.7  |
| 1820 | 36.6  | 20.1  | 56.7  | 32.9  | 16.0  | 48.9  |
| 1870 | 28.1  | 19.9  | 48.0  | 17.1  | 12.1  | 29.1  |
| 1913 | 24.4  | 17.0  | 41.4  | 8.8   | 7.5   | 16.3  |
| 1950 | 21.7  | 14.2  | 38.9  | 4.5   | 4.2   | 8.7   |
| 1973 | 22.5  | 14.8  | 37.3  | 4.6   | 3.1   | 7.7   |
| 2001 | 20.7  | 16.5  | 37.2  | 12.3  | 5.4   | 17.7  |

*Note*: The percentages in this table have been calculated from estimates of population and GDP in Maddison (2003). The data on GDP are in 1990 international Geary-Khamis dollars, which are purchasing power parities used to evaluate output that are calculated based on a specific method devised to define international prices. This measure facilitates intercountry comparisons over time.
*Source*: Maddison (2003).

50 per cent of world income. The percentage shares of China and India, taken separately, fluctuated over the period but, on the whole, were roughly equal. Even in 1820, China and India accounted for 57 per cent of the world population and 49 per cent of world income. There was a dramatic change over the next 150 years. In 1973, the share of China and India in world population was significantly lower at 38 per cent but their share in world income collapsed to less than 8 per cent, which was a small fraction of what it was 150 years earlier. The next 30 years witnessed some recovery. While the share of China and India in world population remained in the range of 37 per cent, their share in world income in 2001 rose to almost 18 per cent. The essential contours of this story are clear enough. Beginning in 1820, the share of China and India in world population declined steadily until 1973 but, over the same period, the decline in their share of world income was much more pronounced. Consequently, during the period from 1820 to 1973, there was a sharp increase in the asymmetries, or disproportionalities, between the shares of China and India in world population and in world income. The partial recovery in their share of world income during the period from 1973 to 2001 has reduced the asymmetry but the disproportionality remains significant. However, this trend suggests a re-entry of China and India into the world economy.

## The present

It is possible to juxtapose this past with the present. Table 5.2 outlines a profile of GDP, population and GDP per capita in China and India, as compared with developing countries, industrialized countries and the world, in 2000 and 2005. It shows that the population of the world is more than 6 billion, of which a little less than 1 billion is in the industrialized countries, somewhat more than 5 billion is in the developing countries and more than 2 billion is in China and India. Thus, 37 per cent of the population in the world and 44 per cent of the population in developing countries lives in China and India. There are two sets of figures on GDP and GDP per capita: at constant prices with market exchange rates and in terms of purchasing power parities. Let us consider each in turn.

At market exchange rates, between 2000 and 2005, the share of China and India increased from 5 per cent to 7 per cent of world GDP and from 27 per cent to 32 per cent of GDP in developing countries. Over the same period, at market exchange rates, GDP per capita in China was about the same as, while GDP per capita in India was less than half, the average GDP per capita in developing countries. It is worth noting that both

Table 5.2 GDP, population and GDP per capita (China and India: 2000 and 2005)

| Country | GDP ($ billion) | | GDP ($ per capita) | | Population (million) | | PPP-GDP ($ billion) | | PPP-GDP ($ per capita) | |
|---|---|---|---|---|---|---|---|---|---|---|
| | 2000 | 2005 | 2000 | 2005 | 2000 | 2005 | 2000 | 2005 | 2000 | 2005 |
| China | 1,198 | 1,890 | 949 | 1,449 | 1,263 | 1,305 | 4,973 | 7,842 | 3,939 | 6,012 |
| India | 460 | 644 | 453 | 588 | 1,016 | 1,095 | 2,402 | 3,362 | 2,364 | 3,072 |
| Total | 1,659 | 2,534 | | | 2,279 | 2,399 | 7,375 | 11,204 | | |
| Developing countries | 6,058 | 7,813 | 1,191 | 1,440 | 5,085 | 5,427 | 18,818 | 25,322 | 3,701 | 4,666 |
| (China and India as % of) | (27.4) | (32.4) | | | (44.8) | (44.2) | (39.2) | (44.2) | | |
| Industrialized countries | 24,542 | 27,148 | 27,304 | 29,251 | 899 | 928 | 25,157 | 27,898 | 27,988 | 30,058 |
| World | 31,756 | 36,352 | 5,241 | 5,647 | 6,060 | 6,438 | 45,144 | 54,573 | 7,450 | 8,477 |
| (China and India as % of) | (5.2) | (7.0) | | | (37.6) | (37.3) | (16.3) | (20.5) | | |

Notes: GDP and GDP per capita, and PPP-GDP and PPP-GDP per capita, are measured in constant 2000 US dollars.
Source: World Bank (2007).

China and India are far below GDP per capita in the industrialized countries and significantly below GDP per capita in the world as a whole. The picture is somewhat different if the comparison is in terms of purchasing power parities. Between 2000 and 2005, the share of China and India increased from 16 per cent to 20 per cent of world PPP-GDP and from 39 per cent to 44 per cent of the PPP-GDP of developing countries. It would seem that, for China and India, these shares in world income are now much more symmetrical with their share in world population. Over the same period, in PPP terms, GDP per capita in China moved ahead of GDP per capita in developing countries, whereas GDP per capita in India was about two-thirds of GDP per capita in developing countries. In this short span of time, both countries moved closer to PPP-GDP per capita in the world, China more than India.

Most growth scenarios for the future are based on an extrapolation of growth from the past. Table 5.3 sets out rates of growth in GDP and GDP per capita, during the periods 1951–80 and 1981–2005, for China and India, in comparison with the world economy, the industrialized countries, the developing countries and regions within the developing world. The figures for the period 1951–80 are based on Maddison data because United Nations data are not available before 1971. The figures for the period 1981–2005 are based on United Nations data because Maddison data are not available after 2001. These two sources are not strictly comparable. For the period 1981–2000, however, data are available from both sources. To facilitate a comparison, Table 5.3 also presents figures on growth rates, during 1981–2000, computed separately from Maddison data and United Nations data. A comparison of the two sets of growth rates, during the period 1981–2000 for which both sources are available, shows that the numbers correspond closely, although there are significant differences in the figures for China where UN data suggest much higher growth rates than Maddison data. Even so, it is reasonable to infer that the growth rates for the periods 1951–80 and 1981–2005, even if computed from different sources, are comparable, with the exception of China, for which some downward adjustment may be needed.

A study of Table 5.3 clearly shows that growth in GDP and GDP per capita during 1981–2005 was much slower than it was during 1951–80. This was so for the world economy, for industrialized countries and for developing countries. Growth in GDP was in the range 4–5 per cent per annum during 1951–80 and in the range of 2–3 per cent per annum during 1981–2005 almost everywhere, except Asia where it was 6 per cent and 4 per cent per annum respectively. Growth in GDP per capita slowed down considerably even in the industrialized countries, from

*Table 5.3*   Growth performance of China and India: 1951–80 and 1981–2005, comparison with country groups and regions (per cent per annum)

| | Maddison data | | United Nations data | |
|---|---|---|---|---|
| | 1951–80 | 1981–2000 | 1981–2000 | 1981–2005 |
| *GDP* | | | | |
| World | 4.77 | 2.64 | 2.72 | 2.95 |
| Industrialized countries | 4.40 | 2.56 | 2.59 | 2.50 |
| Developing countries | 4.84 | 2.65 | 2.74 | 3.04 |
| Latin America | 4.69 | 2.01 | 2.09 | 2.26 |
| Africa | 4.12 | 2.42 | 2.60 | 2.97 |
| Asia | 6.28 | 4.04 | 3.90 | 4.06 |
| China | 5.03 | 7.36 | 9.80 | 9.73 |
| India | 3.57 | 5.68 | 5.54 | 5.79 |
| *GDP per capita* | | | | |
| World | 2.40 | 0.66 | 0.69 | 0.99 |
| Industrialized countries | 3.50 | 2.04 | 2.06 | 1.96 |
| Developing countries | 2.19 | 0.39 | 0.42 | 0.80 |
| Latin America | 2.11 | 0.15 | 0.20 | 0.44 |
| Africa | 1.66 | −0.17 | −0.06 | 0.39 |
| Asia | 2.90 | 1.61 | 1.36 | 1.63 |
| China | 3.01 | 6.01 | 8.46 | 8.51 |
| India | 1.40 | 3.62 | 3.50 | 3.83 |

*Notes*: (a) The growth rates for each period are computed as geometric means of the annual growth rates in that period. (b) The Maddison data and the United Nations data on GDP and GDP per capita are not strictly comparable. (c) The Maddison data on GDP and GDP per capita, which are in 1990 international Geary-Khamis dollars, are purchasing power parities used to evaluate output which are calculated based on a specific method devised to define international prices. This measure facilitates intercountry comparisons. (d) The United Nations data on GDP and GDP per capita are in constant 1990 US dollars. (e) The figures in this table for the world economy cover 128 countries, of which 21 are industrialized countries and 107 are developing countries. (f) Latin America includes the Caribbean.
*Sources*: Maddison (2003) and United Nations (2006a).

3.5 per cent per annum to 2 per cent per annum, but the slowdown was more pronounced for developing countries, from 2.2 per cent per annum to 0.8 per cent per annum. In Latin America and Africa, during 1981–2005, growth in GDP per capita was less than 0.5 per cent per annum, while Asia fared better at more than 1.5 per cent per annum. It is worth stressing that China and India were the exceptions to this worldwide slowdown in growth. In both countries, growth rates in the second period were much higher than the perfectly respectable growth rates in the first period. So much so that, between 1951–80 and 1981–2005,

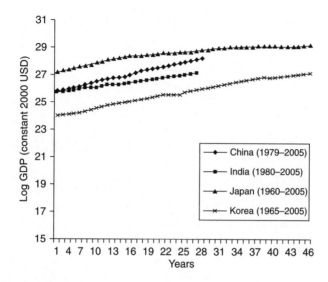

*Source*: World Bank (2007).
*Figure 5.1* GDP growth trajectories in China and India compared with Japan and Korea

average annual growth in GDP per capita almost trebled in both China and India. This was attributable in part to higher GDP growth rates and in part to lower population growth rates.

It might also be worth comparing the growth performance of China and India with the growth performance of other latecomers to industrialization at comparable stages of development. Figure 5.1 attempts such a comparison. It shows the GDP growth trajectories in China starting 1979, India starting 1980, Japan starting 1960 and Korea starting 1965, when rapid economic growth began in these countries. It would seem that China's economic growth performance is discernibly better while India's growth performance is roughly comparable with that of Japan and Korea. Interestingly enough, a comparison of growth in exports of goods and services, in Figure 5.2, reveals that export performance in China beginning 1979 and India beginning 1980 was almost at a par with that in Japan beginning 1960 and Korea beginning 1965, although the export growth in Japan and Korea was discernibly higher in the first decade.

### The future

The construction of future scenarios began with the Goldman Sachs study which attempted to project levels of GDP and GDP per capita

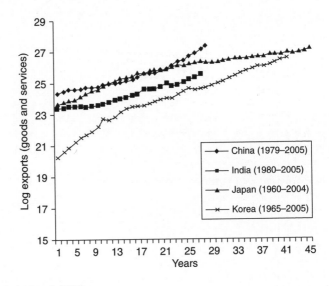

Source: World Bank (2007).
*Figure 5.2*   Export growth in China and India compared with Japan and Korea

for Brazil, Russia, India and China in 2050.[1] In attempting such projections, most exercises assume that growth rates in China and India, as also in the industrialized countries, would remain at levels observed in the recent past. In a more sophisticated exercise that uses simple convergence equations, Robert Rowthorn (2006) projects that, in 2050, at purchasing power parity, the per capita income in China would be 63 per cent of per capita income in the United States, while in India it would be 45 per cent. It is also projected that both China and India should comfortably overtake the United States in GDP measured at purchasing power parity. This catch-up is not confined to PPP-GDP comparisons. The Rowthorn projections show that, even at market exchange rates, by 2050, total output in China would be 60 per cent larger than in the US, while total output in India and the US would be roughly equal.[2]

It needs to be said that these projections suggest broad orders of magnitude rather than precise predictions. Even so, such projections highlight the power of compound growth rates. For growth rates do indeed matter. If GDP grows at 10 per cent per annum, national income doubles in seven years. If GDP per capita grows at 7 per cent per annum, per capita income doubles in ten years. If GDP grows at 7 per cent per annum, national income doubles in 14 years. Growth rates in China and India have been in this range for some time. And growth rates in India have accelerated in the early 2000s. If such growth rates are sustained, their cumulative impact over time is no surprise. However, growth is not simply about arithmetic. In fact, it is about more than economics. Therefore, it is necessary to consider the economic determinants of growth.

In principle, China and India may be able to sustain high rates of economic growth for some time to come for the following reasons. First, their population size is large and income levels are low. Second, their demographic characteristics, in particular the high proportion of young people in the population, which would mean an increase in the workforce for some time to come, are conducive to growth. Third, in both countries, wages are significantly lower than in the world outside, while there are large reservoirs of surplus labour. Fourth, emerging technological capabilities have the potential to support productivity increase. In practice, however, China and India may not be able to sustain their high rates of growth because of constraints that are already discernible. In China, the declining productivity of investment at the margin and the sustainability of the political system are both potential constraints. In India, the crisis in agriculture, the bottlenecks in infrastructure and the limited spread of education in society are potential constraints. Of course, these constraints are illustrative rather than exhaustive. And there are many others in both countries which could slow down the process of growth. Even if growth slows down, however, a catch-up scenario is plausible but it would require a longer period of time.

## Channels of engagement and transmission

The preceding discussion is largely in terms of macroeconomic aggregates. It is also necessary to consider the forms of engagement with the world economy, through which the impact of rapid economic growth in China and India, whether positive or negative, is transmitted elsewhere. The obvious, and most important, channels of transmission are international trade, international investment, international finance and international migration.

### International trade

International trade is, perhaps, the most important form of engagement with the world economy, not only for China and India but also for developing countries. Table 5.4 presents evidence on China's and India's trade in goods with the developing countries and the world as a whole in 2000

*Table 5.4*   Trade flows ($ billion)

| Country | Total exports | | Total imports | | | Exports to developing countries | | Imports from developing countries | |
|---|---|---|---|---|---|---|---|---|---|
| | 2000 | 2005 | 2000 | 2005 | | 2000 | 2005 | 2000 | 2005 |
| China | 249 | 762 | 225 | 660 | | 102 | 317 | 104 | 330 |
| India | 42 | 100 | 52 | 139 | | 17 | 52 | 17 | 45 |
| Total | 291 | 862 | 277 | 799 | | 119 | 369 | 121 | 375 |
| World | 6,444 | 10,441 | 6,642 | 10,712 | Developing countries | 803 | 1,614 | 791 | 1,664 |
| (China and India as % of) | (4.5) | (8.3) | (4.2) | (7.5) | (China and India as % of) | (14.8) | (22.9) | (15.3) | (22.5) |

*Note*: The figures in this table are on merchandise trade, exports and imports, in US$ billion at current prices.
*Source*: UNCTAD Handbook of Statistics On-line (http://stats.unctad.org/handbook).

and 2005. It shows the relative importance of China and India as markets for exports and sources of imports for the world. The share of China and India in world trade, as markets for exports and as sources of imports, doubled in this short span of time from a little more than 4 per cent in 2000 to about 8 per cent in 2005. The share of China and India in the trade of developing countries, both as markets for exports and as sources of imports, also rose rapidly from about 15 per cent in 2000 to almost 23 per cent in 2005. The emerging significance is clear. In 2005, China and India, taken together, accounted for about one-twelfth of merchandise trade in the world and somewhat less than one quarter of the merchandise trade of developing countries. It is worth noting that these aggregate proportions may be somewhat deceptive because, in 2005, China accounted for as much as 85 per cent while India accounted for only 15 per cent of these trade flows.

### International investment

The picture of international investment is different. In the global context, the relative importance of China and India is limited. Table 5.5 sets out evidence on foreign direct investment, inward and outward, in China and India compared with developing countries, industrialized countries and the world. The figures on stocks are for 2000 and 2005, while the figures on flows are annual averages for the period 2001–05.

*Table 5.5* Foreign direct investment: stocks and flows ($ billion)

| Country | Stocks | | | | Flows (average per annum) | |
|---|---|---|---|---|---|---|
| | Inward | | Outward | | Inward | Outward |
| | 2000 | 2005 | 2000 | 2005 | 2001–05 | 2001–05 |
| China | 193 | 318 | 28 | 46 | 57 | 4 |
| India | 18 | 45 | 2 | 10 | 6 | 2 |
| Total | 211 | 363 | 30 | 56 | 63 | 6 |
| Developing Countries | 1,697 | 2,655 | 856 | 1,268 | 225 | 80 |
| (China and India as % of) | (12.4) | (13.7) | (3.5) | (4.4) | (27.9) | (7.5) |
| Developed countries | 4,035 | 7,219 | 5,593 | 9,278 | 476 | 602 |
| World | 5,803 | 10,130 | 6,471 | 10,672 | 727 | 691 |
| (China and India as % of) | (3.6) | (3.6) | (0.5) | (0.5) | (8.6) | (0.9) |

*Source*: UNCTAD Foreign Direct Investment Online Database (http://stats.unctad.org/fdi).

In the early 2000s, China and India accounted for about one-eighth the inward stock of foreign direct investment in developing countries and one-thirtieth of that in the world. During the period 2001–05, China and India accounted for about 28 per cent of inward flows of foreign direct investment in developing countries and a little less than 9 per cent of those in the world. In the early 2000s, China and India accounted for about 4 per cent of the outward stock of foreign direct investment from developing countries and a mere 0.5 per cent of that in the world. During the period 2001–05, China and India accounted for 7.5 per cent of the outward flows of foreign direct investment from developing countries and about 1 per cent of those from the world. It is necessary to recognize that these aggregate proportions may be deceptive because, as with trade, in 2005, China accounted for more than 80 per cent whereas India accounted for less than 20 per cent of this foreign direct investment, whether inward or outward. Even so, it is possible to draw three inferences from this evidence. First, foreign direct investment in, and from, China and India is small as a proportion of both stocks and flows in the world. Second, for China and India, inward foreign direct investment is much more significant than outward foreign direct investment in terms of both stocks and flows.[3] Third, it would seem that China and India are more a competition for, rather than a source of, foreign direct investment for developing countries.

## International finance

International finance is, perhaps, the least important form of engagement for China and India with developing countries in the world economy. In principle, China and India could be potential sources of finance for development through current account surpluses, foreign exchange reserves and foreign aid flows. Let us consider each in turn.

The current account surplus in the balance of payments is significant for China and negligible for India. In China, the current account surplus rose from a modest US$3.3 billion per annum during 1991–95 to US$23.5 billion per annum during 1996–2000, and US$65.6 billion per annum during 2001–05. This current account surplus, as a proportion of GDP, increased from 0.8 per cent to 2.3 per cent and 3.5 per cent, respectively, in the three periods.[4] In India, there was a modest current account surplus of US$2 billion per annum during 2001–05, while there was a current account deficit of US$3.75 billion per annum through the 1990s. The current account surplus, during 2001–05 was the equivalent of just 0.9 per cent of GDP. This contrast is easily explained in a wider macroeconomic context. During the period 2001–05, as a proportion of GDP, gross domestic savings exceeded gross capital formation in China by 3 percentage points, whereas gross capital formation exceeded gross domestic savings in India by 1.7 percentage points.[5] This evidence suggests that China is a potential source of international finance for developing countries but India is not, at least so far.

In the sphere of foreign exchange reserves, however, the similarities are greater than the differences. Table 5.6 outlines the trends in foreign exchange reserves, from 1996 to 2005, for China, India, developing countries and the world. It shows that both China and India accumulated international reserves at a rapid rate during this decade. Between 1996 and 2005, the share of China and India in the total foreign exchange reserves of developing countries more than doubled from 15 per cent to 33 per cent, while their share of foreign exchange reserves in the world as a whole almost trebled from 7.6 per cent to 22.3 per cent. Once again, it is important to note that these aggregates are deceptive because China accounted for more than 80 per cent of the international reserves held by the two countries taken together. The substantial importance of China and India in foreign exchange reserves held by central banks, however, does not quite translate into a potential source of finance for developing countries. This is so for two reasons. First, an overwhelming

*Table 5.6* Foreign exchange reserves (SDRs billion)

| Years | China | India | Total | Developing countries | China & India as % of | World | China & India as % of |
|---|---|---|---|---|---|---|---|
| 1996 | 75 | 14 | 89 | 601 | 14.9 | 1,178 | 7.6 |
| 1997 | 106 | 19 | 125 | 691 | 18.1 | 1,297 | 9.6 |
| 1998 | 106 | 20 | 126 | 706 | 17.9 | 1,282 | 9.8 |
| 1999 | 115 | 24 | 140 | 786 | 17.8 | 1,405 | 9.9 |
| 2000 | 130 | 29 | 159 | 902 | 17.6 | 1,586 | 10.0 |
| 2001 | 172 | 37 | 209 | 1,022 | 20.5 | 1,741 | 12.0 |
| 2002 | 215 | 50 | 265 | 1,127 | 23.5 | 1,890 | 14.0 |
| 2003 | 275 | 67 | 342 | 1,306 | 26.2 | 2,155 | 15.9 |
| 2004 | 396 | 82 | 478 | 1,588 | 30.1 | 2,521 | 19.0 |
| 2005 | 575 | 93 | 668 | 2,035 | 32.8 | 3,000 | 22.3 |

*Note*: The data relate to international reserves held by the Central Banks of countries or country groups at the end of the calendar year.
*Source*: IMF International Financial Statistics Online Database (http://imfStatistics.org).

proportion of these foreign exchange reserves are held in the form of fiduciary deposits or government bonds in industrialized countries, so that actual placements are not put to any strategic use, let alone provide a potential source of finance for development. Second, even these massive foreign exchange reserves are marginal in relation to transactions in international finance, given that daily transactions in foreign exchange in world markets are as large as the foreign exchange reserves held by all the central banks in the world.[6]

The possibilities are much greater in the sphere of foreign aid and development assistance. Both China and India are emerging as donors, with a significant presence in Africa. The thrust of China's aid programmes is development finance, whereas the focus of India's aid programmes is technical assistance. Evidence on foreign aid flows from China and India to developing countries is not readily available. It is clear, however, that it is relatively small as compared with that provided by the industrialized countries.[7] Yet, it is possible that the multiplier effects of aid from China and India may be significant.

## International migration

International migration is, possibly, a significant form of engagement with the world economy for China and even more so for India. In the contemporary world economy, it is possible to distinguish between four categories of cross-border movements of people. The traditional category is emigrants. The new categories are guest workers, illegal migrants and professionals. Both China and India have always been, and continue to be, important countries-of-origin for international migration. Globalization has, however, increased the mobility of labour in the new categories.[8] China and India are also countries-of-origin for such cross-border movements of people.

Remittances are, perhaps, the most important source of development finance associated with international migration.[9] Indeed, for India, remittances are a substantial source of external finance.[10] For China too, remittances are considerable. But China and India export labour to, rather than import it from, other developing countries. Consequently, remittances from China and India simply do not enter the picture as a source of development finance. The engagement of China and India with developing countries, through international migration, is attributable in part to the diaspora and in part to globalization.

The diaspora has historical origins. Following the abolition of slavery in the British Empire, starting around the mid-1830s, for a period of 50 years, about 50 million people left India and China to work as indentured labour in mines, plantations and construction in the Americas, the Caribbean, South Africa, South East Asia and other distant lands.[11] This was probably close to 10 per cent of the total population of India and China circa 1880. The migration from India and China continued, in somewhat different forms, during the first half of the twentieth century, particularly in the period between the two world wars. There is, consequently, a significant presence of the diaspora from China and India across the world, not only in the industrialized countries but also in the developing countries. This is associated with entrepreneurial capitalism, both Chinese and Indian, in developing countries where the migration stream has aged.

The second half of the twentieth century also witnessed significant waves of international migration from India, made up of permanent emigration to the industrialized countries and temporary migration to the oil-exporting countries in the Middle East.[12] The international migration from China, however, was limited during this period. Of course, such migration, particularly to the industrialized countries, is now constrained by immigration laws and consular practices. But the gathering momentum of globalization during the past two decades has led to a significant increase in the new categories of cross-border movements of people. In this sphere, the engagement of India with the world economy is much more than that of China. The advent of globalization, which has also made it easier to move people across borders, is associated with managerial capitalisms, especially with professionals from India who can migrate permanently, live abroad temporarily, or stay at home and travel frequently for business. These people are almost as mobile as capital across borders.

## Implications for developing countries

Globalization is associated with increasing economic openness, growing economic interdependence and deepening economic integration in the world economy. In such a world, growth prospects would be significantly influenced, if not shaped, by the growth performance of lead economies. The discussion that follows asks whether China and India could be new engines of growth, considers the underlying mechanisms, and examines and explores the possible impact on developing countries.

### Engines of growth?

History provides obvious examples. Britain in the nineteenth century and the United States in the twentieth century were engines of growth for the world economy. Statistical analysis for the period since the early 1960s provides confirmation.[13] It is widely accepted that GDP growth in the United States leads GDP growth in the world. A statistical analysis of long-term trends in economic growth, with five-year moving averages for both sets of growth rates, yields a correlation coefficient of 0.82, while a simple lead-lag analysis shows that the US economy leads the world economy by one year. Evidence available also reveals that developing countries, excluding China, follow the trends in world economic growth and, hence, trends in economic growth of the United States. It is worth noting that economic growth in developing countries follows economic growth in the United States with a lag, but with more pronounced swings in cyclical ups and downs.

Rapid economic growth in China and India, if it is sustained at the projected rates, is bound to exercise considerable influence on prospects for the world economy, the industrialized countries and the developing countries. The consequences for the world economy could be positive in so far as these two mega-economies from Asia turn into engines of growth. The impact could also be negative in the form of environmental and labour market consequences. It would mean too much of a digression to enter into a discussion of these possibilities here. Similarly, rapid economic growth in China and India would have an impact on the industrialized countries. This impact, too, could be either positive or negative. Such an analysis, however, is beyond the scope of this chapter.

In any case, the possible consequences of the rise of China and India for the industrialized countries have been considered in the emerging literature on the subject.[14] Therefore, the focus of this chapter is on the implications and consequences for developing countries.

In reflecting on the future, is it possible to think of China and India as engines of growth for the developing world, even if not for the world economy? The answer depends, in large part, on the size of the two economies and their rates of growth. There are some pointers in recent experience. Statistical analysis shows that, since 1980, the Chinese economy also leads world GDP, with a lag of one or two years, although the correlation coefficient is much smaller than that for the United States. This is not surprising. For one, in 2005, China accounted for 5 per cent of world GDP at market exchange rates and 14 per cent of world GDP in PPP terms. For another, GDP growth in China has been in the range of 9 per cent per annum for 25 years. By these criteria, India is not an engine of growth, at least not yet. This is also not surprising. Its economic size is smaller than that of China and its growth rate is not as high. In 2005, India accounted for only 2 per cent of world GDP at market exchange rates and 6 per cent of world GDP in PPP terms. For another, GDP growth in India has been in the range of 6 per cent per annum for 25 years. Even so, India is a potential engine of growth in terms of both attributes.

Rapid economic growth in lead economies drives economic growth elsewhere in the world by providing markets for exports, resources for investment, finances for development, and technologies for productivity. The classic examples – Britain in the nineteenth century and the United States in the twentieth century – provide confirmation of the suggested economic causation and the possible transmission mechanisms. Indeed, during their periods of dominance in the world, both Britain and the United States were engines of growth, insofar as they provided the rest of the world not only with markets for exports and resources for investment, but also with finance for development and technologies for productivity. At this juncture, China is not quite an engine of growth in every dimension. Economic growth in China provides a stimulus to economic growth elsewhere, in large part, as a market for exports. So far, India cannot be characterized as an engine of growth in any dimension, perhaps not even as a market for exports.

## Causation and mechanisms

The economic causation outlined above is necessary but not sufficient. The overall effects of economic growth in lead economies on economic growth elsewhere depend upon: (a) whether such growth is complementary or competitive; (b) whether the direct effects are reinforced or counteracted by the indirect effects; and (c) whether, on balance, the impact is positive or negative.[15]

In principle, economic growth in lead economies may be complementary or competitive to economic growth elsewhere. It may be complementary insofar as it increases the demand for exports, but it may be competitive insofar as it develops alternative sources of supply. It may be complementary if it provides resources for investment or finance for development, but it may be competitive if it pre-empts such resources for investment or finances for development. It may be complementary if it provides technologies to others, but it may be competitive if it stifles the development of technologies elsewhere. This distinction between the complementary and the competitive aspects is widely recognized. However, the distinction between direct effects and indirect effects is less clear because the latter sometimes are difficult to discern, let alone measure. In situations where direct effects are complementary, indirect effects could be reinforcing if complementary, but counteracting if competitive. Some examples might be illustrative.

The direct effects may be complementary if the lead economies, say China and India, provide cheap wage goods to other developing countries, but the indirect effects may be competitive if competition from firms in lead economies, say China and India, squeezes out local firms in other developing countries. The direct effects may be complementary if firms from the lead economies, say China and India, invest in other developing countries, but the indirect effects may be competitive if firms from industrialized countries relocate production and invest in China and India rather than in other developing countries. The direct effects may be complementary if lead economies, say China and India, provide cheaper inputs for manufactured exports from other developing countries, but the indirect effects may be competitive if competition from lead economies, say China and India, squeezes out manufactured exports from other developing countries in the markets of industrialized countries. In principle, then, the impact of economic growth in lead economies on economic growth elsewhere could be positive, or negative, or some combination of both. Therefore, on balance, such impact can be either positive or negative. The outcomes may differ across space and change over time, so that generalizations are difficult.

In this context, it is worth noting that macroeconomic policies in China and India, once they become lead economies, may exercise an important influence on economic growth elsewhere. If such policies are countercyclical, which has been the case for the United States, these would be supportive of economic growth elsewhere. But if these policies are pro-cyclical, which is common in developing countries, these could be disruptive for economic growth elsewhere. Similarly, exchange rates and interest rates in lead economies could exercise a significant influence, either positive or negative, on economic growth elsewhere in the world. For example, an undervalued exchange rate in China, which has persisted for quite some time, constrains the prospects for labour-intensive manufactured exports from other developing countries, thereby limiting the potential demand stimulus to economic growth that could be provided by exports. Similarly, a high interest rate in India, which has been the case for some time, pre-empts possible foreign capital inflows, thereby limiting the potential external finance necessary to support economic growth in other developing countries.

### Possible impact

During the first quarter of the twenty-first century, economic growth in China and India could have a positive impact on developing countries if it improves the terms of trade, provides appropriate technologies and creates new sources of finance for development, whether as investment or aid. Let us consider each in turn.

It is clear that, for some time to come, the positive impact on developing countries would be transmitted through an improvement in their terms of trade.[16] Rapid economic growth in China and India is bound to boost the demand for primary commodities exported by developing countries. The reasons are simple enough. Both China and India have large populations. But that is not all. In both countries, levels of consumption per capita in most primary commodities are low, while income elasticities of demand for most primary commodities are high. This burgeoning demand will almost certainly raise prices of primary commodities in world markets and thereby improve the terms of trade for developing countries. What is more, China already is, and India is likely to become, a source of manufactured goods in the world market. Such manufactures, particularly wage goods, from China and India, are likely to be cheaper than competing goods from industrialized countries. This would also improve the terms of trade for developing countries.

The positive impact of China and India on developing countries through the other potential channels of transmission is not as clear. We do not yet have either the evidence or the experience. In principle, it is possible that China and India would develop technologies that are more appropriate for the factor endowments and the economic needs of developing countries. But it is too early to come to a judgment on this matter. Similarly, China and India are potential sources of finance for development. Their foreign aid programmes, particularly in Africa, constitute a modest beginning. But their contribution in terms of foreign direct investment is limited so far.

The emergence of China and India in the world economy could also have a negative impact on developing countries if the two megaeconomies provide developing countries with competition as markets for exports or as destinations for investment. Let us examine each in turn.

At this juncture, China is clearly the largest supplier of labour-intensive manufactured goods in the world market. Even if not as large as China, India is also a significant supplier. There can be little doubt that manufactured exports from China and India span almost the entire range of manufactured exports in which other developing countries could have a potential comparative advantage. Hence, it is plausible to argue, though impossible to prove that, on balance, China and India possibly have a negative impact on manufactured exports from other developing countries which have to compete with China and India for export markets in industrialized countries. This can change if and when China and India vacate their space in the international trade matrix, in much the same way as latecomers to industrialization in Asia, such as Japan, Korea, Hong Kong, Taiwan and Singapore, vacated their space in the market for simple labour-intensive manufactures for countries that followed in their footsteps. This is not likely, at least in the medium term, because both China and India have large reservoirs of surplus labour at low wages, not only in the rural hinterlands but also in the urban informal sectors.

The evidence presented earlier showed that China and India absorb a significant proportion of inward foreign direct investment in developing countries, both in terms of stocks and flows. Given that the two Asian giants are now among the most attractive destinations for transnational firms seeking to locate production in the developing world, it is once again plausible to suggest though impossible to prove that foreign direct investment in China and India might be at the expense of developing countries. At the same time, the share of China and India in outward foreign direct investment in the world economy, as also from developing countries, is modest in both stocks and flows, so that firms from China and India do not compensate with foreign direct investment in other developing countries.

The less discernible but more significant negative impact of the Asian mega-economies, particularly China, on developing countries is implicit in the unchanged division of labour. For one, China and India might pre-empt opportunities for other developing countries to industrialize through manufactured exports, which is attributable to their surplus labour and low wages that might continue for some time to come. For another, China's present division of labour with the developing world, reflected in the composition of trade flows, is not different from the old North–South pattern of trade, insofar as Chinese imports from the developing world are largely primary commodities, while Chinese exports to the developing world are largely manufactured goods.[17] China's trade with countries in South East Asia is the exception to this rule. But Chinese trade with, and investment in, Africa confirms even more closely to this caricature neocolonial pattern. Such traditional patterns of trade, it should be recognized, can neither transform the structure of production in developing countries nor make for a new international division of labour. Indeed, such trade can only perpetuate the dependence of developing countries on exports of primary commodities without creating possibilities of increasing value added before export or entering into manufacturing activities characterized by economies of scale. Such path-dependent specialization can only curb the possibilities of structural transformation in developing countries. Trade with China and India can sustain growth and support industrialization in developing countries only if there is a successful transition from a complementary to a competitive pattern of trade, so that intersectoral trade is gradually replaced by intrasectoral or intra-industry trade and specialization.

## Concluding remarks

In conclusion, it is worth noting two important limitations of the analysis in this chapter. First, it considers China and India together, which may be somewhat deceptive insofar as China is much larger than India in almost every dimension of engagement with the world economy. Second, it considers China and India as a composite, which may not be entirely appropriate insofar as economic and political rivalry between the countries could exercise a significant influence in shaping the impact on developing countries. Even so, the chapter constitutes an important beginning in a relatively unexplored subject. It is clear that, in times to come, economic development in China and India will have implications and consequences, both positive and negative, for developing countries. The impact, on balance, will depend upon how reality unfolds. But it would also depend on the nature of China's and India's interaction with developing countries, just as it would depend upon what developing countries do to maximize the benefits and minimize the costs associated with the rise of China and India in the world economy. There is, obviously, a strong need for more research on the subject.

## Notes

1. For the methodology and the conclusions, see Wilson and Purushothaman (2003).
2. For a detailed discussion on the model, the data and the results, see Rowthorn (2006).
3. For an analysis of investment and acquisitions by Indian firms abroad, see Nayyar (2008a).
4. See World Bank (2007).
5. These averages for the period are calculated from data reported in World Bank (2007).
6. See Nayyar (2006).
7. During the period 2001–05, net ODA disbursements from DAC countries were US$ 73,200 million per annum, while net ODA disbursements from non-DAC donors were a mere US$ 575 million per annum. For the annual statistics, see http:// stats.oecd.org/wbos.
8. For a discussion of the categories, and an analysis of the changing nature of international migration, see Nayyar (2002).
9. See Solimano (2005) and Nayyar (2008b).
10. For an analysis of the macroeconomic significance of remittances in India, see Nayyar (1994).
11. See Lewis (1977) and Nayyar (2002).
12. For a discussion, see Nayyar (1994).
13. For a more detailed discussion on the statistical evidence and analysis cited in this paragraph, see United Nations (2006b).
14. See, for example, Freeman (2005), Rowthorn (2006) and Singh (2007).
15. For a detailed discussion, see Kaplinsky (2006). The literature on this subject is limited. But the implications and consequences of rapid growth in China and India, for the developing world, are analysed in Kaplinsky and Messner (2008).
16. This proposition is stressed by Kaplinsky (2006), Rowthorn (2006) and Singh (2007).
17. See United Nations (2006b, p. 22).

## References

Freeman, R. B. (2005) 'What Really Ails Europe and America: The Doubling of the Global Workforce', *Globalist*, 3 June.
Kaplinsky, R. (ed.) (2006) 'Asian Drivers: Opportunities and Threats', *IDS Bulletin* 37.
Kaplinsky, R. and D. Messner (2008) 'The Impact of the Asian Drivers on the Developing World', *World Development* 36 (2): 197–209.

Lewis, W. A. (1977) *The Evolution of the International Economic Order*, Princeton: Princeton University Press.

Maddison, A. (2003) *The World Economy: Historical Statistics*, Paris: OECD.

Nayyar, D. (1994) *Migration, Remittances and Capital Flows: The Indian Experience*, Delhi: Oxford University Press.

Nayyar, D. (2002) 'Cross-Border Movements of People', in D. Nayyar (ed.), *Governing Globalization: Issues and Institutions*, Oxford: Oxford University Press.

Nayyar, D. (2006) 'Globalization, History and Development: A Tale of Two Centuries', *Cambridge Journal of Economics* 30 (1): 137–59.

Nayyar, D. (2008a) 'The Internationalization of Firms from India: Investment, Mergers and Acquisitions', *Oxford Development Studies* 36 (1): 111–31.

Nayyar, D. (2008b) 'International Migration and Economic Development', in J. Stiglitz and N. Serra (eds), *The Washington Consensus Reconsidered: Towards a New Global Governance*, Oxford: Oxford University Press.

Rowthorn, R. (2006) 'The Renaissance of China and India: Implications for the Advanced Economies', UNCTAD discussion paper 182, October, Geneva: UNCTAD.

Singh, A. (2007) 'Globalization, Industrial Revolutions in India and China and Labour Markets in Advanced Countries: Implications for National and International Economic Policy', working paper 81, Policy Integration Department, March, Geneva: ILO.

Solimano, A. (2005) 'Remittances by Emigrants: Issues and Evidence', in A. B. Atkinson (ed.), *New Sources of Development Finance*, Oxford: Oxford University Press.

United Nations (2006a) National Accounts Main Aggregates Database, Department of Economic and Social Affairs, New York, available at http://unstats.un.org/unsd/snaama/introduction.asp.

United Nations (2006b) *Diverging Growth and Development, World Economic and Social Survey 2006*, New York: United Nations.

Wilson, D. and R. Purushothaman (2003) 'Dreaming with BRICS: The Path to 2050', Global Economics Paper 99, New York: Goldman Sachs.

World Bank (2007) *World Development Indicators 2007*, Washington, DC: World Bank.

# 6
# China's Impact on Sub-Saharan African Development: Trade, Aid and Politics

*John Toye*

## Introduction

It is a great privilege to be asked to contribute to a Festschrift for Ajit Singh. Ajit's reputation as a fine economist rests in the first instance on his body of work on the economics of corporate takeovers, industrial mergers and associated issues of performance and profitability, which have great relevance for policies of corporate governance. However, in addition to his pioneering research on these issues, he has also written extensively on questions of industrialization and economic development, including growth in developing countries and the effectiveness of development aid. In these areas of development economics, Ajit has been a powerful controversialist, marking out and defending positions that avoid standard Eurocentric presuppositions and take seriously the perspectives of developing countries. Throughout his career, he has provided a challenging counterpoint to the views of mainstream development economists. In a time of intellectual conformity, his has been the voice of unapologetic and creative heterodoxy.

In a recent paper on aid, conditionality and development, Ajit opened up a debate with Jan Pronk on these topics with his customary clarity and force (Singh, 2002, pp. 295–305). Within a brief compass, Ajit covered a great deal of important ground, and did so in a way that invited continuing discussion and debate. This chapter joins that argument, focusing particularly on the vexed question of the use of policy conditionality in aid agreements. I wish to challenge the rather romantic conception of the developing countries, and of the economic relations between them, that tends to surface in the aid-conditionality debate. To do so I shall place heavy emphasis on a global phenomenon that is often neglected, namely the process of economic differentiation among developing countries. I believe that the economic differentiation of developing countries has very important implications for the debate on the effectiveness of aid. Increasingly over the last 50 years, the progress of economic differentiation has blurred the original sharpness of the division between developed and developing countries, and blunted its usefulness in controversies over official development aid.

The stark fact is that, while the economic indicators of the OECD countries have tended to converge, those of the non-OECD countries have sharply diverged, bringing some of them close to OECD levels while others have moved even further away from them. It seems that a country must reach a threshold level of income or skill before international economic convergence via technology transfer can take place (Baumol *et al.*, 1994). The existence of such a threshold, leading to the divergence among developing countries, would open up a new area of potential policy problems, not least when some developing countries begin to provide development aid for others. I intend to explore this issue through the lens of the economic and political relations between the People's Republic of China (PRC) and sub-Saharan Africa (SSA). Perhaps it will be objected that the nexus between these two parties represents an extreme case. So it does, but since about one-third of the people living in low income countries are in sub-Saharan Africa, it has some claim to be worthy of attention in its own right.

Twenty years ago, I drew attention to the economic differentiation of the developing countries, even then putting a dramatic question: 'does the Third World still exist?'. I argued that, while the Third World had a psychological and political reality, based on experiences of colonialism, it has no economic homogeneity – and that was precisely the reason why one-size-fits-all policy formulas such as the neo-liberal consensus could not succeed in inducing widespread development. This is what I said in 1987, with due apologies for repetition:

> The relative position of Africa has worsened steadily during the last twenty years, with the continent as a whole seeing little growth in the 1970s and falls in output in the 1980s ... Economies least affected by the recession of the 1980s were those already growing very fast. Important in this group were the East Asian economies achieving their growth through investment in industries that could produce manufactured export, plus India and China, who were following an inward-looking strategy of industrialization. (Toye, 1993, p. 35)

The structure of what I have to say now is as follows. First, I will note the rhetorical format in which the recent unprecedented expansion of trade and aid cooperation between the PRC and SSA is presented by both parties. This is the familiar rhetoric of South–South cooperation, which speaks of mutual respect and reciprocity in international relations between developing countries. I will suggest that this rhetoric needs to be interrogated in the light of inequalities in the economic situations of the PRC and SSA, some of which I then illustrate. The argument is that the concept of 'developing countries' needs to be unpacked, given the great and growing differences between some of them.

I will then turn to trade and examine the likely effects of increasing SSA–PRC trade. Africa's terms of trade are likely to continue to improve, but the development impact of this economic improvement will be mediated by national political structures and institutions. I will take account of characteristic instruments of the PRC's burgeoning economic diplomacy, specifically the fact that trade and FDI expansion are linked to aid flows. I argue that the availability of Chinese aid without policy conditions will undermine OECD efforts to attach policy conditions to its aid to Africa, and this will have adverse effects on institutional quality, and thus on income distribution and poverty reduction. I will then detail the recent experience of five countries where expanded economic relations with the PRC have had unhelpful consequences for poverty reduction and standards of governance. I briefly speculate on how the PRC's growing economic presence in SSA is likely to play out in the future.

## The PRC and the rhetoric of South–South cooperation

The credibility of Stalin's doctrine that the whole world was divided into two armed camps evaporated soon after his death in 1953. The PRC, under its 'Great Helmsman' Mao Zedong, began to move out of the shadow of the Soviet Union. Mao cancelled previous agreements for Soviet aid, and expelled Russian technical assistance personnel in 1955. Before the Sino–Soviet rift became obvious to the West, the PRC used the Bandung Conference of 1955 to join with India and Yugoslavia at the head of a group of nations that were not aligned to either side of the cold war, but were self-declared neutrals in that conflict, later known collectively as the Third World. Indeed, it was the Bandung Conference that initiated sustained relations between the PRC and selected African countries (Mawdsley, 2007, p. 4). From that beginning, the PRC has taken a twin-track approach to developing countries, on the one hand robustly promoting 'communism with Chinese characteristics' and on the other representing itself as just another developing economy interested in mutual cooperation. It is noteworthy that, of the 76 UN members supporting the PRC's displacement of Taiwan on the UN Security Council in 1971, 26 were African (ibid., p. 5). The memory of Bandung still lingers on, able to be strongly evoked, for example, at the African–Asian summit held in Jakarta in April 2005.

South–South cooperation is often held up as a superior way to promote development, compared with the fraught and conflict-ridden trade and aid relationships between the countries of the developing South and those of the developed industrial North. Several assumptions, both negative and positive, underpin this claim of superiority. The most familiar negative assumption is that North–South relations still remain inherently tainted by the history of imperialism. It is said that the granting of formal political independence did not confer genuine independence on former colonies and that new forms of assistance, such as development aid, were intended to try to create and sustain neocolonial dependence in the South.

Instead of simply following this standard analysis of neocolonial dependence, Ajit has offered us a variation on it. He argues that the cold war provided developing countries with an opportunity to draw the sting of neocolonialism. By playing one side in the cold war off against the other, he argues, developing countries were able to preserve their autonomy over policy and neutralize neocolonial machinations. Further, he sees the preservation of their policy autonomy as the cause of the developing countries' good growth record in 'the Golden Age' (the period 1950–73), which was faster compared both with the colonial period and with the era of policy-conditioned aid that has prevailed since the debt crisis of 1982 (Singh, 2002, pp. 298–9).

This is a bold attribution, for which I would suggest the evidence is far from conclusive. In particular, it is significant that it omits any analysis of what happened during the – in my view crucial – decade from 1973 to 1982. It is silent about the whole sorry story of the oil price rises, stagflation in the OECD countries and the response of developing countries to the ill-advised recycling of petrodollars (for which see Mosley *et al.*, 1995, pp. 4–9). In this decade, serious economic policy mistakes were made by many countries, developed and developing alike. To attribute the debt crisis solely to a change in US monetary policy in the early 1980s, as Ajit seems to do, closes off the question of whether developing countries were exercising wisely what policy autonomy they had before that change occurred.

Apart from that, it is far from clear how much policy autonomy really existed for aid recipients during the cold war. Certainly, when the PRC's aid provision to Africa was strong in the 1960s and early 1970s, it was directed to support only left-wing movements and governments, sometimes by making big infrastructure investments (e.g. the Tanzam railway). This form of ideological aid engagement weakened after the fall of Mao. From then until the turn of the century, Africa mainly figured in Chinese diplomacy as part of the PRC's campaign to isolate Taiwan in the international diplomatic arena. Chinese aid to Africa declined as, under Deng Xiaoping's rule, its strategy directed effort inwards to domestic modernization and growth. Since 2000, however, plans for much greater PRC–Africa exchanges have been made and they are being executed under the rhetorical banner of South–South cooperation.

The PRC–Africa summit meeting held in Beijing in November 2006 was attended by 40 African heads of state and government, and was the largest such gathering ever organized by a foreign power without colonial ties to Africa. The final communiqué announced 'a new type of strategic partnership between Africa and China, featuring political equality and mutual trust, economic win-win cooperation and cultural exchanges'. This was warmly welcomed by African governments. An Ethiopian spokesperson emphasized the complementary nature of PRC–Africa cooperation and South–South cooperation. The Angolan Prime Minister reiterated the need to strengthen South–South cooperation by deepening commercial and economic relations between the PRC and Africa. The Sudanese president praised the ties between Sudan and China as an 'exemplary' case of South–South cooperation.

The positive assumption behind these high-flown statements is that developing countries are in a sufficiently similar situation to each other to generate sincere mutual sympathy and understanding, so that their relations could be better planned, less self-interested and more genuinely cooperative in nature. I shall suggest that, in the instance of the PRC and SSA, this assumption does not survive inspection of the facts.

## The PRC and SSA: some economic comparisons

The assumption of similar situations and shared interests between developing countries is questionable, given the considerable, and growing, heterogeneity of the developing countries, in their natural endowments, their institutions and their cultures. How can cooperation still take place on the basis of equality of respect if, in reality, wide economic disparities separate the would-be partners?

In the context of the PRC and SSA, it may be helpful to review some simple measures of the economic distance between them. There are 47 separate countries in SSA, so there is a considerable heterogeneity within it. Even if we disregard those intra-SSA differences and aggregate all the countries of SSA for the purpose of comparison with the PRC, we still find considerable economic disparities. For example, the area of SSA is two and a half times larger than the PRC, and SSA has just over half the number of the PRC's population. Although this gives SSA a much more favourable land/labour ratio than the PRC, per capita income in the PRC at $1,500 per head is two and a half times that of SSA ( at $601 per head). Part of this difference is accounted for by the higher share of industry in value added in the PRC. In the PRC it is nearly one half, while in SSA it is only one-third, and much of the latter figure derives from the dubious accounting convention that includes resource extraction in the category of 'industry'.

Initial differences in endowments and their productivity have been further enlarged by a powerful and continuing process of economic differentiation over the last 30 years. In 1978, the economic reforms of Deng Xiaoping set the PRC on a path of economic liberalization and accelerated growth. Meanwhile, SSA entered a period of deep economic crisis, followed by stabilization and partial recovery. While the share of industry in value added rose in the PRC, SSA experienced deindustrialization. The increasing divergence between the PRC and SSA was belatedly (and inadequately) recognized by the international community in September 2006, when the PRC's quota in the IMF (which depends on its 'position in the world economy') was increased from 2.5 to 3.73 per cent, and SSA's was reduced from 5 to 2.5 per cent.

The economic differentiation of the PRC and SSA can be illustrated very dramatically by contrasting their respective paths of economic development since 1960. Compare first of all the growth rates of output in the PRC and in 19 African countries for the period 1960 to 2000. Whereas the PRC's economy was growing at just under 3 per cent a year in the 1960s, rising to 10 per cent in the 1990s, SSA's economies grew at over 5 per cent in the 1960s and fell to 2.3 per cent in the 1990s. The PRC's story is one of ever accelerating growth of output, labour productivity, capital per worker and total factor productivity. In the African countries, by contrast, the pace of growth has been progressively slowing and the growth of labour productivity and of total factor productivity have now both turned negative. The contrast between these two growth trajectories – one accelerating since 1960 and the other increasingly faltering – is almost total, according to figures calculated by Bosworth and Collins (2003, p. 122, Table 1).

Key social indicators, such as births attended by skilled health staff, the infant mortality rate and the primary school completion rate have also shown increasing divergence between the PRC and SSA over the past 15 years. In most cases, the widening of these gaps has been caused, not by the stagnation or retrogression of SSA in social terms. (The main exception to this statement is that life expectancy in SSA has fallen as a consequence of the HIV/AIDS epidemic.) The general explanation is that, when social improvements have occurred in SSA, they have been extremely small relative to the very rapid progress that has meanwhile been taking place in the PRC. The percentage of births attended by a skilled health worker almost doubled in the PRC, for example, while in SSA it has scarcely moved at all.

## The growth of PRC–SSA trade

Despite the contrast in their growth trajectories, one accelerating and the other decelerating, trade between SSA and PRC–SSA has been growing rapidly. Worth roughly $1 billion in 1990, SSA's exports to the PRC had risen to $14 billion by 2004. A growth rate of 20 per cent annually between 1990–94 had risen to 48 per cent annually between 1999 and 2004. SSA's imports from the PRC – mainly manufactures, textiles and food grains – reached about $11 billion in 2004 (Broadman, 2007, pp. 79–80). Imports, like exports, have continued to rise spectacularly since then.

The main driver of the growth of SSA's exports to the PRC has been the latter's demand for oil to fuel its economic growth. In 2004, crude petroleum constituted two-thirds of all SSA exports to the PRC. The PRC had been self-sufficient in oil until 1993. Its demand for oil since then, driven by rapid economic growth, has not been matched by equivalent growth in domestic oil supplies. By 2003, the country imported 40 per cent of the oil it consumed, a figure that is predicted to rise to 60 per cent by 2020. At the moment, Africa provides about 25–30 per cent of this imported oil. Angola alone provided half of the total, while another 20 per cent comes from the Sudan. That is to say, that together these two African countries provide 7–8.5 per cent of Chinese oil consumption, while Africa as a whole provides 10–12 per cent. While this is not an overwhelmingly larger share, it is clear that its interruption for any reason would be highly damaging to Chinese growth.

However, the rapid expansion of trade has not altered the basic inequality of the relationship. While SSA's exports to the PRC now account for about 10 per cent of total SSA exports, this constitutes a much smaller share, around 2 per cent, of the PRC's total imports (Broadman, 2007, p. 11). Similarly, although the PRC's FDI in SSA has increased rapidly, the growth has not been reciprocal, and SSA's FDI in the PRC is extremely small. In general, there is a correlation between the export share of GDP and the FDI share (ibid., p. 28).

How, from the present position, is the trade relationship between the PRC and SSA likely to develop in the future? The changes will be the combined result of two economic processes:

1. The continued removal of barriers to trade, leading to a once-for-all increase in participation by the PRC in world import and export markets (including SSA). This change will bring the prices of traded goods into closer alignment with the trading countries' comparative advantages.
2. The growth of the PRC economy at a faster rate than those of its trading partners, leading to a continuous increase in its weight in the world trading system. This process will also alter the prices of traded goods, leading to changes in countries' terms of trade.

In this book, Adrian Wood argues for the usefulness of a modified version of the Heckscher-Ohlin theory in trade analysis. In this framework, as modified by Wood and Mayer (2001, pp. 370–1), comparative advantage is determined by the relative abundance of factors of production, the relevant factors taken to be land and labour disaggregated by skill, instead of the classical factors of homogeneous labour and capital. As previously indicated, SSA is relatively abundantly endowed with land, while the PRC is, relative to Africa, somewhat better endowed with skilled labour, a disparity that is likely to increase as rapid growth occurs. These comparative advantages indicate the tendencies that can be expected as trade barriers fall and the PRC grows more rapidly that SSA. Falling trade barriers will further expose the current comparative disadvantage of SSA's manufacturing industries, especially in labour-intensive manufacturing, so that earnings of workers with basic education in urban areas are likely to fall. Some of that real income loss will be compensated by the greater availability of cheap consumption goods imported to the urban areas from the PRC.

Apart from these effects, export competition in third-country markets is unlikely to be severe in general, but it will be damaging in a few country cases. Given the large differences in factor endowments, export overlap is the exception, not the rule. As one would expect, measures of the extent of overlap between the PRC's export patterns and those of SSA countries are lowest for the large oil producers like Nigeria and Sudan, and highest for countries like South Africa, Namibia, Kenya and Lesotho, where relatively unsophisticated forms of manufacturing have already been established (Jenkins and Edwards, 2006, Table 3). In recognition of South Africa's vulnerability to Chinese competition, the PRC has already negotiated a voluntary limit of Chinese exports of textiles to South Africa.

Finally, rapid economic growth in the PRC will bid up its demand for land-based primary products, in which Africa has a comparative advantage. This will continue to turn the terms of trade in SSA's favour, a trend that is already evident. On a base of 2000 = 100, SSA's terms of trade overall had risen to 121 by 2004/05. Terms of trade improvements had been even greater for oil exporting countries, such as Angola (134), Sudan (157), Gabon (144) and Nigeria (125). Oil producers will not be the only beneficiaries. The PRC's demand for non-ferrous metals has driven up the world prices of these commodities more recently, with gains for the Democratic Republic of the Congo (DRC) and Zambia. The same thing might happen also to food commodities, including livestock and meat products. Africa's meat exports are constrained by problems of reaching international veterinary health standards, but these could be lower in the Chinese market. However, on the whole there is little evidence so far to suggest that a process of African export diversification – even within the category of primary commodities – has resulted from the rapid expansion of trade relations with the PRC.

The way in which improvements in the terms of trade filter through to affect the average level and distribution of real incomes in SSA will depend on many factors. These include the system of land property rights and the pattern of ownership of land rights. Where the national government is the relevant owner, what matters is the quality of the institutions responsible for government expenditure, including transfers. Summary indices of institutional quality show that SSA ranks low relative to other regions (Wood, 2003, pp. 187–8 and Table 8).

As Wood and Mayer have observed, 'the most serious problems of natural-resource-based development are not economic, but political, and in particular that resource rents are often appropriated by social or political elites with little interest in the broad-based development of their countries' (2001, pp. 392–3). At least two distinct mechanisms are at work to undermine institutional quality. One derives from the pressure which governments that own resource rents are under to defend themselves against would-be usurpers. The ever-present concern to survive skews government spending in favour of the military, police and intelligence services, and it leads to the militarization of politics and to the political exclusion of opposition forces. The other undermining mechanism derives from the effect of natural resource rents in insulating the government from the need to engage politically with its own population. The government has a weak incentive to tax its population, and correspondingly a weak incentive to grant widespread political representation in return for receiving tax revenues. The countervailing pressure on it for developmental spending on education, health and social services has no channel. These two mechanisms can be mutually reinforcing (Moore, 2007, p. 21, n. 32).

Some of the empirical work testing the relation between government possession of natural resource wealth and institutional quality has run into measurement problems. When the correct measure of such wealth – the element of rent – is used, the negative statistical association with institutional quality emerges in the regression results. If high institutional quality is necessary for ensuring an efficient and equitable distribution of terms of trade gains, the prospects for widespread distribution of the gains from trade are bleak. In my view, institutional quality is precisely what is likely to be eroded in some SSA countries, as a direct consequence of greater PRC–SSA cooperation, and the practice of bundling together deals on trade, investment and aid. I shall elaborate on this claim in the following section.

## Trade/FDI/aid bundling and its dangers

As the world markets for primary commodities – but especially oil supplies – continue to tighten as a result of increased demand from the PRC, it becomes less likely that such trade will be conducted at arm's length at spot prices and more probable that such trade will be negotiated as part of a larger set of long-term contracts, including offers of soft loans, FDI and technical assistance on favourable terms. The incentive to lock in commodity trade by means of various forms of aid will be strong.

The PRC's scramble for influence and resources in Africa since 2000 has involved the use of various linked policies, which though basically familiar also have some distinct Chinese characteristics:

1. Acquisition of stakes in oil companies in 20 African nations, at a cumulative cost of around $15 billion.
2. Chinese FDI in Africa grew from $20 million in 1998 to $6 billion in 2005. Much of this is done by state-linked companies that can be persuaded to accept risks that private enterprise companies would decline. The destination of Chinese FDI has so far been largely, but

not exclusively, related to resource extraction, with Sudan and Nigeria the major beneficiaries in 2004.
3. Much FDI (as well as aid) is directed to building low-cost infrastructure. Construction often involves the use of Chinese labour, which may not be repatriated after project completion. Up to 100,000 Chinese labourers may be working in Africa, and the low cost of construction may be the result of low labour standards. However, infrastructure projects are hard to fund from Western bilateral and multilateral sources.
4. By 2004, the PRC provided $2.7 billion in aid to Africa, up from $107 million in 1998. This aid is in the form of loans, with most of the expenditure tied to procurement from the PRC. However, if the Chinese government judges the bilateral relationship to be satisfactory, it is frequently willing to forgive repayment of the loan.

The PRC's practice of bundling trade, FDI and aid, and offering them to SSA countries in a series of package deals, is driven by the desire to lock in their major African suppliers of natural resources. A typical deal of this kind was negotiated with the DRC in mid-2007. It is worth $5 billion in total, and breaks down into $2 billion for revitalizing mines held by the DRC government and the remainder for constructing a 3,400 km highway and a 3,200 km rail link, both between mining areas and export outlets. The DRC would repay initially in shipments of copper and cobalt, then with mining concessions for nickel and gold. The concessional element in the financing arrangements is not transparent. Western aid donors have just put in place an $8 billion debt forgiveness package, but have held off from investing in new infrastructure projects because of concerns about corruption and the slow speed of economic reform.

Deals like the PRC's with the DRC are a response to increasing competition among major nations to secure supplies located in Africa – competition driven by the United States and India, among others. Aid is used as a sweetener in a package of measures to try to bind strategic allies more closely and secure supplies of materials crucial to the national economy. For example, 67 per cent of the PRC's infrastructure investment between 2001 and 2006 went to the three oil-producing countries of Nigeria, Angola and Sudan.

This resurgence of tied aid follows a decade, the 1990s, when after the cold war, aid from the OECD countries began to be reformed on more rational and altruistic principles. In the 1980s, aid was still an instrument of the cold war, and the OECD-DAC (Development Assistance Committee) countries were faced by the Soviet bloc's Council for

Mutual Economic Assistance (CMEA). From 1989, the ending of the cold war ushered in a period of much reduced geopolitical contest. By the mid-1990s, the Western nations and their international organizations, the World Bank and the OECD almost completely dominated the international aid scene. They provided 98 per cent of all official aid, according to the calculations in Manning's recent article (2006, p. 372, Figure 1).

Having achieved a virtual monopoly of aid giving, the OECD nations took the opportunity to adopt more rational and altruistic aid policies than they had embraced during the cold war. Evidence of this can be found in their public commitment to poverty reduction as the overarching objective of aid in the early 1990s, followed by the setting of explicit and time-bound targets (the Millennium Development Goals, or MDGs) for poverty reduction. Further evidence was the DAC donors' commitment to increasing the proportion of their GNP devoted to aid, its progressive untying from national procurement and (admittedly small and inadequate) improvements in donor coordination.

This was also a time when the use of policy conditionality in aid-giving increased, and the opportunity was taken to extend its reach from the economic policies to the political arrangements of the recipient. Policy conditionality is no doubt, formally speaking, another form of aid-tying. However, the nature of the tie is quite different in purpose, in that it is intended to benefit the recipient, and not just the donor. In that sense, it is a more altruistic form of aid-tying than had been practised by Western donors in the past. Questions certainly remain about whether aid donors have sufficient local knowledge to make their policy change conditions succeed in delivering the anticipated economic benefits. The decidedly mixed experience of the 1990s has induced greater humility into the ambitions of Western donor agencies, fortunately.

In the context of political conditions attached to aid, the intention of bilateral donors was to encourage a switchover from single party regimes to multiparty systems with regular elections. The aim of both bilateral and multilateral donors was to try to advance a policy agenda of raising standards of governance – including increasing the transparency of government action and strengthening mechanisms for enforcing government accountability, because better governance was believed to be conducive both to faster development and the more effective use of aid to that end. Both of these seem worthwhile aims (even if not without their own complicated problems), and aid conditionality is a legitimate – if not necessarily effective – means to promote them. After all, the country that is offered aid on terms to which it objects fundamentally always has the option to turn it down. No country can be forced to accept aid of which it disapproves.

What is the alternative to political conditions attached to aid? It is to give aid regardless of the nature of the recipient regime and of the uses which it makes of the aid. To choose that alternative is to ignore the welfare of the people of the recipient country and of the taxpayers of the donor country. The PRC currently seems to be willing to give aid to SSA without attaching any conditions relating to the nature of the political regime, institutional improvement, good governance or human rights. The probable consequences are not only that many African countries will seek to substitute Chinese aid for OECD aid, but also that Western attempts to continue to attach governance conditions to their own aid will be undermined. The problem is not just that the proportion of OECD to non-OECD aid will decline. It is also that the effectiveness of OECD aid conditionality will evaporate, since it depends in an important way on the absence of alternative sources of aid finance that omit these types of conditions. If we think of Western aid donors as a cartel that has formal and informal agreements between members about the terms and conditions on which its aid is made available, then the PRC is outside the cartel and can compete with it unfettered by the restraints that cartel members have imposed on themselves. Indeed, the PRC advertises this feature of its aid when it emphasizes, as a key aspect of South–South cooperation, non-interference in the internal affairs of other countries and respect for their sovereignty. In this new lending environment, it is easy to see that the impetus to aid-related institutional reform in SSA will weaken, if not completely stop.

## Five country cases of PRC–SSA cooperation

Now there will be many who, on hearing this, will shout 'hurrah!' and look forward to the dawning of a new era of 'policy autonomy'. Yet before we all throw our hats in the air, it may be worthwhile to pause for a moment to consider how well the purposes of aid-giving will be served. To do this, we need some normative criteria. Ajit himself has endorsed the principle that aid should be allocated according to need, and that because of the existence of moral hazard, it is right for aid donors to have regard as well to performance indicators of poverty reduction, such as the percentage of children in primary school, and so on, in their allocation decisions (Singh, 2002, p. 302). (This in itself seems to me to imply a certain degree of policy conditionality.) At the same time,

Ajit opposes aid conditionality applied to issues of good governance. He says:

> Changes in governance must be left as far as possible to the internal processes of these countries, unless there are compelling reasons for the international community to be involved as in the case of genocide or widespread violation of human rights. (Singh, 2002, p. 301)

In his view, genocide or the widespread violation of human rights are compelling reasons for intervention, and thus provide the justification (albeit limited and exceptional) for policy conditionality to include issues of governance. I shall not put my own arguments for Ajit's two principles here, but will take them as illustrative of the type of propositions about aid that would command widespread assent.

Let us now review briefly what has been happening in five SSA countries that have been in the forefront of PRC–SSA cooperation, bearing these two principles in mind.

### Angola

In 2002, armed conflict in Angola came to an end with the death of Joseph Savimbi, providing an opportunity for donors to offer aid to rebuild the country after a long civil war. One of the obstacles to rebuilding was pervasive corruption that frittered away the inflow of aid funds. Transparency International ranks Angola as one of the most corrupt countries in SSA. The IMF decided to try and persuade the Angolan government to adopt a set of measures to reduce leakages from the oil revenues and ensure that more oil money went into social services to the general public. Ministers at first seemed to favour the idea of IMF loans linked to increased transparency of government revenues and intensive monitoring of spending. In early 2005, an agreement with the IMF on these lines seemed imminent. But then the Angolan government broke off talks with the IMF and announced that it would be receiving loans for oil industry reconstruction from the PRC. These loans and credits were worth $5 billion, and had no conditions about improved transparency and monitoring.

### Chad

To unlock the revenues from its oil resources, Chad has constructed a pipeline through Cameroon, a project which the World Bank helped to finance. One of the conditions of the deal was the passage of the

Petroleum Revenue Management Law, requiring that some of the oil revenue would be placed in a special fund and used to improve social welfare provision. The oil started to flow through the pipeline at the end of 2003, but at the end of 2005 the Chadian government reneged on that condition, in order that President Idriss Déby could create a war chest to fight Chadian rebels, who were being supported by the Sudanese government.

In January 2006, the World Bank suspended existing disbursements and threatened to cut off future assistance, although it subsequently agreed to negotiate new arrangements with Chad. The Déby government then turned to Sudan's patron, the PRC. It has held out the prospect that it would evict the existing pipeline partners Chevron Corp and Petronas in favour of Chinese oil companies, if the PRC persuaded the Sudanese government to stop supporting the anti-government rebels.

## Kenya

Western aid donors had a troubled relationship with the corrupt government of Daniel arap Moi, and hoped for better times when Mwai Kibaki's coalition won the elections of December 2002. However, relations between Western donors and the Kibaki government deteriorated quickly in the wake of more high-profile corruption scandals, and the Kenyan government faced World Bank and IMF criticism of its failure to implement a comprehensive anti-corruption strategy. John Githongo, the official responsible for bringing anti-corruption cases to court, was obstructed in his work by top political figures and left Kenya for exile in the UK.

In April 2006, the PRC's President Hu Jintao visited Nairobi and agreed a £7 million grant and £35 million loan. The Kenyan government denounced Taiwanese independence in any form, and granted the Chinese state oil company, China National Petroleum Corporation (CNOC), the right to explore for oil in six blocks covering 115,000 square kilometres in north and south Kenya. Raphael Tuju, Kenya's foreign minister, said: 'you can call it a scramble for Africa, but [it is] a scramble for Africa with which we are willing negotiators'.

## Sudan

In 1996, the CNOC purchased a 40 per cent share in Sudan's Greater Nile Petroleum Corporation, and transformed the moribund energy sector into Sudan's leading export industry, with the PRC as the top export destination. A humanitarian crisis erupted in Darfur in 2003 as a result of the activities of the Janjaweed militias, which killed an estimated 200,000 people and displaced from their homes a further two million. The government of Sudan has been accused variously of 'genocide' and 'ethnic cleansing by proxy'. The PRC used its permanent seat on the UN Security Council to block all resolutions opposed by the Khartoum government of President al-Bashir. Most recently, between January 2006 and August 2007, the PRC blocked the deployment of an enlarged UN peacekeeping force to replace the small African Union force of 7,000. Chinese arms manufacturers have continued to sell heavy weaponry (including fighter jets) to Sudan even when UN sanctions were in place, and Sudanese government planes have been engaged in aerial bombardment in Darfur.

## Zimbabwe

In the 1970s, the Chinese provided aid for the ZANU forces of Robert Mugabe to unseat the white settler rulers of the then Rhodesia. Thirty years later, President Mugabe's government, despite its human rights violations and its consequent pariah status, has been allowed to purchase at least 12 jet fighters from the PRC. In addition, all Zimbabwe's internal flights are now undertaken with Chinese passenger aircraft. Despite the desperate state of Zimbabwe's economy, the PRC has also made the government a $900 million loan, which has helped to pay off part of its arrears to the IMF, and prevent its expulsion from that body. Chinese cash and military supplies were given in exchange for the right to buy up large stakes in Zimbabwean utility companies (electricity and rail) and also extensive mineral rights.

Politically, President Mugabe has been enabled to resist international pressure to conduct serious negotiations with the opposition parties. Although at the instigation of President Mbeki of South Africa, some meetings between the Zimbabwe government and opposition took place in 2007, little of real substance was discussed ahead of the elections held in early 2008. When Mugabe came second to Morgan Tsvangirai in the first round of the presidential ballot and began a campaign of violent intimidation of Tsvangirai's supporters, the PRC maintained its arms shipments to Zimbabwe. They were foiled only by the spontaneous action of docks workers in South Africa and Angola.

In summary, the facts of these five country cases are sufficient to fuel concerns that Chinese aid to SSA is not being allocated according to need, is not requiring any accountability in terms of poverty reduction and is, in a number of important cases, being deployed in support of regimes that systematically abuse the human rights of their populations.

## Outlook

The PRC's scramble for African natural resources is likely to continue, and even intensify, in the immediate future. In December 2006, Chen Yuan, Governor of the China Development Bank (CDB), announced plans to put more resources into Chinese enterprises that wish to expand in the energy and minerals sectors overseas. The CDB is already the world's largest development institution by the criterion of assets, but now it wants to expand from 4 per cent the share of its loans financing projects abroad. Venezuela, Russia and central Asia are some of the likely destinations, but another likely target is SSA, where Chinese enterprises already have a substantial presence. The PRC is in the process of negotiating with five African countries special 'economic cooperation zones', in which it remits all taxes on the investors. Two have been awarded to Zambia and Mauritius, and Tanzania, Liberia, Nigeria and Cape Verde are competing for the other three.

Can the damage that some cases of PRC–SSA cooperation are doing to poverty-targeted aid and human rights be mitigated? There are various ways in which they might be alleviated. The first possible scenario is growing disenchantment in SSA with Chinese-style South–South cooperation. There is some evidence of this in Angola. It has been claimed that infrastructure projects funded by Chinese loans have excluded Angolan firms from competing for any part of the work, while the use of imported Chinese labour means little additional employment is generated for the local population. The quality of some of the infrastructure has also been criticized. Also, in Zambia's 2006 presidential elections, the challenger, Michael Sata, attacked Chinese investment in the country, alleging poor labour practices in Chinese-owned copper mines. Although Sata lost the election, he seemed to reflect some genuine grassroots concerns. Such disenchantment may become more widespread.

A second possible scenario is that the PRC becomes disenchanted with SSA as an energy source. This might be because the Chinese are not yet fully aware of the risks that all oil companies operating in Africa are exposed to, exemplified by the situation in the Niger delta. The attack on Chinese oil workers in the Ogaden region of Ethiopia in April 2007 might perhaps be a catalyst of greater caution. Alternatively, the Chinese government might have worries that the sea-borne supplies from SSA might not be as secure as land-based supplies, leading them to switch to land-based sources that it considers more secure, possibly from Russia or the Middle East. This second possibility might not seem very plausible and there are not at the moment many signs of this happening.

A third possibility is that the PRC succumbs to diplomatic pressure to converge towards Western FDI and aid practices. The World Bank and the European Investment Bank see current Chinese practices as a threat to their loan business. The World Bank has publicly criticized Chinese banks for ignoring human rights and environmental standards when lending to developing countries in Africa. Philippe Maystadt, the EIB President, has expressed similar concerns. Raising these issues directly with Chinese officials has brought no positive response so far. Nevertheless, it is possible that some convergence towards existing Western loan and aid standards will gradually occur.

Evidence that the PRC may not be entirely comfortable with the role of sustaining regimes that abuse human rights and create instability in SSA first came from US public statements about recent changes in the PRC's position on the Darfur crisis. These claimed that, since a meeting between President Hu Jintao and President Omar al-Bashir of Sudan in November 2006, the PRC has been urging Sudan to cooperate with the UN plan for an enlarged UN peacekeeping force in Darfur. In August 2007, the UN did finally pass a resolution to establish such a force, without it being vetoed by the PRC. Whether the enlarged force of 26,000 can be mustered, and will be adequate to bring peace and stability to Darfur, are still moot points. The PRC's acceptance of it is in any case a definite concession to the wishes of the wider international community, and may signal that the Chinese government can be expected to make some further accommodations to international opinion in the run up to the 2008 Olympic Games in Beijing, even as the scramble for African natural resources intensifies.

## Conclusion

It is time to inject an overdue dose of realism into the debate on the use of policy conditionality in aid agreements. The claim that policy conditionality has failed is often heard, but that is because it is one of those half-truths with which people of very different persuasions all find it possible to agree. There surely have been failures, owing to incentive incompatibility being designed into the aid contract. I was among the early critics who pointed out how and why particular ways of including policy conditionality in aid contracts failed to achieve what the designers intended them to achieve. However, this kind of criticism is logically distinct from a rejection of the instrument of policy conditionality in all its shapes and forms.

As previously stated, I do not subscribe to the view that developing countries have always used well such policy autonomy as they have had. Some countries certainly have, and they have been rewarded with accelerated development, but many others have not, and they have been unable to make much progress. Further, the failure to use existing policy space well can often be explained by the nature of the country's political structures, which act as internal constraints, even when external constraints are absent. Unfortunately, there is no simple categorization of these constraining political structures. Such is the porosity of political institutions, constraining structures can appear in 'democratic' as well as 'authoritarian' forms. The issue therefore is not one of insisting on the adoption of particular Western-style 'democratic' political governance structures.

The issue is about preventing aid from doing harm to the people whom it is intended to assist. Most people oppose genocide and the abuse of human rights, and acknowledge that these practices are by no means a monopoly of developed nations. By implication, attaching political conditions to offers of aid may be necessary and desirable in the future. Aid conditionality of all kinds cannot be objectionable in principle, if one can conceive of circumstances under which it could be used to achieve something desirable. The complete rejection of aid conditionality seems to be based both on an over-pessimistic estimate of the intentions of Western aid donors, and on an over-romantic view of developing countries, and the economic relations that exist between them. As I have tried to show in this chapter, the romantic view certainly does not apply when the relevant regions are as highly differentiated as the PRC and SSA are.

This conclusion gives me no comfort, in that I sincerely wish that the rhetoric of South–South cooperation could be taken at face, and that the harmony that it assumes to reign between developing countries did in fact prevail. Perhaps, one day, it will. Until then, however, one's critical faculties must stay alert to the realities confronting the 300 million poor people of Africa.

## References

Baumol, W. J., R. R. Nelson and E. N. Wolff (eds) (1994) *Convergence of Productivity*, New York: Oxford University Press.

Bosworth, B. P. and S. M. Collins (2003) 'The Empirics of Growth: An Update' *Brooking Papers on Economic Activity*, 2: 113–79.

Broadman, H. G. (2007) *Africa's Silk Road. China and India's New Economic Frontier*, Washington, DC: World Bank.

Jenkins, R. and C. Edwards (2006) 'The Asian Drivers and Sub-Saharan Africa', *IDS Bulletin* 37 (1): 23–31.

Manning, R. (2006) 'Will "Emerging Donors" Change the Face of International Co-operation?', *Development Policy Review* 24 (4): 371–85.

Mawdsley, E. (2007) 'China and Africa: Emerging Challenges to the Geographies of Power', *Geography Compass* 1: 1–17.

Moore, M. (2007) 'How Does Taxation Affect the Quality of Governance?', IDS working paper 280, Institute of Development Studies, Brighton.

Mosley, P., J. Harrigan and J. Toye (1995) *Aid and Power: The World Bank and Policy-conditioned Lending*, London: Routledge.

Singh, A. (2002) 'Aid, Conditionality and Development', *Development Policy Review* 33 (2): 295–305.

Toye, J. (1993) *Dilemmas of Development*, Oxford: Blackwell.

Wood, A. (2003) 'Could Africa be like America?', *Annual World Bank Conference on Development Economics 2003*, Washington: World Bank.

Wood, A. and J. Mayer (2001) 'Africa's Export Structure in Comparative Perspective', *Cambridge Journal of Economics* 25: 369–94.

# 7
# The Contradictions of Capitalist Globalization*

*Peter Nolan*

## Capitalist rationality

The bourgeoisie, during its rule of scarce one hundred years, has created more massive and more colossal productive forces than have all the preceding generations together. Subjection of Nature's forces to man, machinery, application to industry and agriculture, steam-navigation, railways, electric telegraphs, clearing whole continents for cultivation, canalisation of rivers, whole populations conjured out of the ground – what earlier century had even a presentiment that such productive forces slumbered in the lap of social labour?

(Marx and Engels, *The Communist Manifesto*)

Since ancient times the exercise of individual freedom has been inseparable from the expansion of the market, driven by the search for profit. This force, namely capitalism, has stimulated human creativity and aggression in ways that have produced immense benefits. As capitalism has broadened its scope in the epoch of globalization, so these benefits have become even greater. Human beings have been liberated to an even greater degree than hitherto from the tyranny of nature, from control by others over their lives, from poverty, and from war.

## Capitalism and coordination

Adam Smith, through his famous metaphor of the 'invisible hand', provided a vivid characterization of the rationality of the competitive market

---

*This chapter presents in compressed form the arguments in my book *Capitalism and Freedom: The Contradictory Character of Capitalist Globalisation*, London: Anthem Press, 2007.

economy. The essence of the market mechanism is a 'non-zero sum game' in which the participants are able mutually to benefit through specialization and exchange. In Smith's view, the invisible hand of marketplace competition between firms not only stimulates efficiency through gains from specialization and exchange, but also stimulates technical progress through competition among specialist capital goods makers. During the 500 years or so before Adam Smith published the *Wealth of Nations*, this mechanism had stimulated the immense technical progress of the Scientific Revolution. As large capitalist firms emerged at the end of the nineteenth century, a new coordination mechanism came into being, namely the so-called 'visible hand' of planning within the large modern corporation. Giant capitalist firms combined internal planning with intense interfirm competition. In the recent phase of the Global Business Revolution, the nature of the large firm has again changed radically. The extent of the division of labour has widened dramatically in this period. The boundaries of the firm have shifted, with a greatly increased array of inputs of goods and services procured from specialist suppliers. Simultaneously, the boundaries have become 'blurred', with functions of control and coordination exercised by the extending of the core systems integrators across the boundaries of the legally defined firm. Giant oligopolistic systems integrators continue to compete intensely with each other.

### Finance and development

The liberalization of international capital movements enabled a large increase in the flow of foreign direct investment in developing countries, rising from $23 billion in 1990 to $211 billion in 2004. Multinational firms wish to benefit from lower costs of production and from close proximity to fast-growing markets. The expansion of the production facilities of multinational firms in developing countries has stimulated the expansion of their supply chains close at hand, in order to minimize costs through 'just-in-time' supply. Global firms tend increasingly to lower their costs by using global platforms for their products and procuring inputs globally, even though they are produced and supplied locally. This has encouraged the emergence of common technologies in the operations of multinational companies across the world. These processes have stimulated rapid modernization of large swathes of the economy in developing countries.

Liberalization of inflows of short-term capital has helped to stimulate a rapid expansion of stock market capitalization in developing countries, rising from 19 per cent of their aggregate GDP in 1990 to 44 per cent in 2005. The increased role of the stock market helped to improve corporate governance, facilitate mergers and acquisitions, and broaden the sources of capital away from bank lending.

The period of the Global Business Revolution witnessed a revolutionary transformation of financial firms. An explosive round of mergers and acquisitions resulted in the creation of a small group of super-large global financial firms, such as HSBC, Citigroup, JP Morgan Chase, and Bank of America. These giant firms benefit from large economies of scale in the procurement of information technology systems, in risk spreading across a wide range of economies, in the attractiveness of high quality human resources in the sector, and in the high standards of corporate governance imposed by regulators in high-income countries. Across large parts of Latin America and Eastern Europe, international banks have undertaken extensive acquisitions, and now dominate the financial sector. The World Bank believes that 'transition economies that have been willing to cede majority control of their banks to foreign interests have enjoyed higher growth rates than their neighbours'.

Advances in mathematical modelling of financial markets has contributed to greatly improved capabilities for risk evaluation in financial institutions. A wide range of new financial products has been devised, notably the vast array of derivative products that distribute risk far more deeply in the financial system. As a result the global financial system has become so 'thick' as to be nearly indestructible. It has survived a succession of financial crises in this period, including the Mexican, East Asian, Russian, Long Term Capital Management, and Argentinean crises, as well as the shock of 9/11, which is a vivid testimony to the greatly improved robustness of the global financial system in this epoch.

## Competition, industrial concentration and technical progress

Economists have tended to polarize around their view of the inherent tendencies of competitive markets in relation to industrial concentration. The main body of 'mainstream' economists believe that interfirm competition is analogous to the 'trees in the forest', with large firms constantly being out-competed by small, nimble new entrants. It widely thought that this process has become even more powerful in the epoch of modern information technology, which has made the world of industrial competition 'flat', with unprecedented opportunities for small and medium-sized firms to out-compete large firms. An alternative, non-mainstream view has argued that the inherent tendency of capitalism is towards industrial concentration due to the opportunities for large firms to benefit from economies of scale and scope.

The period of capitalist globalization since the late 1970s has provided an opportunity to test scientifically the predictive qualities of the contrasting theories. During this period the brakes on the operation of market forces, which existed for much of the twentieth century, have been progressively removed. This period has seen the most explosive episode of mergers and acquisitions that capitalism has ever witnessed. In each industrial sector, a small group of widely recognized companies occupy the 'commanding heights' of their respective sectors, accounting for a one-half or more of the total global market. This is the visible part of the 'iceberg' of industrial concentration. However, the pressure from these leading systems-integrator firms has cascaded down across the supply chain, forcing intense consolidation of their supplier firms, which in turn exercise pressure upon their own supply chain. The result is that in the invisible part of the iceberg of industrial concentration, 'below the water level', there also has emerged a high degree of industrial concentration at a global level.

The core of the world's technical progress takes place within a relatively small group of companies that are the leaders in their respective industrial sector, and which struggle with each other to produce new and better products. The UK's Department of Trade and Industry estimates that the top 1,250 companies (the 'Global 1250') spend around US$433 billion annually on research and development. This is the core of the world's technical progress. The expenditure on research and development is 'strongly concentrated by country, sector and company': the top 100 firms account for 62 per cent of total expenditure undertaken by the Global 1250, while the bottom 150 account for just 1.3 per cent. One of the most important characteristics of the period of capitalist globalization is that intense oligopolistic competition persists throughout the upper reaches (at least) of the supply chain in almost all industries. Oligopolistic competition during capitalist globalization has witnessed the most rapid and dramatic technical progress the world has ever seen. As we shall see this has contributed to huge advances in human freedom.

## Capitalism and the expansion of human freedom

The epoch of capitalist globalization has witnessed an unprecedented advance in the liberation of human beings from the tyranny of nature. Far from mankind perceiving that it faced a danger of oil supplies running out, technical progress in the epoch of capitalist globalization has been so rapid that, at $70 per barrel, it was supposed that oil reserves were to all intents and purposes infinite, including the belief that oil could be obtained from existing fields through better extraction techniques, from coal (coal liquefaction), from tar sands, from shale oil and from 'gas in crystals'.

Pressure from market forces has stimulated a tremendous reduction in the amount of primary energy needed to produce a unit of final product. In 1990 the world produced US$3.5 (at constant prices) of GDP per kilogramme (oil equivalent) of primary energy consumed. By 2001 this had increased to US$4.2, an increase of one-fifth. Technical progress in a number of related areas has created the possibility to use existing technologies which can stabilize global carbon dioxide emissions at their current levels if suitable regulations and changes in patterns of consumption can be achieved. These include constructing more nuclear power stations, improved building techniques, wind turbines, reforestation, carbon sequestration from fossil-fuel-fired power stations, photovoltaic cells and the replacement of coal-fired power stations with gas. Transport technologies have changed at high speed in recent decades under the impetus of intense oligopolistic competition between automobile, truck, train, aeroplane and ship makers. New technologies of vehicle construction, engine design, materials use and integration of new information systems have led to greatly reduced vehicle weight, fuel consumption and maintenance, alongside greatly continuous improvement in vehicle reliability and safety. The period of capitalist globalization has seen a dramatic decline in the costs of transporting both people and goods. It has witnessed a revolution in telecommunications. In developing countries, the number of cell phones per thousand people rose from zero in 1990 to over 100 in 2002, and is continuing to rise at high speed alongside a continuous fall in the price of both mobile phones and telecommunications services. The emerging epoch of converged communications, combining voice, data and video, is witnessing an even greater revolution in communication technologies, with huge implications for people's daily lives in both rich and poor countries.

The period of capitalist globalization has seen a rapid advance in the level of urbanization. The share of the urban population in developing countries rose from 24 per cent in 1965 to 42 per cent in 2002. Urbanization has allowed large changes in people's daily lives. Young people in general, and women in particular, have much greater autonomy from their family, especially their parents. The opportunities for employment is broadened dramatically when compared with those in villages. Urban areas provide greater opportunities for advancing personal skills through formal and informal education. They also provide greater opportunities for groups of people to establish autonomous organizations.

During the epoch of capitalist globalization, developing countries were able to take advantage of being latecomers to absorb modern technology and capital from high income countries. Rates of growth of GDP per capita in low income countries have been faster than in high income countries. There is evidence of a reduction in overall measures of income inequality. The Gini coefficient of global income inequality, using Purchasing Power Parity dollars and weighted by country population, is estimated to have fallen from 0.55 in the1970s to 0.50 in 2000.

For people in developing countries the most important developmental goal is freedom from absolute poverty. The World Bank estimates that during the epoch of capitalist globalization, the proportion of people in developing countries living on less than US$1 per day (at constant prices) fell from 40 per cent in 1981 to 19 per cent in 2001. During the period of capitalist globalization, tremendous progress has been achieved in human health. Average global life expectancy rose from 56 years in 1970/75 to 65 years in 2000/05. This achievement was made possible in part by technical progress in medical equipment and medicines, as well as by advances in food production, including improved seeds and farm equipment, and better functioning food markets, including advances in information technology to spread knowledge more effectively and transport systems to distribute food better.

From a global perspective, peace is the most important goal. As early as 1794, Immanuel Kant visualized the logical possibility of a global 'cosmopolitan' political structure. The vision of a cosmopolitan consciousness was at the heart of Karl Marx's view of the progressive character of capitalist globalization. In the epoch of this capitalist globalization, national economic boundaries have been broken down on an unprecedented scale. International trade as a proportion of global GDP rose from 40 per cent in 1990 to 55 per cent in 2004. The large corporation has become increasingly an international entity in terms of its markets, its ownership, its management and its language of internal communication. Between 1995 and 2004, there were over 800 cross-border mergers and acquisitions worth over US$1 billion. In other words, over 800 firms that were formerly based in a given country 'gave up their passports' for that of another country. Former leading 'national champions' now often are led by foreigners and have more shares owned by foreigners than by those of the country in which they have their headquarters.

English has become the common language of most international firms. Capitalist globalization has helped to create a global culture among the mass of the population. Total tourist arrivals, facilitated by cheap air travel, increased from 450 million in 1990 to over 700 million in 2004.

English has established itself as the common language of the global mass media. International sports events such as the Olympics and the World Cup unite vast swathes of the world's population.

An interconnected, cosmopolitan world has come into being in the epoch of capitalist globalization. It is hard to imagine that such a world could experience a major military conflict.

## Capitalist contradictions in the epoch of the Global Business Revolution

It was the best of times, it was the worst of times, it was the age of wisdom, it was the age of foolishness, it was the epoch of belief, it was the epoch of incredulity, it was the season of Light, it was the season of Darkness, it was the spring of hope, it was the winter of despair, we had everything before us, we had nothing before us. (Charles Dickens, *A Tale of Two Cities*)

Capitalist freedom is a two-edged sword. In the epoch of capitalist globalization, its contradictions have intensified. As human beings have taken to new heights their ability to free themselves from fundamental constraints through the market mechanism, so they also have reached new depths in terms of the uncontrollability of the structures they have created. Global capitalism has created uniquely intense threats to the very existence of the human species at the same time that it has liberated humanity more than ever before from fundamental constraints. The contradictions of capitalist globalization comprehensively threaten the natural environment. They have stimulated a ferocious international struggle to secure access to scarce resources. They have produced an extraordinary concentration of business power in the hands of a relatively small number of firms headquartered in the high-income countries. They have contributed to intensified global inequality within both rich and poor countries, and between the internationalized global power elite and the mass of citizens rooted within their respective nations. They have produced a world of potentially extreme financial instability. Behind these contradictions looms the threat of nuclear warfare.

### The environment

In 1962 Rachel Carson's book, *The Silent Spring*, warned of the potentially destructive consequences for the natural environment if human beings continued to treat it as a resource to be exploited rather than as a complex living ecology of which they are merely one part. Her fears have come to fruition. The tropical rain forests are the home to by far the majority of animal and plant species. Over the past two decades, serious deforestation has taken place in developing countries, especially in tropical areas. Between 1990 and 2005, Brazil and Indonesia alone experienced a combined annual decline in their forested area of over 46 million square kilometres (0.5 and 1.6 per cent per annum respectively), amounting to 56 per cent of the total world decline in forested areas. Less than 1 per cent of the world's oceans are protected from overfishing. It is estimated that the proportion of 'collapsed species' rose from zero in 1950 to 40 per cent in 2003, and will reach 100 per cent by 2050 unless drastic action is taken to conserve the global commons of the high seas.

Across large parts of the developing world, expansion of the capitalist market economy is associated with a long phase of intensification of environmental deterioration. Poor countries find it hard to avoid the transition from 'poor and clean' to 'large and dirty', before they can advance towards a situation of being 'rich and clean'. For example, airborne particulates in Cairo are 159 micrograms per cubic metre and 99 micrograms in Beijing, compared with just 22 micrograms in New York. China is not only the home to the most dynamic part of the global economy, but also contains 16 of the world's 20 most polluted cities. A high priority for developing countries is to attempt to solve their own urgent pollution problems, which arise from a lack of coordination of the market economy.

The high-income economies are locked into a pattern of production and consumption that is profligate in the use of fossil fuels. At its heart is the system of transportation of goods and people based on trucks and automobiles. The developing countries have an average of less than 50 motor vehicles per 1,000 people compared with over 800 in the United States. The high-income countries consume 5,400 kilograms (oil equivalent) of primary energy per capita, compared with 1,400 kilograms in the middle-income countries and 500 kilograms in the low-income economies. Prior to 1800 emissions of carbon dioxide are estimated to have been 260 parts per million (ppm). These increased to 397 ppm in 2005, and, in the absence of strict controls, are predicted to reach 800 ppm in 2100. It is now recognized by almost all scientists that the path of development followed by today's high-income countries would be unsustainable if it were generalized to the developing countries. It is critically important for the sustainability of life on the planet to find a new development path in which the market mechanism is brought under collective control.

Oil is critically important to the current pattern of market-led development. It will take decades to displace oil with new sources of commercially viable primary energy, such as solar power or large-scale construction of nuclear power stations. The vast bulk of the world's oil supplies are located in the Middle East. There is a serious possibility of conflict over access to these oil supplies. It will take decades also to produce commercially viable technologies for carbon sequestration. In the absence of such technical progress, there are serious possibilities of international conflict between high income and developing countries over global warming. The high-income countries produced most of the accumulated stocks of carbon dioxide, but developing countries will produce an increasing share of the increments to world carbon dioxide output. Developing countries produce only small amounts of carbon dioxide per capita even though their contribution to the total increments of carbon dioxide production is high and rising. Moreover, the citizens of developing countries live in highly polluted environments, so that solving serious domestic pollution problems is regarded by most citizens as more important than solving the world's pollution problems.

## The challenge of the Global Business Revolution

As we have seen, contrary to the predictions of mainstream economists, the period of capitalist globalization has witnessed a dramatic process of merger and acquisition and industrial consolidation. Leading firms have been able to take advantage of economies of scale in procurement, research and development, branding and human resource acquisition. Alongside the explosive consolidation of business power in the modern sector of the global economy, there exists a sea of small- and medium-sized firms across the developing world that use labour-intensive techniques to produce low quality, low value-added goods and services for poor people.

After more than two decades of the Global Business Revolution, business power is concentrated in the hands of firms with their headquarters in the high-income countries. Despite large changes in the nature of the large firm in this period, most of their shareholders and senior managers also are from the high-income countries. Although developing countries account for over 84 per cent of the world's population, firms from these countries account for less than one-tenth of the Fortune 500 and the FT 500. Moreover, most of these are state-owned firms in the financial services and the natural resource and telecommunications sectors, which operate in protected domestic markets.

Research and development is a critical component of long-term competitive capability in the modern sector. We have already noted that the Global 1250 group of firms stands at the centre of global technical progress. Within this group, firms from the top ten countries, all high-income countries, account for 94 per cent of the total. The IT sector is by far the most important. The Global 1250 contains 225 IT hardware companies – of which 62 per cent are headquartered in the United States – and 111 software and computer service companies – of which 71 per cent are also headquartered in the United States. Five small European countries (Switzerland, the Netherlands, Sweden, Finland and Denmark), containing a total of 43 million people, have 112 firms in the Global 1250. The 'BRIC' countries (Brazil, Russia, India and China) contain 2,704 million people, but have a combined total of only 12 firms in the Global 1250.

The world of industrial competition that has emerged in the period of the Global Business Revolution is not 'flat'. Rather it is profoundly unequal. If developing countries are to nurture their own large, globally competitive firms, they have to devise new forms of industrial policy appropriate to the challenges of this period. Success in this endeavour will in its turn pose a challenge for policy-makers in the high-income countries. They have devoted a great deal of energy during the period of capitalist globalization to establishing an international competitive environment in which support for 'national champion' firms has been removed. This flies in the face of the policies that they themselves pursued during the only early modern industrialization experience. Without exception they protected their infant industries, which gave them the breathing space to catch up with the world's leading firms at that time.

## Inequality

Capitalist globalization has been extending its reach for over two decades. One should now be able to judge accurately the implications of capitalist globalization for the worldwide class structure. A distinct global elite has emerged. Its members inhabit the upper reaches of global corporations. They constitute a tiny fraction of the world's population and earn exceptionally high incomes. They share an international culture based around a common language, English. They read the same newspaper (the *Financial Times*) and share common values. They stay in the same global hotels. They buy the same globally branded luxury goods. They own residences in several countries. Their children attend the same international private schools and finish their education at the same global elite universities. They attend the Davos Economic Forum. They have less and less attachment to a particular country.

The long-term trends in global inequality are unambiguous.[1] If global inequality is measured in terms of the average per capita income of countries (using the PPP exchange rate, unweighted by population) then the Gini coefficient more than doubled from 0.20 in 1820 to around 0.52 in the 1980s. As we have seen, there is some evidence that there has been a small decline in global inequality in recent decades, with broad agreement that this is almost entirely due to China's rapid growth. The estimates which suggest some decline in global inequality in the recent past use unweighted average per capita income for each country.

Attempts have been made to estimate global inequality incorporating data on inequality within countries. These reveal no trend change in global inequality in recent decades. They also show a far greater extent of global inequality than alternative measures. In 1998, using the purchasing power parity (PPP) exchange rate, and incorporating intercountry measures of income distribution, the Gini coefficient of global income distribution is estimated to have been 0.64, with the top 10 per cent receiving 50 per cent of global income. This level of inequality is 'perhaps unparalleled in world history': 'If such extreme inequality existed in smaller communities or in a nation-state, governing authorities would find it too destabilizing to leave it alone, or revolutions or riots might break out' (Milanovic, 2007). Using the official exchange rate to convert national income data to a common standard reveals an even greater extent of global inequality. Using this measure, the global Gini coefficient in 1998 was no less than 0.80, with the top 10 per cent accounting for 68 per cent of total global income.

The United Nations World Institute for Development Economics Research (WIDER) has recently completed a meticulous study of the distribution of global wealth in the year 2000. It estimates that the total global amount of household wealth is US$125 trillion, which is three times the total amount of global GDP. It estimates that the Gini coefficient for the distribution of household wealth is 0.89. The top 2 per cent of households account for 50 per cent of the total and the top 10 per cent account for 80 per cent of the total. The bottom 50 per cent account for 1 per cent of the total. That the world of capitalist globalization has produced such a fantastically unjust distribution of accumulated wealth is cause for deep reflection.

The integration of global markets has had profoundly contradictory results for the citizens of the high-income countries, including the

United States. On the one hand, it has helped to raise real incomes due to the falling real price of imported consumer goods. On the other hand, it has helped to increase inequality. The liberalization of capital and product markets since the 1980s has opened up a vast world of low-priced labour across the 'transition' and 'developing' countries. Global labour markets are being integrated mainly through the migration of capital to poor countries and through the export of goods and services from poor to rich countries. This places intense pressure for international equalization of wages and conditions of work through the operation of the 'law of one price'. These pressures add greatly to the impact of technological change, which has replaced a wide segment of white-collar office jobs that demanded modest skills, while demand for unskilled jobs in the service sector, such as restaurants, retail and domestic help, has surged. From the 1960s to the early 1980s, the income share of the top decile of the US population was stable at around 32–33 per cent but thereafter it rose to around 43–44 per cent in 2000–02, which was the same income share that they received in the 1920s and the 1930s. The share of the top 1 per cent of the distribution rose from less than 8 per cent in the late 1960s and 1970s to around 15–17 per cent at the end of the 1990s. There is widespread public angst across the whole political spectrum about the growth of inequality within the United States, and its relationship to globalization.

Developing countries also are in the throes of widespread increases in inequality, closely linked with their integration into the global capitalist economy. The presence of large pockets of multinational firms within fast-growing low and middle-income countries has 'brought the twenty-first century' to these countries in terms of employment and remuneration, with pay and conditions of work determined by global standards. However, those employed in these conditions constitute only a small fraction of the non-farm population. Surrounding them is a vast and far larger sea of urban informal sector employment, for which pay and conditions of work are set by the standards of the rural under-employed masses, not by international markets. During the 'Lewis phase' of economic development a fundamental constraint is set to the growth of real wages for urban unskilled labour by the availability of unlimited supplies of under-employed rural labour. Over the past two decades, income inequality has increased within fast-growing developing countries. In East Asia, inequality has increased significantly over the last several decades. For example, in China, the Gini coefficient of urban income distribution rose from 0.16 in 1978 to 0.34 in 2002, while the overall Gini coefficient rose from 0.30 to 0.45 in the same period. In Latin

America, inequality increased almost uniformly in the 1980s, though the deterioration was less pronounced in the 1990s.

## Finance

Financial markets have an inherent propensity towards speculation and asset price bubbles. Keynes famously warned of the dangers of financial speculation: 'Speculators may do no harm as bubbles on a steady stream of enterprise. But the position is serious when enterprise becomes the bubble on a whirlpool of speculation. When the capital development of a country becomes a by-product of the activities of a casino, the job is likely to be ill-done' (Keynes, 1936, p. 159). The initiating factor in speculative bubbles is typically the optimism generated by a feeling that the economy has entered a 'new era'. No period has created a greater sense of a new era than the past two decades of capitalist globalization.

Once the speculation process gets under way, powerful positive feedback loops drive markets ever higher. Monetary expansion is endogenous to the economic system. In spite of the efforts of monetary authorities to control the supply of money, it has tended to expand in periods of asset price inflation to finance speculation. Credit is extended on the basis of increased collateral asset prices, which supports still further increases in asset prices, and still further credit expansion. In the period of capitalist globalization, the volume of new 'money' that is being created through speculation in newly developed financial instruments dwarfs the 'real' economy. At the end of 2006, central bank 'power money' amounted to around 10 per cent of global GDP, but to just 1 per cent of total global liquidity. So-called 'broad money' amounted to around 122 per cent of global GDP, but still accounted for only around 11 per cent of total global liquidity. Securitized debt amounted to around 142 per cent of global GDP, but still accounted for just 13 per cent of total global liquidity. Derivatives, which didn't exist 20 years ago, now amounted to no less than 802 per cent of total global GDP, and fully 75 per cent of total global liquidity. In other words, 'cyber money' now amounts to more than eight times the total global output of goods and services.

The period of capitalist globalization has witnessed a powerful decline in the real price of goods and services alongside an unprecedented global asset bubble, fuelled by the huge increase in money in its myriad forms. The asset bubble has been self-reinforcing, with speculation driving up asset prices in a vicious cycle around the world. It has affected almost all assets, including equities, property, energy, raw materials, agricultural products, bonds and works of art. In the high-income economies, the asset prices bubble, especially that in property, has formed the foundation for an explosive growth of credit to fund both speculation and current consumption. The level of household debt in the US has risen remorselessly, from 60 per cent of household income in the mid-1980s to over 120 per cent in 2004.

The global financial system is now deeply integrated across national boundaries, far more deeply even than the integration of production systems. The massive extent of repacking and sale of debt means that debt is far more deeply distributed throughout the economy than was the case before the Global Business Revolution. This provides a source of stability and enhances the ability of the financial system to ride out relatively small-scale crises, but it means that the whole global financial system is far more susceptible to a giant financial crisis should it erupt.

The transition from primarily national to global markets has not been accompanied by a strengthening of international regulatory governance. The IMF, the institution that is supposed to guide the global financial system, has been described as a 'rudderless ship in a sea of liquidity'. The problem for regulators has been exacerbated by the fact that the global financial system has developed instruments of such great complexity and at such a high speed that no one understands how to regulate the whole system, even assuming that the political mechanisms existed to do so.

There is a palpable sense of deep unease among policy-makers. In 2007, at a variety of different meetings, deep fears were expressed by a wide range of financial system regulators about the absence of control over the global financial system consequent upon the new forms of liquidity creation, due to their complexity, absence of regulatory oversight and their international nature. Kenneth Rogoff, former chief economist at the IMF, issued an alarming warning about the absence of global governance over the financial system:

> Whatever happened to all the grandiose plans for improving the global financial architecture? Over the past couple of years, all introspection seems to have vanished. Instead, the policy community has developed a smug belief that enhanced macroeconomic stability at the national level combined with financial innovation at the international level have obviated the need to tinker with the system... There is no problem that markets cannot solve... Contrary to market perceptions, global central banks have only very limited instruments for dealing with a genuinely sharp rise in global volatility, particularly one that is geo-politically induced. (*Financial Times*, 8 February 2007)

## Explosive interaction

The contradictions of capitalist globalization are capable of explosive interaction, possibly even erupting into open warfare. The United States has a stock of 8,000 active or operational nuclear warheads, with an average destructive power that is 20 times that of the Hiroshima bomb, which killed around 200,000 people. Of these nuclear weapons, 2,000 are on hair-trigger alert, ready to be launched at 15 minutes warning. The United States has never endorsed the policy of 'no first use'. Robert McNamara, former US Secretary of Defense, believes that the world has never faced a greater risk of nuclear warfare. The US Government regards nuclear weapons as central to its military strategy for 'at least the next several decades'. This provides an intense incentive for other nations to either expand their existing arsenal or develop nuclear weapons if they do not already possess them. McNamara characterizes the US nuclear weapons policy thus: '[It is] immoral, illegal, militarily unnecessary, and dreadfully dangerous. The risk of an accidental or inadvertent nuclear launch is unacceptably high.' The only rational policy, in his view, is to 'move promptly towards the elimination – or near elimination – of all nuclear weapons'. It is an extraordinary fact that in the midst of the 'Golden Age' of capitalist globalization, the world's dominant capitalist country should have the most terrifying, and steadily advancing, weaponry at the centre of its military strategy. The British Astronomer Royal, Lord Rees, believes that 'the odds are no better than fifty-fifty that our present civilization on Earth will survive to the end of the present century'.

## Summary and conclusions

Capitalist freedom to compete has been at the heart of human progress since the dawn of human civilization. In the current epoch of capitalist globalization, the pace of progress has reached a new highpoint, with unprecedented advances in technology stimulated by the invisible hand of competition, led by giant oligopolistic firms battling for a leading position on global markets.

However, capitalist freedom is a two-edged sword. In the current period of capitalist globalization, these contradictions have reached new depths that threaten the very survival of the human species. Capitalist freedom to pollute and consume exhaustible resources has led to a deep threat to the global environment. It has led also to the possibility of international conflict over global warming and over access to exhaustible resources, especially fossil fuels. It has resulted in an unprecedented concentration of business power, with oligopolies established deep into the value chain of a wide range of industries. It has resulted in unprecedentedly high levels of inequality in the distribution of income and wealth at a global level, and intensified inequality within both rich and poor countries. It has resulted in the construction of an anarchic global financial system, which has produced an asset bubble of unprecedented dimensions. The collapse of the bubble could lead to a global financial, economic and socio-political crisis analogous in severity at least to that of the 1930s.

If human beings are to resolve the contradictions of capitalist globalization, it is urgently necessary to establish global mechanisms to contain the tiger of unconstrained global capitalism. However, to do so requires cooperation between real nations, with real national interests that often diverge from each other. It also requires cooperation between groups of nations at different levels of economic development. The richer group of countries have many interests in common that often diverge from those of the developing countries. For most human beings, 'global' is not their framework of reference or source of identity. For most people, apart from the family and religion, the 'nation' is the primary source of identity and the main forum within which they have a political voice. Although the forces of capitalist globalization are increasingly international, the national interest of citizens and national governments remains an immensely potent force.

A central issue in humanity's attempt to grope a way forward in this extraordinarily dangerous time is the relationship between the world's dominant power, the United States, and the two most powerful unified cultures, China and Islam, which each contain around 1.3 billion people, totalling around two-fifths of the world's population. The capability of human beings cooperating in order to ensure a sustainable future will stand or fall on these relationships. If their engagement is confrontational rather than constructive, the prospects for humanity are bleak. Many people within each of these cultures believe that there is an unavoidable 'clash of civilizations', between the West on the one hand and China and Islam on the other. In fact, there is no fundamental clash between Western capitalism and the civilizations of China and Islam. Despite their differences in culture, political structure and belief systems, it is the common elements in the long-term evolution of socio-economic systems of China, Islam and the West that are the outstanding features when viewed from the perspective of the early twenty-first century and the swelling tide of globalization.

In both the East and the West, in both the medieval and the modern world, private property, extension of the market and pursuit of profit have been the central forces stimulating human ingenuity to achieve technical progress. Both in China and in the Islamic world, in both medieval and modern times, intellectuals and political leaders have wrestled with the conundrum of attempting to 'civilize' capitalism and establish a harmonious, stable society. In China this took the ideological form of Confucianism and the attempt since the 1980s to construct a form of Chinese socialism that 'learns from the past in order to serve the present'. In the Islamic world, in both medieval and modern times, the dominant discourse for taming and civilizing the market has been the Islamic faith, based on the Koran. Both China and the Islamic world have a rich potential contribution to make in resolving the contradictions inherent in the nature of capitalist globalization.

Modern capitalist globalization began in the 1970s. The removal of constraints on the operation of the market mechanism has proceeded remorselessly across the whole world. The first 'wild' phase of modern capitalist globalization is drawing to a close, as the intensifying multiple contradictions become ever more apparent. The resolution of these multiple contradictions necessitates globally coordinated regulation of the capitalist system. As the 'wild animal' of global capitalism becomes ever larger and more powerful, it becomes ever more important that human beings, who have given birth to and nurtured this animal, establish a moral framework to regulate its activity, and thereby prevent the wild animal from devouring its creator, humanity. In order to resolve the contradictions of capitalist globalization, there is no choice other than to grope towards international cooperation. Such cooperation is necessary in order to avoid a global ecological disaster. It is necessary in order that both rich and poor countries reach a mutual understanding about the challenges that globalization poses for the distribution of income and wealth in their respective countries. It is necessary in order that both rich and poor countries reach a mutual understanding about the challenges posed by the explosive concentration of business power consequent upon the global business revolution. It is most urgently necessary in order to establish collective control over the global financial system.

The capitalist system is the product of the collective exercise of human intelligence. The way in which people choose collectively to exercise that intelligence is governed by their ethics. Ethics are the 'Pole Star' to guide humanity on its journey through history. The possibilities for a sustainable future for human beings is, in turn, deeply related to human beings' psychological needs. There have, since ancient times, been sharply polarized views of what the fundamental needs of human beings are and what the ethical systems are that correspond to those needs.

The contradictory character of human psychology has been recognized since the great thinkers of antiquity. One may interpret Homer's great legends, *The Iliad* and *The Odyssey* as concerned, respectively, with the 'life instinct' and the 'death instinct'. The former was a joyous celebration of human creativity and the pleasure of the human voyage of discovery. The latter was a remorseless pageant of horror and mutual destruction by men motivated by 'heroism'. Sigmund Freud, the founder of modern psychology, also came to the conclusion that the fundamental driver of human psychology was the struggle between the constructive, loving, life instinct ('Eros'), and the destructive, selfish, death instinct ('Thanatos'). The life instinct came from man's sense of his place within an infinite realm of being. The death instinct came from man's deepest fears, especially the fear of death itself. The death instinct inclined people to distrust and compete with their fellow beings, while the life instinct inclined people to trust and cooperate. In the wake of the horrors of the First World War, Sigmund Freud posed the question of the survival of the human species in stark terms:

> The fateful question for the human species seems to me to be whether, and to what extent, their cultural development will succeed in mastering the disturbance of their communal life by the human instinct of aggression and self-destruction . . . Men have gained control of the forces of nature to such an extent that with their help they would have no difficulty in exterminating one another to the last man. They know this, and hence comes a large part of their current unrest, their unhappiness and their mood of anxiety. And now it is to be expected that the other of the two 'Heavenly Powers', eternal Eros, will make an effort to assert himself in the struggle with his equally immortal adversary. But who can foresee with what success and with what result? (Freud, 2001, p. 145)

If humanity cannot find a mean, its prospects for survival are bleak. The destruction of human civilization may arise either from the internal self-destructiveness of extreme free market individualism, or from the nihilistic response of those excluded and angered by the globalization of the free market.

The challenges that are faced by human beings are the product of people's own purposive activities, expressed mainly through the economic system. It is within their collective power to resolve these contradictions. The very depth of the challenges they now face may shock them into the action necessary to ensure the survival of the species. Alongside human beings competitive and destructive instincts are their instincts for species survival through cooperation. However great the challenge may be, human beings have the capability of solving the contradictions that are of their own making. It may only be the approaching 'final hour' which finally forces human beings to grope their way towards globally cooperative solutions. The falling of the dusk, as humanity looks into the abyss, may be the final impulse to produce the cooperative solution that is immanent within the unfolding of global capitalism: 'The owl of Minerva spreads its wings only with the falling of the dusk' (Hegel, 1952, p. 13).

## Note

1. Milanovic (2007) provides a summary of the recent evidence on the global distribution of income. He is Lead Economist at the World Bank's Research Department's unit which deals with poverty, income distribution and household surveys.

## References

Freud, S. (2001 [1930]) *Complete Works of Sigmund Freud*, vol. xxi, London: Vintage.
Hegel, G. F. (1952 [1820]) *The Philosophy of Right*, Oxford: Oxford University Press.
McNamara, R. (2005) 'Apocalypse Soon', *Foreign Policy*, May/June.
Milanovic, B. (2007) 'Globalisation and inequality', in D. Held and A. Kaya (eds), *Global Inequality*, Cambridge: Polity Press.

# 8
# Europe's Future: Income Convergence to Fight Unemployment

*James K. Galbraith*

## Introduction: the European paradox*

Why does – why should – any country wish to join the European Union? The answer is plain: to become European. And what does that mean? If it means anything, surely the European dream is to be stable, democratic and prosperous, with a touch of the 'social model' that is supposed to distinguish Europe from the United States. This is obvious, and not only that: it is spelled out explicitly in the founding documents of the Union.

For the presently less-prosperous and quite poor regions of the European Union (EU) to the east, becoming European requires that they catch up toward the living standards prevailing in the west. It does not require equality. Living standards in Poland will never (probably!) equal those in Germany, because the industrial and financial core of Europe will never (probably!) move from Germany to Poland. But the EU, as a project, does require that the gap between Poland and Germany narrow over time. It also requires that the dramatic gaps that separate wage levels in Estonia and Bulgaria from those in Spain or the Czech Republic be narrowed, even as the Spaniards and Czechs reduce the gaps separating their countries from the truly rich.

*This paper is adapted from 'Maastricht 2042 and the Fate of Europe: Toward Convergence and Full Employment' an essay prepared for the Friedrich Ebert Stiftung and jointly published by the Levy Economics Institute. I thank Enrique Garcilazo of the OECD, Michael Dauderstaedt of the Friedrich Ebert Stiftung, and the many members of the University of Texas Inequality Project team. Several parts are adapted from work published elsewhere and originally written with support from the Carnegie Scholars Program. The work of UTIP can be found at http://utip.gov.utexas.edu.

This we may call the imperative of income convergence. This chapter explores that imperative over a relatively long time, stretching out to the 50th anniversary of the Maastricht Treaty in 2042. Will that landmark be truly a golden jubilee, or will it prove to be nothing more than a sour footnote in the record of a failed endeavour? This question is facing Europe today. The answer will depend, in part, on whether the income convergence imperative is recognized and realized between now and then.

Mathematically, the convergence imperative imposes a simple condition: growth of wages and incomes must be inversely proportional to present wage rates. This does not mean the rich must stagnate. It means that the incomes and wages of the rich must grow more slowly than those of the less rich, and those of the poor should grow the most rapidly of all. The achievement of equal growth rates across regions is not good enough. Equal growth rates preserve proportionate differences, in which case absolute differences grow over time.

For some time, the force of foreign direct investment has been bringing the start of convergence to some of the accession countries of the EU-25; for instance, the Czech Republic and Hungary. Thanks to appreciating currencies, wages in these countries have been rising quite rapidly – when measured in euros. But this process is not very visible to those actually in the countries, and it is unlikely to complete the job, for two reasons: investment booms tend to peter out; and once a country joins the eurozone, exchange-rate based convergence will stop. It has already stopped for some poorer regions of the present eurozone, for which the convergence project is also far from complete. Over the long run, therefore, convergence of real wages and incomes will not just happen. It must be made to happen. And that means it must be part of an economic policy agenda for Europe.

But here we encounter a problem. Consider the economic policy prescription being advanced across Europe, under the unanimous advice of national governments, the EU, international institutions such as the International Monetary Fund (IMF) and the Organisation for Economic Co-operation and Development (OECD), the media and, of course, a phalanx of economists, most of them safely protected by academic tenure. These are the projects of *policy convergence*, dictated by the Maastricht Treaty, and of 'labour market reform' – aimed, it is said, at reducing the mass unemployment that afflicts so much of Europe today.

Policy convergence is not income convergence. It is, rather, the business of hitting particular, and ultimately arbitrary, budget targets under the diktat of the European Commission. In an article in *The Times* dated

26 October 2006, the journalist Anatole Kaletsky described the effects of recent steps toward policy convergence in Europe:

> In Italy the Government is on the brink of collapse because of Signor Prodi's insistence on implementing tax increases and budget cuts demanded by ... the EU Economic Commissioner, under the terms of the Maastricht Treaty. In Hungary, the riots began a month ago because the Prime Minister showed his contempt for democracy by publicly admitting that he had 'lied, morning, noon and night' about the tax increases and public spending cuts that he had promised [the EU] before a recent election – and after the election was over, he naturally felt that his promises to Brussels were far more important than the ones he had made to Hungarian voters. The resulting budget cuts of 7 per cent of GDP over two years would be roughly equivalent in Britain to closing down the entire NHS. And Hungary, remember, is being forced to do this to comply with the Maastricht Treaty, without even being admitted to the eurozone.

'Labour market reform' is part of the agenda of policy convergence, and is utterly pervasive, if sometimes less distinct than fiscal policy convergence. In broad outline, labour markets are supposed to operate under the guidance of supply and demand, with supply curves sloping upwards (mostly) and demand curves sloping downwards (always). If unemployment exists, the cause must lie in a failure of the real wage to adjust to its equilibrium value. Perhaps technological change and other factors have cut demand for workers equipped with relatively limited skills. To restore full employment, wages paid to such workers must fall. This can be accomplished by weakening unions, cutting job protections and unemployment benefits or otherwise dismantling market power that rash democratic governments have allowed to accumulate in the hands of the unskilled. The form of labour market reform that is demanded varies from country to country, since some countries (such as Spain and Italy) have historically favoured job-tenure protections (which do not impose accounting costs on the state budget), while others place more emphasis on unemployment benefits, training and a compressed distribution of wages. But the substance always consists of kicking out the props from under such remnants of worker power, whatever form it takes.

In the medium term, the project envisages that the EU should become flexible enough to reach levels of inequality characteristic of a 'dynamic' capitalist economy. For this, many Europeans see a model – when they gaze across the Atlantic at the United States. Thus, the American model stands as the template for the degree of inequality that must be achieved in order to enjoy full employment.

A second truism of current economic discussion is globalization. Everyone knows that the boundaries of the economy are no longer at the national frontier. We live in a global economy and workers must therefore face the harsh reality that they compete not only with their compatriots, but with all workers of similar productivity, wherever they are. This reality must be doubly true within the confines of the EU, which lacks even the modest between-country protective barriers of other times and places.

This truism carries an implication. We observe, first, that unemployment and underemployment are typically higher in the peripheral regions of Europe, including in the accession countries, than in the relatively prosperous core countries. We observe also that in many of the accession countries, educational attainment is comparatively low. According to the logic of supply and demand, this must mean that the productivity of the accession countries does not justify, or at best barely justifies, the wages that workers presently make in those countries. It therefore cannot justify rapid wage increases.

Now consider what could happen when unskilled workers in France accept pay cuts, as the doctrine of labour market reform dictates that they must. If workers in Poland fail to follow suit, then in relative terms they must lose competitiveness vis-à-vis their low-skilled counterparts in France. If Poland had been attracting jobs from France due to lower unit labour costs, some of that benefit may be lost. Faced with wage cuts in France and to maintain position, it follows that the Poles must also reduce their wages relative to what they would otherwise be. So speaks the logic of globalization, combined with the logic of labour market reform. Unfortunately, the consequence of this logic – like that of the Maastricht criteria – is income divergence and, in the limiting case, even declining pay rates in the poorer regions of Europe.

This is the European paradox. European ideals require income convergence. But the logic of European policy imposes income divergence. Once the present phase of investment-driven convergence passes, pressure for divergence must fall heavily on the poorer countries. Of course, pay is the largest part of income, and income is the most important determinant of living standards. It follows that the application of labour market reform in Europe must mean slower growth of incomes and living standards in poorer regions, including the periphery of old Europe and the accession countries. Logically, one is entitled to fear especially that the accession countries will discover that European economic policies work to obstruct their rise toward a fully European living standard.

Actual European policy cannot operate indefinitely in this way. It is mathematically and humanly certain that unless income gaps between rich and poor countries decline over the long run, there will be increasing migration of the poor to the rich. Sooner or later, if incomes do not converge strongly, this migration will develop into a full-scale convergence of populations. For practical economic purposes, some of the poorer countries will cease to exist, except as tourist destinations and sources of migrant labour. The richer countries will become either melting pots – admitting all European citizens to full political rights – or ethnic oligarchies (modern versions of apartheid South Africa). In either case, both groups of countries will completely lose their present characters, for good.

And the other possibility, if European economic policy were to follow the programme of labour market reform qua globalization to its end, is that the EU will disappear. The EU is already politically stagnant. It has lost its grip on the idealism that it had as recently as 20 years ago, and the union is engendering a nationalist and xenophobic backlash in many places. Kaletsky warns of this explicitly:

> The political consequence of this asymmetry of power is growing disillusionment in the East, not only with the EU but even with the concept of parliamentary democracy. The economic effect of forcing Central Europe to abide by deflationary policies designed for the mature economies of the eurozone is the weak demand growth and mass unemployment experienced by the accession countries. This unemployment has been the main driving force behind the huge flow of labour out of Central Europe. And that flood of workers, in turn, has provoked the hostile and ultimately self-defeating rhetoric of the British Government against Bulgarian and Romanian immigrants.

A lesson of the past two decades is that, when failed states collapse, the effects can be economically catastrophic, as they were in the Soviet Union, or violently catastrophic, as in Yugoslavia. Europe is not yet a state, but it is not immune to one catastrophic possibility or the other.

The European project must be saved. It must be saved, most of all, from itself. And this means that the paradox of Europe must be overcome. The question is how to do it. An answer requires a re-examination of underlying economics. This will be a surprising exercise for many readers and, perhaps, a difficult one, because breaking free of the ingrained logic of supply-and-demand economics or the grip of factual preconceptions is not easy. It will be, in short, an exercise in the spirit of Ajit Singh's work, in which theory can and must meet the test of fact. For, contrary to theory, supply-and-demand economics do not rule the labour market. And, in fact, the United States does not represent the ultimate example of high inequality in its pay structure, compared to modern Europe.

## The economics of inequality and unemployment

In this section, I argue the following propositions: the theory of unemployment underlying the policy doctrine of labour market reform is fallacious, and its implication that jobs are purchased with inequality is incorrect. Across Europe, the opposite relationship holds: countries and regions, which are *more* egalitarian, systematically enjoy *less* unemployment. This is not an anomaly, but entirely in accord with correct principles of economics.

The claim that the United States has a more unequal pay structure than that of Europe is false. All calculations that purport to verify this claim have been based on comparisons between the entire United States and individual countries of Europe. These calculations invalidly compare a large country with many small ones, and they exclude consideration of large inequalities that exist between European countries. When these inequalities are added in, the pay structure of the United States emerges as more egalitarian than that of Europe. And the American pay structure is dramatically more egalitarian when pay is measured geographically across states and regions.

As widely believed, moving Europe toward American levels of employment means moving Europe toward American levels of inequality. But to achieve this goal, inequalities within Europe must be *reduced*. That is because they are actually lower in the United States than in Europe, once one takes account of the international differentials inside Europe.

This is the resolution of the European paradox. No contradiction exists between the ideal of European equality and an efficient economic policy resulting in full employment. Nor is there any contradiction between the lessons of US experience, correctly measured, and what is good for Europe. The contradiction is only between the policies that are required and what, so far, the political, academic, media and business elites of Europe have believed. Most of all, the rigidities that must be overcome exist in the mindset of European policy-makers.

## Why the conventional theory of unemployment in Europe is wrong

The problem of unemployment in Europe is vexed by a theory-driven predisposition to blame it on defects of labour market structure and then to go out in search of particular rigidities to blame. A great part of the economic literature follows this pattern, but the result has been a wild goose chase. Repeated attempts by the most committed advocates of the rigidities doctrine have failed. National differences of labour market institutions cannot effectively explain the existing pattern of variations in unemployment. Garcilazo (2005) provides an exhaustive survey of those differences, including examination of the underlying datasets used to measure differences in institutions across European countries. These datasets are of very low quality and they do not inspire confidence in empirical generalizations that might be drawn from them.

In a review of the empirical literature, Baker *et al.* (2004) show that the entire power of institutional explanations for unemployment differences across Europe rests on one fact. It is true that centralized collective bargaining and union density are associated with unemployment. But the effect is that stronger unions are associated with less – not more – unemployment. This effect does not support the rigidities doctrine.

Let's examine the flexibility hypothesis in more depth. Why do people become unemployed? Unemployment did not exist in pre-industrial society. Unemployment, as we know it, emerged with the Industrial Revolution, took its definition from American statistical practices in the late 19th century, and became a mass phenomenon – worthy for the first time of concentrated attention from economists – in the Great Depression of the 1930s. Why?

It makes no sense to point to the creation of unemployment insurance (UI) and similar institutions as a cause for the rise of unemployment. UI was not invented before unemployment. Equally clearly, the standard supply-and-demand diagram, with wages set above the market-clearing levels, cannot account for the emergence of unemployment in the industrial age. Real factory wages in the 19th century were not protected by laws or by unions. Real wages were low, as any reader of Marx or Dickens knows. Moreover, many workers had other options. If they migrated from Europe to the slums of New York City, they could still move on, after a short time, to the west. Yet, in many cases, they did not. Instead, they formed, more or less willingly under the circumstances, the 'reserve army of the unemployed'. And that army remained, even though industrial production grew rapidly and the time was not one of depression or stagnation in output and demand. Why?

The textbook view holds that even though real wages were very low, they were nevertheless too high. Since the workers most likely to face unemployment in this model are those who are the least productive, it follows that wages for the least productive workers should have fallen, in order to give each worker a job commensurate with his or her skills. This can only lead to a greater inequality in wages than existed previously. The calls heard in Europe for 'increased flexibility' today are of the same type. They are calls for increased pay inequalities, as a direct route toward full employment equilibrium.

And yet, it is almost always possible (in principle) for an unproductive worker to let his or her wages fall. Out-of-work academics know this very well: they become consultants. Ex-graduate students can wait at tables. Secretaries become temps. Former farm boys can (in the most extreme cases) go back to the farm. Or they can work off the books, mowing lawns and weeding gardens.

If they accept unemployment instead, it may be because such inferior jobs stand in the way of one's chances of finding better work. At any rate, given the existence of an informal sector, dropping wages in the more formal sectors to the levels of the informal sector cannot be a solution, except insofar as it discourages people from leaving the informal sector. If productivity is determined by the capital stock (human and physical) available to workers, then cutting wages only amounts to a transfer of the surplus from inframarginal workers in the high-wage sectors to their employers.

A satisfactory theory of unemployment must deal with a world in which the options of organized and informal employment both exist. It must be valid for the developing (which is to say, pre-industrial and industrializing) countries and also for the post-industrial world. Indeed, it is only when both types of employment are recognized explicitly that one can make sense of the phenomenon of unemployment and the empirical relationship between unemployment and pay. What, then, is that theory?

A half century ago, Simon Kuznets (1955) argued that inequality would rise in the early stages of economic development and transition to industrial growth. The reasons were concrete. New urban centres were places of concentrated income and wealth. The differential between incomes in these centres and those in the countryside became significant as cities grew; and that disparity would only decline later as the proportion of the population remaining in the countryside shrank. This dynamic was not the entirety of the theory behind Kuznets's famous inverted-U relationship between income and inequality, but it was surely the most significant single factor.

John Harris and Michael Todaro (1970) offered a model that captured these characteristics in a neoclassical paper aimed mainly at development economists. In the model, workers migrate from a low marginal-product rural sector to cities, where minimum wages are imposed, and accept a high probability of sustained unemployment, in exchange for a low probability of getting jobs and enjoying the resulting rise in income. The equilibrium condition is that the expected value of the gain is equal to the cost incurred in leaving rural employment; this condition entails substantial equilibrium unemployment.

From this, a positive monotonic relationship between inequality and unemployment emerges. As development starts, the riches of the city become magnets for the rural poor. No one on the farm can find an urban industrial job without pulling up stakes and heading to the city. Everyone with initiative does this, particularly if a shock to farm incomes suddenly makes the inequality worse.

But the number of jobs cannot keep up. And so, no matter how rapidly cities grow, mass unemployment is inevitable for a time. It will only end when the rural population is absorbed or emigrates. It can only be contained (as in modern China) by a pass system regulating who may live in the cities. And it can only be regulated, effectively, by measures that provide strong incentives to stay in the countryside or in the smaller cities and towns. (Social security systems, which provide common money incomes to retirees and therefore higher real incomes to those living where staples are cheap, are an example of such an incentive, one that works effectively to this purpose in the United States.)

While Harris and Todaro focused on East Africa, their argument is also adaptable for post-agricultural societies. From the standpoint of the individual worker, the decision to risk unemployment depends on two parameters: the difference between current income and the hoped-for improvement; and the probability of attaining that improvement. The former can be measured by the inequality of wages. The greater the existing inequality, the greater the potential rewards. The latter depends in part on the rate at which new higher-wage employments are offered.

Thus, as outlined above, *pay inequality causes unemployment*. It is not the only cause, certainly, but it matters. Unequal societies should have more unemployment than egalitarian societies. Mobility barriers across regions will help determine how far workers are willing to go to look for jobs, and where unemployment is actually found. Thus, in the relatively unified United States, with a single federal unemployment insurance system, one would expect the highest unemployment in or around the richest places. In Europe, where welfare states remain national and the loss from moving across national frontiers is relatively high, one might expect the unemployed of (say) Poland to congregate in Poland.

Is their unemployment voluntary or involuntary? In this theory, the distinction has lost its meaning, for it is purely a matter of perspective. From the standpoint of the individual worker, there is always a choice – to risk unemployment or not to risk it. In this sense, unemployment is voluntary. But, at the same time, from the larger standpoint of society, the aggregate volume of unemployment is endogenous. And at least one critical variable – the inequality of the wage structure – is subject to policy control. Since unemployment can be reduced by policy without changing the underlying preferences of the workforce, then, by Keynes's definition, it is involuntary, in spite of having been individually chosen.

Finally, a dynamic element may be added to the discussion. I draw on Meidner and Rehn (1951), whose work underpinned the conceptualization of the Swedish model. They pointed out another consequence of inegalitarianism in the structure of pay: it permits technologically backward firms to maintain competitiveness, despite higher unit costs, by paying their workers less than more progressive firms. Thus a high degree of inequality in the wage structure would be associated with a weak degree of technological dynamism and, over time, a lower average productivity and standard of living than would otherwise be the case.

Deliberate compression of wage differentials puts the technological laggards out of business. It therefore releases labour. But with active labour-market policies (providing retraining for displaced workers) and a policy of strong aggregate demand, the end result can be an expansion of capacity by the technologically progressive firms. Some of the unemployed can then be absorbed in the expanding, advanced industries. And many more can be maintained in subsidized, low-productivity employment – either public or nominally private sector – essentially paid for by the surplus created in the high-productivity firms. In this way, egalitarian societies enjoy efficient use of all their labour resources, high absolute living standards and competitive advantages over societies that allow markets to adjust wages to an existing structure of relative productivities.

In short, it is not just that full employment tends to reduce inequality. It is also that inequality produces unemployment. The more unequal the structure of pay facing an individual worker, the greater the likelihood that he or she will choose the lottery of unemployment over the certainty of an impoverished and miserable life.

Inequality, however, is a feature of society. It is not a characteristic of the individual, but of the environment within which the individual lives. And this raises a question of crucial importance that is entirely overlooked in the literature. What are the boundaries of the environment? Are they purely local? Are they national? Or are they continental in scope?

This is a subjective matter, but it is clear that, as economic barriers fall between regions and countries, and as communications improve and discrimination decreases, individual horizons must necessarily expand. This process has been going on in Europe for 50 years – it is in many ways the essence of European integration. And given the theoretical proposition just stated (relating the perception of inequality to unemployment), it is immediately obvious that European integration poses a huge conundrum for European employment.

For the further one looks in any direction across Europe, the greater the inequality one observes. It follows that the more Europe integrates, the greater the problem of unemployment, unless drastic measures are taken to reduce interregional inequalities. This is the basic economic logic of a convergence strategy.

## Inequality and unemployment in Europe

Europe experiences different levels of inequality at different levels of geographic aggregation. In many parts of the continent, local or national inequality is low. Scandinavians and Germans take pride in the economic equality within their borders, and with reason. However, wage differentials between European countries are high. Average income (in nominal terms and common currency units) in Spain is only about 60 per cent of that in Germany – comparable to the average differential between American blacks and whites. It follows that making a correct prediction of the unemployment rate expected from any given level of inequality depends critically on drawing analytical boundaries in an economically and socially relevant way. In principle, we must gauge inequality across the geographic and political range of individuals. And this problem is complicated by the fact that, at a given moment in time, different groups may experience different geographic (as well as occupational) horizons.

In this sense, Poland today is no longer an independent labour market but a province of greater Europe. The unemployed are not the unemployed merely of Poland, but the unemployed of all Europe. They are not only the low-wage workers seeking to escape the countryside for Warsaw or Kraków, but also the low-wage workers who cannot find jobs across the vast differentials separating Poland from Germany. Today, they may live in Poland because barriers to international mobility still exist, they have not yet located jobs or they don't qualify for German welfare. If one has to be unemployed, then it is better to be jobless near home.

But if international inequalities are not steadily reduced, a new wave of emigration from the peripheries into the centre of Europe is inevitable. And at that point, both Poland and Germany would cease to be national units in their present sense. They would become merely geographic boundaries with wholly floating populations – as is the case today for US states – except that they would lack the easy political integration enjoyed by mobile Americans.

Conceição *et al.* (1999) found that, in general, European countries with less inequality enjoy more employment. Galbraith and Garcilazo (2004) have extended this work by introducing new measures of inequality across 159 European provinces annually for 15 years, and showing the degree of inequality within provinces and the degree to which each province contributed to inequality in Europe as a whole. Their findings are consistent with the theory that regions with lower inequality and higher average incomes enjoy systematically less unemployment across Europe. Galbraith and Garcilazo have also shown that, on balance, institutional differences between the major countries of continental Europe (except Spain before the recent decline in unemployment there and, to a very modest extent, the United Kingdom and the Netherlands) are not major predictors of differences in average unemployment rates. These findings are all inconsistent with the national labour market–rigidities framework.

In sum, both national and provincial measures of inequality support an augmented version of the Harris-Todaro view that unemployment depends on the expected value of gain from accepting a ticket to search for higher wages. They are equally consistent with the view that wealthy countries avoid unemployment most effectively; not by liberalizing their labour markets, but by subsidizing low-productivity workers to stay in their jobs. As Conceição *et al.* (1999) argued, the efficiency gains from this strategy can be astonishingly large and propel an egalitarian country with mediocre productivity, such as Denmark, into the forefront of the world competition for a high standard of living.

## The case of the United States

A widespread European belief holds that the American model stands as the template for the degree of inequality that must be achieved in order to enjoy the American level of full employment. I endorse this belief. In my judgment, the forces that determine employment must operate on similar principles everywhere. For example, in a given state of technology, there must be a particular relationship between pay inequality and unemployment. There is no compelling reason why this relationship should differ between the United States and Europe. It follows that there likely does exist an 'optimal' structure of pay inequality associated with maximum employment. Since the American employment experience is plainly better – a point no one disputes – it follows that good employment policy for Europe would seek levels of pay inequality characteristic of those found in the United States.

Readers will naturally object on the common sense ground that 'everyone knows' that overall American society is grotesquely unequal, while Europeans retain values of solidarity, which impart rigidities to their wages. So how can this argument possibly reconcile low unemployment in the United States with high unemployment in Europe?

Part of the answer is that the relevant inequalities are of wages, the reward for work. They do not include inequalities of other forms of income, including income from property and capital. In the American case, measurement is contaminated by a very wide range of highly unequal, non-wage incomes. Moreover, those inequalities grew dramatically in the late 1990s, in particular, and they were a function of the speculative bubble at that time. Capital gains were intensely concentrated by industry and location. As Galbraith and Hale (2006) show, the between-counties component of the surge in income inequality in the late 1990s was accounted for almost entirely by increasing income in just five of 3,150 counties overall: New York, New York; King County, Washington (Seattle); and three counties in northern California (Santa Clara, San Francisco and San Mateo).

Pay inequalities can be measured directly and they are relevant to a theory of labour-market adjustment. Comparable measures of industrial pay inequality for Europe and the United States can be drawn from the OECD's Structural Analysis dataset; the relevant calculations were made by Conceição *et al.* (1999). They show that inequalities in industrial pay, measured across sectors in the United States, are comparable to the upper end of the national European range. They are not materially higher than in, say, Spain or Italy. And when one takes account of the large differentials between European country averages, intersectoral industrial pay inequalities are actually larger in Europe than in the United States.[1]

An even more direct and updated comparison of between-regions pay inequalities uses measures of total payroll and total employment for 215 European regions and all 50 US states, plus the District of Columbia (Galbraith, 2007). The measures are made comparable by presenting them in the form of Gini coefficients, which are calculated on the arti-ficial assumption that every person within a state or region enjoys the same average income. This comparison is not, nor is it intended to be, a full comparison of inequalities within the United States or across Europe. However, for a theory of unemployment, interregional inequalities are particularly important. They measure, quite directly, the incentive for long-distance economic migration and therefore the incentive to expose oneself to the risk of unemployment in order to gain the possibility of a high-income job. By comparison, inequalities within close geographic quarters may represent nothing more than the incentive to commute (e.g. by train between the suburbs and downtown Paris, or by subway from the Bronx to Manhattan).

The results are striking. A European cross-regional Gini coefficient is about 0.235, or more than twice the value across the American states (0.101). Across continental distances, average European incomes are dra-matically more unequal than are those in the United States. It is true that in Europe cost-of-living differences between regions are likely to be large, so that real-wage inequalities are smaller than the nominal earnings dif-ferentials. Nevertheless, for the purposes of a theory of unemployment, it is nominal earnings differentials that matter.

For a person contemplating long-distance migration, a key consider-ation is whether the nominal income available in a rich country can provide a decent living standard, not in the rich country but in the poorer region whence the migrant comes and where his or her family likely remains. Typically, migrants are willing to endure cramped and deprived conditions in their place of work, precisely in order to maxi-mize the incomes sent back to their homes, where purchasing power is magnified by low living costs. Hence, nominal inequalities – for exam-ple, between Andalucía and Madrid, the Algarve and Paris, or Poland and Frankfurt – drive both the competition for low-skilled jobs in the rich regions and, to a very substantial extent, the unemployment rates.

Furthermore, one can reasonably expect that cost-of-living differ-entials across Europe will decline over time. As markets continue to integrate, the traded-goods components of living costs will tend to equal-ize, leaving only the non-traded goods components (whose price levels depend on local wage levels – including rents – and the intangible ele-ments of the living standard) as separating the costs of living in richer and poorer regions of Europe. Absent convergence of nominal wages and convergence of living costs will produce further divergence of real living standards. Convergence policy must, therefore, deal with nominal differentials, as expressed in the common currency unit.

## The mechanics and policies of convergence

What would it take to reduce the degree of interregional inequality across Europe to American levels by 2042, the 50th anniversary of the Maastricht Treaty? An illustrative answer can be obtained by calibrating relative growth rates across sectors within regions, using Eurostat's REGIO dataset for 215 European regions and 16 economic sectors in each region.[2] The results are shown in Figure 8.1. The map gives the annual compound growth rate of average wages for each region that is required to achieve an American degree of regional earnings convergence by 2042. Values range up to 7 per cent per year – a high but by no means historically unprecedented figure.

Since convergence *per se* has no effect on the prices of traded goods produced in the high-wage, high-productivity regions, there is no reason to expect that it would affect traded-goods prices and therefore the conventional measures of price inflation in traded goods. Nor should convergence induce any wage spirals among workers in richer countries, so long as the purposes of policy were well understood, agreed upon and respected in practice. Convergence is not designed to catapult Spain (say) ahead of France: its purpose is only to reduce the gap between them.

Convergence would raise effective demand emanating from the low-wage regions. It would raise the demand for traded goods produced elsewhere in Europe, and therefore help to absorb unemployed labour in the traded-goods producing centres. And it would raise the demand for (white-market) service employment in the converging countries, absorbing labour *in situ* at increasingly tolerable and ultimately attractive wages. Convergence would reduce incentives to economic migration and reduce pressures on labour supply in the richer countries, even as unemployment fell in the poorer regions.

In the final analysis, Europe would approach full employment in harmony and solidarity, without serious inflation. With confidence that this policy can, in fact, succeed at that objective, opposition to broadening the scope of European integration and governance should melt away. A convergence policy, I suggest, is the only way to achieve this goal and preserve the European ideal in the face of debilitating challenges of unemployment, immigration and social dislocation that are attendant on the manifest failure of European economic policy so far.

But what specific policies will do the work that must be done? One must be careful. Would raising the minimum wage in Germany to a higher fraction of the average, for example, be an effective way to reduce inequalities (and therefore unemployment) in Europe? It would not. For the intersectoral differences within the labour markets of the German

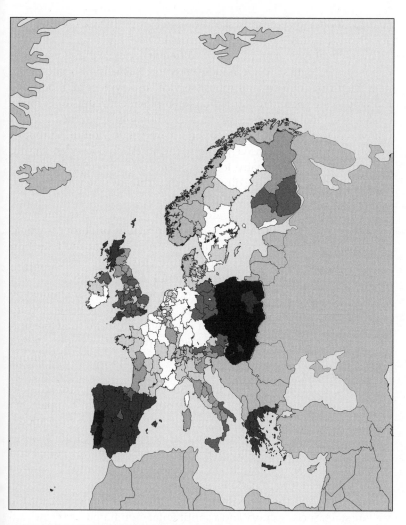

Growth rate to meet convergence criteria

■ 5.7% to 7.4% (36)   ■ 3.3% to 3.8% (36)   ▨ 2.9% to 3.1% (35)

■ 3.8% to 5.7% (37)   ▨ 3.1% to 3.3% (31)   □ 0% to 2.9% (40)

*Figure 8.1* Distribution of economic growth rates required to bring Europe's regions to American income equality by 2042, the 50th anniversary of the Maastricht Treaty

*Source*: Bureau of Labor Statistics, Employment and Earnings, and author's calculations.

*Lande* are not among the most significant in Europe. In fact, these regions are already among Europe's lowest inequalities.

Pay inequality in Europe is of a different kind. Within individual regions, it is highest where middle-class jobs (usually associated with manufacturing industry and robust service employment at good wage rates) are scarce or absent. Structural unemployment festers in Europe's dualistic regional economies, where a few good jobs are in the mix with many undesirable ones. These economies exist mainly on the European periphery and very extensively among the accession countries. Raising minimum wages in Germany does nothing to create middle-class jobs in the periphery or relieve the difference separating average wage levels in Germany from those of Poland or Spain.

It follows that an egalitarian growth policy – with directed measures to raise relative growth rates in the poorer regions of Europe – would be the single most powerful medium-term measure for the reduction of European unemployment. Some instruments for this policy already exist. Regional funds are a proven, powerful tool, especially for smaller countries. They could and should be expanded. But they are limited by the capacity of direct state action. They are also strongly biased toward infrastructure improvements (which pay high wages) and therefore limited in their effect on employment. New instruments are required, and the most practical steps that would generate convergence within Europe involve personal income.

This is an old story in the United States. The Deep South (the old Confederacy) was much poorer than any other region except Appalachia until recent times, and marked by much deeper unemployment. Periodic crises, such as the Dust Bowl of the 1930s, sparked mass migration – the Okies and Arkies to California, and the blacks from Mississippi and Alabama to Chicago and Detroit. These migrations eventually spurred projects directed toward national economic convergence.

In the New Deal, the United States began the process of federalizing the welfare state. Social security and a continental minimum wage came into being in the 1930s. A national industrial development policy grew out of deliberate federal investment decisions during wartime mobilization in the 1940s. A national transportation network was built in the 1950s. Federally funded health care for the elderly and the poor (Medicare and Medicaid) was achieved in the 1960s. Richard Nixon's administration contributed General Revenue Sharing (although this programme alone did not survive the Reagan counter-revolution of the 1980s and no further progress has been made since that time). Nevertheless, the continental integration of social welfare policy in the United States today is much farther along than in Europe (e.g. the Deep South and Appalachia are no longer especially poor). Continental integration, not flexible labour markets, accounts for America's relative success against entrenched structural unemployment.

As economic integration now encompasses all of Europe, the EU needs to follow the earlier American example. More social democracy and a more unified social democracy is the answer to European unemployment. The EU must identify specific measures and prove the model with bold experiments.

One useful, practical step that is fully consonant with economic justice would be the creation of a European Pension Union, which would move the base incomes of the elderly toward convergence. There is no just reason why the retired elderly in the poor countries of a unified Europe should be paid on the income standard of their own nation and suffer the indignity of poverty in old age, compared to fellow Europeans who worked no harder or longer than they did. Minimum pensions should be set on a standard governed by the average productivity of Europe as a whole, and any differentials should be paid to individuals by direct transfers through the EU.

The economic burden of these and similar measures needs to be understood carefully. It need not be, as many suppose, a matter of taxing Germans to support Portuguese. Rather, as there exist unemployed human capital assets in Portugal, the appropriate step is to create a liability that will permit employment in Portugal. A pension supplement scheme – placing purchasing power in the hands of the elderly in Portugal – will mobilize latent resources in Portugal. It has no other important economic effects. In fact, there is no need to tax Germans to do it. A deficit run at the European level is perfectly justifiable, so long as overall unemployment remains high. The interest on the deficit can be paid, in effect, from the eventual increase in Portuguese national income.

Beyond these examples of effective redistributive policy (which could be multiplied, particularly by emulating the role of the non-profit sector in US job creation), the larger problem of relative growth rates needs to be addressed. This is substantially a macroeconomic problem and, accordingly, a new and plainly Keynesian understanding is necessary of how aggregate income convergence might be achieved.

The readily available macroeconomic policy instruments in Europe are now reduced to a single measure: a lower interest rate. But there is no way to impose low interest rate policy on the European Central Bank (ECB), no very practical way to target the policy to the European periphery, and no guarantee that lower interest rates (if they worked at all) would, in fact, foment income convergence. If monetary stimulus were to help the rich countries of Europe more than the poor, inequalities could rise.

The active role of monetary policy in a convergence strategy is therefore somewhat limited. Indeed, convergence would be all too easy to reverse at any time by raising interest rates and transferring income from debtors (the relatively poor) to creditors (the relatively rich). This must be prevented. Rather than relying on central bank policy to lead the process, a major strategic objective must be, simply, to limit the degree to which the ECB can undermine it.

As already noted, some of the accession countries have recently enjoyed a surge of foreign direct investment, whose benefits are transferred to the whole population through a rise in the exchange rate. How far this process will go remains to be seen, although obviously if these countries ever join the euro, it will stop. At that point, more direct policies will be needed to keep the convergence process underway, and while the monetary mechanism that brought such benefits to Spain might be repeated, it is not certain that it will be as the necessary financial institutions and credit market conditions may not arise on their own.

And so we turn to fiscal policy. An effective, targeted, growth-producing, fiscal policy is required. This means running deficits, but in such a way as to help reach the larger goals. This might be achieved by revising the Stability and Growth Pact, and by permitting the EU to run fiscal deficits and issue Eurobonds, which would support the incomes of lower-income persons and regions, and the strategy of convergence. This is what the United States usually does, or tries to do, in a slump. Such a radical change, however, presupposes a development of European federalism and Keynesianism on a scale that is not presently on the cards. An alternative would be to rewrite the Stability and Growth Pact to permit *any* country of the EU to run deficits greater than 3 per cent – the current limit excepted only in deep recessions – so long as unemployment *on average* in Europe is higher than a threshold value. The point here is that it does not matter which country runs deficits and provides stimulus. Since the European economies are integrated, the resource-using effects will be felt everywhere.

## Summary and conclusion

The conquest of mass unemployment in Europe will require a comprehensive strategy of regional convergence, which ensures that the necessary expansion of aggregate effective demand is dispersed over the

European continent in such a way as to provide jobs, raise incomes and reduce migration incentives in the relatively poorer European regions. Such was the experience of the United States in the twentieth century, beginning with the New Deal and ending as a credit expansion, underpinned by fiscal federalism and a long-term, structural policy of interregional convergence, that brought full employment without inflation. This was a happy experience while it lasted. And it contains a plethora of useful, unexpected and unexploited lessons for Europe.

Europe has not plunged itself into needless wars nor grossly neglected its public capital formation, and so, except for its dysfunctional structures of governance and rigid economic ideas, the continent is objectively well-positioned to exploit these lessons. They are just not the lessons that most Europeans expect to find when casting a glance in the American direction. And Europeans will not find them until they come to understand the actual circumstances far better than conventional economics has taught them. In this respect, an open mind, inquiring spirit and rigorous attention to the facts are required. These are the defining characteristics of Ajit Singh's work, and they are the appropriate inspiration for coming to grips with this problem.

## Notes

1. Hourly pay inequalities within industries in the United States may be larger than indicated by the data, thus blunting the intersectoral comparison. (Obvious examples of pay inequalities are the well-known abuses of CEO pay in the United States.) My experience with these comparisons is, generally, that the same order of difference prevails within and between industries. Another reason why US unemployment fell so far below European levels may lie in superior search mechanisms in the language-unified and computerized United States. It may be easier for low-wage services workers in America than in Europe to search for better jobs without actually leaving their current ones. To the extent that this is true, the US service sector may be sheltering many underemployed people who would be openly unemployed in Europe. However, I do not have estimates of this situation; it is also not obvious that underemployment is worse than unemployment.
2. To test the impact of the missing data for Germany, I estimated the missing observations by assuming that the wages and employment in German regions by sector bear the same relationship as those in France. The simulations did not change significantly, so my calculations here do not include this adjustment.

## References

Baker, D., A. Glyn, D. Howell and J. Schmitt (2004) 'Labor Market Institutions and Unemployment: A Critical Assessment of the Cross-Country Evidence', in

D. Howell (ed.), *Fighting Unemployment: The Limits of Free Market Orthodoxy*, New York: Oxford University Press.

Conceição, P., P. Ferreira and J. K. Galbraith (1999) 'Inequality and Unemployment in Europe: The American Cure,' *New Left Review* 237, September–October: 28–51.

Galbraith, J. K. (2007) 'Maastricht 2042 and the Fate of Europe: Toward Convergence and Full Employment', *Levy Economics Institute Public Policy Brief* 87, November 2006. Published separately by the Friedrich Ebert Stiftung, International Policy Analysis Unit, March 2007.

Galbraith, J. K. and E. Garcilazo (2004) 'Unemployment, Inequality, and the Policy of Europe, 1984–2000', *Banca Nazionale del Lavoro Quarterly Review* LVII (228): 3–28.

Galbraith, J. K. and T. Hale (2006) 'American Inequality: From IT Bust to Big Government Boom', *The Economists' Voice* 3 (8).

Garcilazo, E. (2005) 'Regional Labor Markets, Unemployment, and Inequality in Europe', PhD dissertation, University of Texas at Austin, December.

Harris, J. R. and M. P. Todaro (1970) 'Migration, Unemployment and Development: A Two-Sector Analysis', *American Economic Review* 60 (1): 126–42.

Keynes, J. M. (1936) *The General Theory of Employment, Interest, and Money*, London: Macmillan.

Kuznets, S. (1955) 'Economic Growth and Income Inequality', *American Economic Review* 45: 1–28.

Meidner, R. and G. Rehn (1951) *Fackföreningrsrörelsen och den Fulla Sysselsättningen*, Stockholm: LO.

# 9
# Heckscher–Ohlin in Theory and Reality*

*Adrian Wood*

## Introduction

At the start of 1965, in my first year as an undergraduate at Cambridge, Robin Marris took leave to join the new Labour government's Overseas Development Ministry, and Ajit Singh replaced him as my supervisor. Some time in the spring or summer, Ajit set me to work on international trade. My essay, now alas lost, was a scathing critique of Heckscher–Ohlin theory, based mainly on reading about Samuelson's formalization of Ohlin. The long list of assumptions required to make the theory work seemed absurd, as I stated with all the arrogance of youth. Ajit's comment on its cover page was 'too polemical'.

Two decades later, I came back to Heckscher–Ohlin (H–O) theory in search of a way of analysing the effects of rapidly growing imports of manufactures from developing countries on the labour markets of developed countries. This line of research yielded a book (Wood, 1994a) and led me on to other related research into the determinants of manufactured exports from developing countries. Indeed, H–O has been at the core of almost all my academic work for over 20 years.

How can this be explained? Was what I wrote for Ajit completely wrong, or is there some way of reconciling it with my subsequent H–O enthusiasm? The answer seems to me to be that the essay was misdirected: my criticisms were actually of the formal theorizing of Samuelson, but I aimed them at H–O in general, failing to appreciate the empirical power of the less formal theorizing of Heckscher and Ohlin (which

---

*This chapter draws on earlier work with Enrique Aldaz-Carroll, Ed Anderson, Kersti Berge, Kate Jordan, Jörg Mayer, Trudy Owens, Cristobal Ridao-Cano, Alasdair Smith and Paul Tang.

I can see from a rereading of Samuelson's articles that he himself did appreciate).

Happily, I now have the chance to resubmit my essay to Ajit – to write what, with the benefit of 40 years of hindsight, I should have written back in 1965. I shall argue that most trade economists have got H–O wrong: they believe that it works well in theory but badly in reality, whereas the opposite is closer to the truth – H–O works well in reality but badly in theory. (The title of this chapter, incidentally, is similar to that of Leamer 1995, acknowledging another important intellectual debt.)

To elaborate this argument I will discuss the empirical decline of nearly four decades into which Leontief sent H–O in 1953, before addressing its recent empirical revival. I will review the problems of the standard Samuelsonian formalization of H–O theory, then outline a modified formalization that fits the evidence better.

## Empirical decline

The origins of H–O theory were empirical. Heckscher was an economic historian, and his seminal 1919 formulation of the theory was stimulated by a dispute with Wicksell about the policy implications for Sweden of transatlantic trade. Ohlin's 1933 book *Interregional and International Trade* was likewise firmly and frequently based on observation of actual patterns of trade.

From the 1950s to the 1980s, however, H–O had a hard time empirically. Although Leontief's (1953) disproof of the theory was effectively challenged by Leamer (1980), further econometric work yielded little support for H–O theory and many inconsistent findings (for surveys, see Wood, 1994a, section 3.5.2; Leamer and Levinsohn, 1995). Vanek's (1968) articulation of the theory in terms of factor content provided a new way of testing it, but the results of the fullest such test of H–O's empirical accuracy, by Bowen *et al.* (1987), were discouraging.

In retrospect, these unfavourable empirical results seem to me to have arisen from three misunderstandings of the theory.

### 1. Confusing relative with absolute magnitudes

Like all theories of comparative advantage, H–O is about relativities (indeed, double relativities): a country 1 that has more of factor A, relative to factor B and relative to country 2, will produce and export more of factor-A intensive good X, relative to factor-B intensive good Y and relative to country 2. This says nothing about absolute magnitudes: country 1 might have more of factor A than country 2, and yet export less of good X, because its technology was uniformly inferior to that of country 2.

A problem with many of the tests, and in particular with those based on the Vanek reformulation, was that they examined relationships between absolute magnitudes which depended on the implicit assumption that all countries had the same levels of technology (or total factor productivity).[1] That this assumption is wildly misleading had long been recognized by development economists, but it became increasingly better documented by statistical analysis of the causes of cross-country differences in per capita income (from Krueger, 1968 to Hall and Jones, 1999).

The significance of this assumption for tests of H–O theory was emphasized by Trefler (1995). He showed that, if allowance is made for uniform cross-country differences in technology, H–O theory provides a better explanation of the facts. The assumption of uniformity matters: if cross-country differences in technology vary among sectors, comparative advantage is affected also by Ricardian considerations (Harrigan, 1997). Even uniform differences, moreover, make H–O a more modest theory than some earlier tests supposed: it cannot explain the absolute amounts of goods that countries export or import, but only the amounts of some goods relative to other goods.[2]

## 2. Working at the wrong level of aggregation

H–O theory cannot provide a complete explanation of trade, even in relative terms and even abstracting from government policies. For Ricardian reasons, as mentioned, a country that is particularly efficient at producing some good will export that good, even though its mixture of factor endowments gives it no special cost advantage. Economies of scale are also important, especially in explaining the large volume of trade that occurs among countries with similar factor endowments, and in explaining the fine details of the composition of trade.

H–O works best at a high level of aggregation, with a few broadly defined goods (primary products and labour-intensive manufactures, for example) and a few broadly defined factors that are used in all sectors (labour, land and skill, for example). To try to use an H–O model with a few factors to explain more detailed patterns of trade, as many tests have done, is to ignore the standard theory (in which models with more goods than factors are indeterminate) and to invite empirical disappointment, since the effect on comparative costs of differences in factor endowments tends to be swamped by other influences. But to extend an H–O model to include many more, sector-specific factors is to risk trivializing H–O into saying, as Samuelson (quoted by Robinson, 1964) joked, 'that the export of tropical fruit from the tropics is due to the prevalence of tropical conditions there'.

The contribution of H–O theory is thus to provide a broad-brush explanation of major features of the pattern of world trade, especially among countries with widely varying endowments, and of their consequences for domestic factor markets. Even at this level, H–O is necessarily an incomplete explanation – other forces are also at work – but it is at this level that it is most useful. An important implication, however, is that aggregation problems are inevitable in applying H–O theory: both goods and factors are far from homogeneous, which, as noted by Davis and Weinstein (2001) as well as by Schott (2003), requires unusual care in the design of empirical work and in the interpretation of its results.

## 3. Treating capital as a factor of production

Samuelson, who understood capital theory, was careful to make the two factors in his H–O models labour and land. Most textbook presentations, however, make capital the second factor, and most empirical tests of H–O theory have likewise treated capital as a factor of production, measuring its stock in each country as the cumulation of past investment. This approach is questionable, both theoretically and empirically, as was emphasized by Joan Robinson (1964) at about the time I was being taught by Ajit and as I subsequently explained more fully (Wood, 1994a, section 2.2; 1994b). The main empirical difficulty is that capital is internationally mobile: machines are traded, buildings can be put up anywhere in a year or two and finance flows around the world on a massive scale. This mobility matters because – as is clear intuitively and is shown formally by Ethier and Svensson (1986) – the factors relevant to the H–O explanation of trade in goods are only those that are internationally immobile.

Capital is not, of course, perfectly mobile. The prices even of traded capital goods differ somewhat from country to country – a fact with which recent empirical work has grappled (Eaton and Kortum, 2001; Debaere and Demiroglu, 2003). Obstacles to capital flows also cause interest rates in some countries, particularly developing ones, to diverge persistently from world levels. But as a first empirical approximation it is reasonable to suppose that, as a result of mobility of both capital goods and finance, there is little variation among countries in the 'rental' rate of capital (the real interest rate times the price of capital goods). And in capital theory it is a country's rental rate that determines how cheaply it can produce capital-intensive goods, defined as those with high capital-output ratios.[3] So if rental rates are similar in most countries, there should be little variation among countries in comparative advantage as between more and less capital-intensive goods. Most tests of H–O theory, however, have measured this aspect of comparative advantage by the size of a country's stock of capital goods, relative to its other factor endowments – a ratio that varies widely among countries – which helps to explain why they have often yielded peculiar results.

A simple solution is to drop capital from the list of H–O factors, as I have done in my own research. But this raises two questions, of which the first is, if capital is left out, what do we put in its place? Part of the answer is land (or natural resources), but an even bigger part is skill (or human capital). Education, training and knowledge are vital factors of production, there is wide variation among goods in skill intensity, and skill endowments vary widely among countries because of barriers to international mobility (though barriers are lower for some countries and for some types of skilled workers, of which more later). The second question is, if we leave non-human capital out of the explanation of trade, where do we put it in our model, since it is clearly of vital importance for production? The answer is to make it one of the determinants, along with technology, of the productivity of the immobile factors.

## Empirical revival

Since about 1990, partly because of recognition of the misunderstandings outlined above, the reputation of H–O theory as an explanation of how the world works has improved substantially. It still has detractors, and even among its supporters debate continues about the areas and respects in which it is helpful. But H–O has played a major role in two areas of recent empirical work: the effects of trade on wages; and variation in the structure of exports and output.

### Effects of globalization on wage inequalities

In Wood (1994a), which got a good review from Ajit (Singh, 1995), I suggested an H–O connection between several facts: rapid growth of manufactured exports from the East Asian tigers to developed countries; reduced wage inequalities in the tigers; and increased wage inequalities and unemployment of unskilled workers in developed countries. My model had two countries (North and South), two factors (skilled and unskilled labour) and two goods (skill-intensive and labour-intensive manufactures). Reduction of barriers to trade had caused the North to specialize in the skill-intensive good, reducing the demand for unskilled workers, and vice versa in the South.

This suggestion, on a sensitive subject, precipitated an avalanche of other work, some supportive, some highly critical. Most of the contributions were about the developed-country story (I surveyed the first wave of these in Wood, 1998). Some critics argued that I had misinterpreted the theory (more on this below). Others argued that, although rising wage inequality was consistent with an H–O explanation, the relative demand for unskilled workers had declined mainly because of changes in technology unrelated to trade. The 'trade versus technology' debate was lively, but eventually ran out of steam, partly for lack of conclusive evidence and partly because the answer did not affect the policy implications.

Some subsequent critics, including Ajit (Singh, 2003), argued that after the 1980s the behaviour of wage inequalities in developed countries ceased to be consistent with either the trade or the technology explanations, since the relative wages of unskilled workers ceased to fall (Anderson, 2001). This could be rationalized in H–O terms: the North had become fully specialized in skill-intensive manufactures and its labour-intensive manufacturing sector had been extinguished, so that no further harm could be inflicted on its unskilled workers. But this rationalization was not satisfactory, as Ajit noted, because imports from developing countries continued to grow. Moreover, the biggest change in wage inequality in developed countries since the early 1990s has been among skilled workers: a small group at the top has pulled rapidly away from the rest, for which there does not seem to be an H–O explanation.

My simple H–O story about trade narrowing wage inequalities in the South has come under fire too. Although it fitted the facts of East Asia in the 1960s and 1970s, it seemed to be contradicted by the experience of Latin America in the 1980s and 1990s (Robbins, 1996; Wood, 1997). Evidence for other developing regions and countries was sparse, but it, too, suggested a mixed picture (Anderson, 2005). Part of the variation can be explained in H–O terms: only in some developing countries is unskilled labour the abundant factor and hence predicted to gain from openness to trade; in other developing countries the abundant factor is land or (in upper-middle-income ones) skilled labour. But even in some countries where unskilled labour is the abundant factor – Vietnam, for example – wage inequalities have risen.

Ajit's (Singh, 2003) explanation of changes in unskilled relative wages in the North is changes in labour market institutions, macroeconomic conditions and social norms, all of which surely contributed. Changing institutions are a plausible explanation also for rising inequality in Southern countries such as Vietnam. But my own explanation for most of the anomalies – wage changes which cannot be explained in H–O terms – in both North and South is falling travel and communications costs, which enable highly skilled Northern workers to operate globally, raising their wages and those of many Southern workers, but depressing the wages of most other Northern and some Southern workers (Wood, 2002; Anderson *et al.*, 2006).

The debate about globalization and wage inequality, both recently and historically (Williamson, 1997), has attracted a lot of attention to H–O theory, which remains the only analytical framework that links trade and labour markets. But what has been the effect on its empirical credibility? Opinions differ; but my impression is that most people now see H–O as part of a complete explanation and as the main explanation of parts of the outcome. In any event, that is my view, but I also recognize that, as with trade more generally, H–O is not the whole story, for which it is essential to combine it with other sorts of explanation (as in Wood, 2002).

### Effects of endowments on sectoral structure

A fundamental aim of H–O theory is to explain the pattern of trade, and in this regard its empirical reputation has been revived recently by the work particularly of Trefler (1995), Harrigan (1997), Davis and Weinstein (2001) and Schott (2003). In my own work, with various co-authors, I have tried to respond to all three of what I described above as the earlier misunderstandings of H–O theory: by assuming sectorally uniform differences in technology among countries; by working at a high level of aggregation; and by omitting capital as an H–O factor of production.

Figure 9.1, an earlier version of which was in Wood and Berge (1997), is the simplest possible illustration of a strong H–O relationship. For all countries with populations of more than one million for which the necessary data are available in 1990, it plots the ratio of their manufactured exports to their primary exports against the ratio of their skill (or human capital) endowment to their land endowment, both ratios being logged. Skill is measured by the total number of years of schooling in the adult population and land by the area of the country: these measures are far from perfect, not least in their lack of control for variation in land quality (Wood and Mayer, 2001, section 1.3), but their imperfections make the strength of the relationship in the figure even more remarkable.

The H–O interpretation of the positive slope of the line in this figure is that there is a difference in the relative factor intensities of manufacturing and primary production. Manufacturing is more compact than agriculture and needs a more educated labour force: its production technology involves a higher ratio of skill to land.[4] Because of their different factor intensities, a country's comparative advantage as between these two sorts of goods depends on its relative endowments of skill and land.

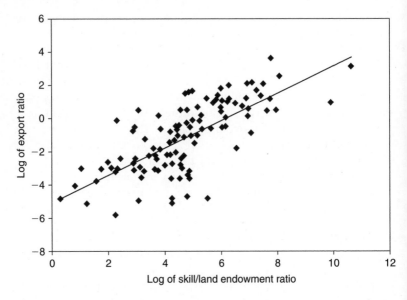

*Figure 9.1*   Cross-country variation in manufactured/primary export ratio, 1990
*Source*: Calculated from data in Wood and Mayer (2001); for more details of the variables, see the notes to Table 9.1 (in this figure, manufactures are NM and primary products are BP). The line is that of the first regression in Table 9.1.

The exports of countries with high ratios of skill to land are concentrated on manufactures, while countries with low ratios of skill to land export mainly primary products.

Table 9.1 contains more H–O regressions, drawn from Wood (2003, Table 3), which contains a fuller explanation and references to related articles. The first regression is the one shown in the figure. The second improves on it by separating the skill/land ratio into two separate ratios, skill/labour ($h$) and land/labour ($n$), which allows for differing labour intensity as well as skill/land intensity, and by including a country size variable (population, $p$), which allows for economies of scale in manufacturing. The ratio of manufactured to primary exports tends to be higher in countries which have more skill per worker and less land per worker, and which are bigger.

The next two regressions in the table explain cross-country variation in the ratio of processed to unprocessed primary exports and in the ratio of skill-intensive to labour-intensive manufactured exports. In both of them, the coefficients on skill per worker are positive and significant: processing requires more skill than unprocessed primary production, as

*Table 9.1* Cross-country regressions explaining export and output structures, 1990

| Dependent variable | Intercept | Coefficients on independent variables | | | | R-squared | Number of countries |
|---|---|---|---|---|---|---|---|
| | | *h/n* | *h* | *n* | *p* | | |
| *Export ratios* | | | | | | | |
| NM/BP | −5.01 | 0.82 | | | | 0.53 | 111 |
| | (−13.3) | (11.2) | | | | | |
| NM/BP | −7.43 | | 1.44 | −0.57 | 0.27 | 0.62 | 111 |
| | (−9.0) | | (7.1) | (−6.3) | (2.9) | | |
| PP/NP | −4.78 | | 1.49 | −0.13 | 0.10 | 0.40 | 111 |
| | (−5.5) | | (6.9) | (−1.4) | (1.0) | | |
| NMH/NML | −3.70 | | 1.59 | −0.07 | 0.01 | 0.38 | 69 |
| | (−4.1) | | (6.2) | (−0.8) | (0.1) | | |
| *Output ratio* | | | | | | | |
| BM/NP | −2.64 | 0.50 | | | | 0.46 | 96 |
| | (−9.2) | (8.9) | | | | | |
| BM/NP | −3.27 | | 1.30 | −0.28 | 0.03 | 0.60 | 96 |
| | (−5.6) | | (8.6) | (−4.4) | (0.4) | | |

*Notes*: NM = narrow manufactures (SITC 5–8 less 68); BM = broad manufactures (ISIC manufacturing); BP = broad primary products (SITC 0–4 plus 68); NP = narrow (unprocessed) primary products (ISIC agriculture and mining); PP = processed primary products (BM less NM); NMH = skill-intensive manufactures; NML = labour-intensive manufactures; $h$ = skill per worker (average adult years of schooling); $n$ = land per worker (square kilometres per adult); $p$ = total adult population (thousands). All variables in natural logarithms. All regressions estimated by OLS. t-statistics in brackets.
*Source*: Wood (2003, Table 3); for information on the coverage of NMH and NML, see Mayer and Wood (2001, Table 1).

does more skill-intensive manufacturing, so that countries with more skilled workforces export relatively more of these sorts of items. But the coefficients on land per worker are insignificant, because there is little difference in land-intensity between processed and unprocessed primary production, and between skill-intensive and labour-intensive manufacturing, so that these dimensions of export structure are largely unaffected by variation across countries in land/labour endowment ratios.

The final two regressions in the table refer to output structure, rather than to export structure: their dependent variable is the ratio of manufacturing to primary net output (value added). The dividing line between manufacturing and primary is not the same as in the export regressions (in the output data, processed primary products are part of manufacturing, and in the export data are part of primary), but the results are similar. The manufacturing to primary output ratio tends to be higher in countries with higher endowments of skill per worker and with lower endowments of land per worker.

All these regressions leave unexplained around half of the cross-country variation in the sectoral structures of exports and output, and there is room for debate about the choice of variables and method of estimation. But the relationships are qualitatively robust to variation in country coverage and choice of year (for example, essentially similar in 1960: Wood and Berge, 1997, Table 1B), and variations in coefficient size by region and year are economically illuminating (Wood and Mayer, 2001, p. 379). Thus, H–O theory, appropriately applied, provides a powerful empirical explanation of important aspects of the pattern of world trade.

## Theoretical problems

Samuelson's formalization of H–O theory, refined later by other economists, is of compelling elegance and usefulness as a tool for analysis and teaching. H–O–S, to use a briefer label, is in the words of Bliss (2007) 'to an international economist what a sharp knife is to a chef'. Its $2 \times 2 \times 2$ version is in every textbook, and its five theorems (Heckscher–Ohlin, factor price equalization, Stolper–Samuelson, Rybczynski and reciprocity) are taught to every graduate student – rightly so. But it also has problems (illuminatingly reviewed, in more technical detail than could be accommodated here, by Deardorff, 2006).

The commonest objection to H–O–S – as in my original essay for Ajit – is its long list of unrealistic assumptions (Ajit, too, criticizes them in Singh, 2003; while Leamer, 1984, p. 45, describes them as 'incredible'). But I now think that they are not the main problem. Only one really matters, which is non-reversal of factor intensities: the simple H–O principle of factor-A abundant countries exporting factor-A intensive goods would be unhelpful if the relative A-intensities of goods often varied with the level of relative factor prices (and with endowments). But factor intensity reversal seems rare, at least when the theory is applied at a high level of aggregation.[5]

The other assumptions matter less. Deviations from them just make the relationships imprecise – reducing the $R^2$ of regressions – and some of them can be allowed for in estimation (as, for example, with non-constant returns to scale in Table 9.1). If H–O theory is about relativities, as argued above, technology does not need to be identical in every country – only to vary among countries in a roughly neutral way.

Consumer preferences do not need to be strictly homothetic or to be identical in every country. Competition in product markets does not need to be perfect – prices must just be linked in some way to costs of production – and institutional imperfections in factor markets can be incorporated into the theory.

The basic problem with H–O–S is therefore not that its assumptions are unlikely to be exactly satisfied: it is the way in which the model behaves even when its assumptions *are* exactly satisfied. In several respects, its predictions diverge widely from readily observable features of the real world.

A glaring example is that factor prices are not equalized, as Robinson (1964) stated in the title of her article, Leamer (1984, pp. 11–12) noted two decades later, and Bliss (2007) another two decades later describes as 'always a cause of embarrassment'. This is not quite so serious as it seems: if the quality of technology varies among countries, then absolute factor prices must also vary – which accounts for most of the variation in wage rates which Robinson and Leamer noted. What is a problem, though, is that *relative* factor prices are not equalized, and that their variation across countries is correlated with endowments – factors are relatively cheaper where they are relatively more abundant, despite countries being open to trade. For example, the relative wage of skilled workers is lower in developed than in developing countries, and land rents are lower, relative to wages, in the US than in Japan.

There are two ways, in H–O–S, to explain why relative factor prices vary with relative factor endowments, but both these cures seem as unattractive as the disease. One is to assume that there are fewer goods than factors, but that too seems unrealistic: if the definition of factors is limited to inputs that are used in most sectors (as distinct from sector-specific factors), there are thousands more goods than factors. The other cure is specialization – trade causing countries to produce only one good (in the two-good version of the theory) or no more goods than there are factors (in higher-dimensional versions). But as Deardorff (2006) emphasizes, which particular subset of goods is produced is in theory hypersensitive to small changes in prices. In reality, moreover, countries are manifestly not highly specialized: most countries produce most goods, albeit in widely varying quantities.

Another glaring (and related) problem is that the H–O–S description of how the world works is highly sensitive to its choice of dimensions – meaning the numbers of goods and factors in the model. The $2 \times 2 \times 2$ model paints one picture of reality, in which (within limits) factor prices are equalized and both countries produce both goods in quantities that depend on their endowments. If the numbers of goods and factors are increased in parallel (higher-dimensional 'even' models), things unsurprisingly get much more complicated. More worrisome are the effects of uneven numbers of goods and factors. If the number of factors exceeds the number of goods, factor prices cannot be equalized. If the number of goods exceeds the number of factors, the structure of output becomes either indeterminate or unrealistically specialized.[6]

This asymmetry seems fatal for using H–O–S to explain reality. As Samuelson was well aware (1953, para. 14), aggregation of goods and factors is both unavoidable and arbitrary. I argued above that H–O is most useful at high levels of aggregation. A model whose predictions vary dramatically with small changes in how the data are aggregated is thus unhelpful. It is also actively misleading, since the behaviour of the world from which the data are drawn obviously does not vary with how the data happen to be aggregated.

Some of the problems of using H–O–S to interpret reality surfaced in the debate about trade and wages in developed countries. Using the $2 \times 2$ version of the model, trade economists argued that all that mattered were prices: trade could reduce the relative wages of unskilled workers only by reducing the prices of labour-intensive goods relative to skill-intensive goods; changes in imports, exports and sectoral output were irrelevant (Lawrence, 1996; Leamer, 2000). In defence of my use of trade flows in factor content calculations and of my idea of defensive innovation, I appealed to another version of the model, arguing that the North had moved from 'manufacturing autarky' to complete specialization in skill-intensive goods (Wood, 1998). Regardless of who was right, this choose-the-version-that-suits-your-case approach to the theory was intellectually unsatisfactory.

It is also hard to make sense, in the H–O–S framework, of the regression results in Figure 9.1 and Table 9.1. At first sight, the upward slope of the regression line in Figure 9.1 is a Rybczynski relationship between the relative outputs of two goods and the relative endowments of two factors. On closer inspection, though, this interpretation is not sustainable. The slope (an elasticity) is less than unity, and is only about one-half for the output ratio, while Rybczynski predicts magnification – an elasticity greater than unity. In H–O–S theory, moreover, the line should slope upwards only over the range in which country endowment ratios lie between the factor intensity ratios of the two goods: on either side of this range, countries should produce only one of the goods, a pattern of which there is no trace in the figure.

The puzzle deepens with examination of the NMH/NML (or the PP/NP) regression in Table 9.1. The insignificant coefficient on the land per worker variable in each of these regressions was attributed above to the small difference in land intensity between the two goods. But if this were genuinely a Rybczynski relationship, a small difference in land intensity would have the opposite effect: it would make the elasticity (absolutely) larger, because adjusting the demand for land to match changes in its supply would require more of a shift in the relative outputs of the two goods than if the difference in land intensity between the goods were large.

## Theoretical revival

These odd properties of H–O–S – its sensitivity, both to changes in dimensionality, as emphasized above, and to small changes in prices, as emphasized by Deardorff (2006) – stem largely from an assumption that does not even appear in the usual 'incredible' list, because it is common to most trade theories and not special to H–O–S. It is that goods prices in an open economy are determined by world market prices (sometimes referred to as 'the law of one price').

The internal prices of an open economy may be affected also by tariffs, as famously analysed by Stolper and Samuelson, but unless tariffs change, internal prices move in lock-step with world prices. Internal prices depend, too, on transport and other trade costs, but these are almost always modelled as proportional wedges, like *ad valorem* tariffs.[7] Demand is thus infinitely elastic: depending on whether its production cost for a tradable good is above or below the world price adjusted for trade costs, a country either sells nothing or it sells as much as it can produce. In this sense, at the individual country level, H–O–S is a model without a demand side.

### Trade costs reduce demand elasticities

Introducing demand inelasticity – inverse relationships between relative goods prices and relative outputs – yields more robust and realistic H–O models. The question is how to explain the demand inelasticity in an economically plausible way. The usual approach, used by Trefler (1995) as well as by computable general equilibrium (CGE) modellers, is to follow Armington (1969) in recognizing that foreign and local varieties of goods are imperfect substitutes. But to get demand elasticities down to realistically low levels, CGE modellers need to assume that national varieties are worse substitutes for one another than is suggested by the casual observation of trade theorists (who remain unconvinced). To achieve realistically low elasticities, CGE models also assume, without clear theoretical foundations, imperfect substitutability for firms between home market sales and export sales, and sometimes also world prices that decline with quantities exported, which in reality is rare.

A better explanation for low demand elasticities is provided by trade costs, viewed in a way that differs from the standard proportional wedges and is more realistic (Wood, 2008a).[8] The essential point is that the relative costs of trading any pair of goods do not, in practice, vary among countries in proportion to the relative costs of producing them. Physical features of goods tend to make the costs of trading them similar for all countries: a good that is heavier than another good has this property in every country. Trade costs vary among countries with, for example, their locations, the efficiency of their ports and their trade policies. But relative trade costs are largely independent of relative production costs – there is no general reason why a country that can produce one good more cheaply than some other good should also be able to trade it more cheaply than the other good.

Because relative trade costs are largely independent of relative production costs, relative purchaser prices (the sum of production costs and trade costs) vary less across countries than do relative production costs – a lot less, because trade costs are large (170 per cent of production costs is the developed-country average in the survey by Anderson and van Wincoop, 2004). The relative demand for goods is to some degree inelastic with respect to relative purchaser prices, since (as already mentioned) buyers view goods from different countries as imperfect substitutes. The effect of trade costs is to lower further the demand elasticity that matters for H–O theory – how much the relative quantities of goods sold vary with the relative prices that producers receive.

To put the point algebraically, define the purchaser price, $p_j$, as the sum of the producer price, $c_j$ (which in equilibrium equals production cost), and the per-unit trade cost, $t_j$. The elasticity of relative demand with respect to relative producer prices for a pair of goods, $j$ and 1, can then be written as

$$\varepsilon_{j1} = \frac{\tilde{\varepsilon}_{j1}}{1 + \tau_{j1}} \qquad (1)$$

where $\tilde{\varepsilon}_{j1}$ is the elasticity of substitution in demand with respect to relative purchaser prices, and $\tau_{j1}$ is the average ratio of trade costs to producer prices $(t/c)$ for goods $j$ and 1. The producer price elasticity, $\varepsilon_{j1}$, is lower than the purchaser price elasticity, $\tilde{\varepsilon}_{j1}$, to a degree which depends on the size of $\tau_{j1}$.[9] For equation (1) to make sense, the purchaser price elasticity, $\tilde{\varepsilon}_{j1}$, must be less than infinite. The equation also holds only approximately when the trade cost ratios ($\tau_j$ and $\tau_1$) differ between the goods. But it conveys simply a proposition of general relevance (discussed at length in Wood, 2008a), which is that trade costs damp producer price elasticities of demand. It also allows openness to be a matter of degree, as in reality, rather than qualitatively different from 'closedness'.

## A modified H–O–S model

The H–O–S model can be modified to allow for demand inelasticity. Wood (2008b) follows Jones (1965) in expressing all variables as proportional changes in relative amounts (ratios of outputs of different goods and of endowments of different factors). The effect of proportional changes (denoted by hats) in the relative endowments of a pair of factors, $v_i$ and $v_1$, on the relative outputs of two goods, $q_j$ and $q_1$, is described by the following equation:

$$\hat{q}_j - \hat{q}_1 = \varepsilon_{j1}(\theta_{ij} - \theta_{i1})\varphi_{i1}(\hat{v}_i - \hat{v}_1) \tag{2}$$

There can be any number, $m$, of factors and hence $(m-1)$ additive terms on the right-hand side, each with factor 1 as numéraire and referring to one of the other factors ($v_2$ and $v_1$, $v_3$ and $v_1$, and so on). There can also be any number, $n$, of goods and hence $(n-1)$ of these equations, each with good 1 as numéraire and referring to one of the other goods ($q_2$ and $q_1$, $q_3$ and $q_1$, and so on).

The composite elasticity $\varepsilon_{j1}(\theta_{ij} - \theta_{i1})\varphi_{i1}$, which is a slope coefficient in the sorts of regressions shown in Table 9.1, is the product of three elasticities. The first, $\varepsilon_{j1}$, is the effect of changes in relative producer prices on relative sales of the two goods in world markets, derived from equation (1) above. The middle term is the effect on relative production costs (and hence on relative producer prices) of changes in relative factor prices, which depends on the shares of the non-numeraire factor $i$ in the costs of producing the two goods ($\theta_{ij} - \theta_{i1}$): its sign depends on the direction of the difference in factor intensity between the goods (which determines the sign of the composite elasticity – both $\varepsilon_{j1}$ and $\varphi_{i1}$ have negative signs, which cancel). The third elasticity, $\varphi_{i1}$, is the effect on relative factor prices of changes in relative endowments. It summarizes a more complicated relationship:

$$\varphi_{i1} = \left[ \sum_{j=1}^{n} (\lambda_{ij}\sigma_{iji} - \lambda_{1j}\sigma_{1ji}) + \sum_{j=2}^{n} (\lambda_{ij} - \lambda_{1j})\varepsilon_{j1}(\theta_{ij} - \theta_{i1}) \right]^{-1} \tag{3}$$

where, as in Jones, $\lambda_{ij}$ is the share of the economy-wide supply of factor $i$ that is used by sector $j$, and $\sigma_{ijk}$ (following the notation of Smith and Wood, 2005) is the elasticity of the input of factor $i$ into good *j* with respect to the price of factor *k*. The two terms reflect the two mechanisms by which changes in relative factor prices can bring relative factor demands into line with relative factor supplies: the first is through changes in technique (or detailed product mix) in each sector; the second is through changes in the sectoral mix of outputs of different factor intensities.[10] Equation (3) is inverted because the stronger are these two mechanisms (and hence the larger are the two corresponding terms), the smaller is the change in relative factor prices required by a change in relative endowments. The equation is defined so as to have a positive sign, like an ordinary elasticity of substitution.

This model has the basic H–O property that the relative outputs of goods of different factor intensities vary among countries with their relative factor endowments, but it is more realistic and more robust than the standard form of H–O–S. It allows relative factor prices to vary among countries with their relative factor endowments, it behaves in the same way with any numbers of goods and factors, and it does not predict extreme specialization in production. It is also consistent with the regressions in Table 9.1, both in its form (constant-elasticity relationships between goods ratios and factor ratios) and in its substance (elasticities can be less than unity, and their absolute sizes vary directly with the differences between the factor intensities of goods – measured by $\theta_{ij} - \theta_{i1}$).

This gain in realism comes at a price: trade costs have been added, so there are more variables (but this can be seen as a benefit, since trade costs should be an integral part of any theory of trade); and the algebra is somewhat more complicated than in the standard H–O–S model. Nor can this or any other formalization escape from the fact that higher-dimensional H–O models are inherently complicated and can potentially generate a wide variety of outcomes: to get clear analytical results, simplifying assumptions are needed (Bliss, 2007, ch. 6). For example, in equation (3) changes in the relative endowments of each pair of factors are assumed to have negligibly small effects on the relative prices of all other pairs of factors. This greatly simplifies the model, but one needs to watch out for cases in which this assumption would be seriously misleading.

The modified H–O–S model presented here is also simplified in other ways. Equation (1) is elaborated in Wood (2008a) to distinguish between home sales and exports. The effects of changes in world prices, and in tariffs and trade costs, also need to be spelled out, and the properties of the model explored in more detail. Some of this is done in Wood (2008b), but the model as outlined above is sufficient to illustrate that allowing for the effects of trade costs on demand elasticities permits H–O theory to be formalized in ways that avoid the most unrealistic properties of the standard H–O–S model.

## Conclusions

My view of H–O now is thus vastly more positive than in my long-ago essay for Ajit. A modified formalization of the theory can convey its intuition without any obvious inconsistency with reality. Appropriately interpreted, moreover, H–O theory provides a basis for illuminating empirical work on the pattern of trade and its interactions with labour markets. H–O is only part of the trade story, but would be hard to replace.

Since 1965, I have followed Ajit into development, another field in which H–O is illuminating. Development economists have never liked H–O: its assumptions seem unrealistic, its approach seems static and its policy implications seem unhelpful. But the assumptions are not really a problem (as I have argued above), the theory can be articulated in a more dynamic way, and useful lessons for development policy can be drawn from it (Wood, 2003).

H–O is of special relevance to two big development issues on which Ajit has written. One is structural change – involving industrialization in particular, but also services (Dasgupta and Singh, 2007). The other is differences in the development experiences of broad regions, most notably East Asia compared to Africa and Latin America (Singh 1993, 1999). On both these issues, Ajit has rightly emphasized the role of policy choices, but variation among regions in patterns of structural change has been powerfully shaped also by differences in their factor endowments, particularly of land relative to labour. H–O is only one element of the theory of development, just as it is only one element of the theory of trade, but in both fields it is a useful element.

## Notes

1. The tests also assumed, unrealistically, that all countries were equally open to trade.
2. As is clear in Jones's classic (1965) reworking of the Samuelsonian formalization of H–O.
3. By contrast, most tests of H–O theory focus on the ratio of the rental rate to the wage rate, and assume the appropriate measure of capital intensity to be the capital–labour ratio. This approach is misleading, as explained in Wood (1994a, pp. 38–40, 75–8).
4. Mining, which is also part of primary exports, is different in its factor intensities from agriculture, but also has a lower skill/land ratio than manufacturing.
5. A notable exception is electronics, of which exports are of high skill intensity in developed countries and low skill intensity in developing countries, as a result of the aggregation of different sorts of items into a single statistical category.

6. Samuelson (1953) argued that the apparently indeterminate outcome might be determinate if countries had similar factor endowments or there were small transport costs (see also Leamer, 1984, pp. 17–18).

7. The literature on trade costs is surveyed by Anderson and van Wincoop (2004). A more recent H–O–S model of a single open economy with proportional trade costs is Markusen and Venables (2007).

8. That non-proportional trade costs reduce demand elasticities is shown in a narrower context by Hummels and Skiba (2004). Aldaz-Carroll (2003) suggests that elasticities are reduced by unit costs of trade that rise with the quantity sold (at the margin, sales must be made in ever more distant and difficult markets). Rising trade costs are suggested as a possible way of improving the realism of H–O models also by Deardorff (2006).

9. A higher value of $\tau_{j1}$ lowers $1/(1 + \tau_{j1})$, which is the average share of the producer price in the purchaser price and so is also the weight of producer price changes in purchaser price changes: for example, if trade costs were equal to producer prices ($\tau_{j1} = 1$) and hence the producer prices accounted for half the purchaser price of a good, a 20 per cent rise in the producer price would cause a 10 per cent rise in the purchaser price; but if trade costs were double producer prices ($\tau_{j1} = 2$), the share of the producer price in the purchaser price would be only one-third, so that a 20 per cent producer price rise would cause only a 6.7 per cent purchaser price rise.

10. In a standard H–O–S model, $\varphi_{i1}$ would be zero and $\varepsilon_{j1}$ would be infinite. Factor prices would not vary with endowments, and (within a cone of diversification) changes in output mix would fully absorb variation in endowments, without changes in technique.

# References

Aldaz-Carroll, E. (2003) 'Getting Things in Proportion: Essays on the Development and Application of Heckscher-Ohlin Trade Theory', DPhil thesis, University of Sussex.

Anderson, E. (2001) 'Is the Unskilled Worker Problem in Developed Countries Going Away?', Department of Economics working paper 2001/06, Keele University.

Anderson, E. (2005) 'Openness and Inequality in Developing Countries: A Review of Theory and Recent Evidence', *World Development* 33: 1045–63.

Anderson, E., P. Tang and A. Wood (2006) 'Globalisation, Co-operation Costs and Wage Inequalities', *Oxford Economic Papers* 58: 569–95.

Anderson, J. and E. van Wincoop (2004) 'Trade Costs', *Journal of Economic Literature* 42: 691–751.

Armington, P. (1969) 'A Theory of Demand for Products Distinguished by Place of Production', *IMF Staff Papers* 16: 159–78.

Bliss, C. (2007) *Trade, Growth, and Inequality*, Oxford: Oxford University Press.

Bowen, H., E. Leamer and L. Sveikauskas (1987) 'Multicountry, Multifactor Tests of the Factor Abundance Theory', *American Economic Review* 77: 791–807.

Dasgupta, S. and A. Singh (2007) 'Manufacturing, Services and Premature Deindustrialisation in Developing Countries', in G. Mavrotas and A. Shorrocks (eds),

*Advancing Development: Core Themes in Global Economics*, London: Palgrave Macmillan.

Davis, D. and D. Weinstein (2001) 'An Account of Global Factor Trade', *American Economic Review* 91: 1423–53.

Deardorff, A. (2006) 'Needs and Means for a Better Workhorse Trade Model', powerpoint slides for Graham Lecture, Princeton University, available at http://www-personal.umich.edu/~alandear/writings/Graham.ppt.

Debaere, P. and U. Demiroglu (2003) 'On the Similarity of Country Endowments', *Journal of International Economics* 59: 101–36.

Eaton, J. and S. Kortum (2001) 'Trade in Capital Goods', *European Economic Review* 45: 1195–235.

Ethier, W. and L. Svensson (1986) 'The Theorems of International Trade with Factor Mobility', *Journal of International Economics* 20: 21–42.

Hall, R. and C. Jones (1999) 'Why do Some Countries Produce so much more Output per Worker than Others?', *Quarterly Journal of Economics* 114: 83–116.

Harrigan, J. (1997) 'Technology, Factor Supplies, and International Specialisation: Estimating the Neoclassical Model', *American Economic Review* 87: 475–94.

Hummels, D. and A. Skiba (2004) 'Shipping the Good Apples Out? An Empirical Confirmation of the Alchian-Allen Conjecture', *Journal of Political Economy* 112: 1384–402.

Jones, R. (1965) 'The Structure of Simple General Equilibrium Models', *Journal of Political Economy* LXXIII: 557–72.

Krueger, A. (1968) 'Factor Endowments and Per Capita Income Differences Among Countries', *Economic Journal* 78: 641–59.

Lawrence, R. (1996) *Single World, Divided Nations*, Paris: OECD.

Leamer, E. (1980) 'The Leontief Paradox Reconsidered', *Journal of Political Economy* 88: 495–503.

Leamer, E. (1984) *Sources of International Comparative Advantage*, Cambridge: MIT Press.

Leamer, E. (1995) 'The Heckscher-Ohlin Model in Theory and Practice', Princeton Studies in International Finance 77, Department of Economics, Princeton University.

Leamer, E. (2000) 'What's the Use of Factor Contents?', *Journal of International Economics* 50: 17–49.

Leamer, E. and J. Levinsohn (1995) 'International Trade Theory: The Evidence', in G. Grossman and K. Rogoff (eds), *Handbook of International Economics*, vol. 3, Amsterdam: Elsevier.

Leontief, W. (1953) 'Domestic Production and Foreign Trade: The American Capital Position Re-Examined', *Proceedings of the American Philosophical Society* 97: 332–49.

Markusen, J. and A. Venables (2007) 'Interacting Factor Endowments and Trade Costs: A Multi-Country, Multi-Good Approach to Trade Theory', *Journal of International Economics* 73: 333–54.

Mayer, J. and A. Wood (2001) 'South Asia's Export Structure in a Comparative Perspective', *Oxford Development Studies* 29: 6–29.

Robbins, D. (1996) 'Evidence on Trade and Wages in the Developing World', technical paper 119, OECD Development Centre.

Robinson, J. (1964) 'Factor Prices not Equalized', *Quarterly Journal of Economics* 78: 202–7.

Samuelson, P. (1953) 'Prices of Goods and Factors in General Equilibrium', *Review of Economic Studies* 21: 1–20.

Schott, P. (2003) 'One Size Fits All? Heckscher–Ohlin Specialisation in Global Production', *American Economic Review* 93: 686–708.

Singh, A. (1993) 'Asian Economic Success and Latin American Failure in the 1980s: New Analyses and Future Policy', *International Review of Applied Economics* 7: 267–89.

Singh, A. (1995) 'Review of "North–South Trade, Employment and Inequality"', *Economic Journal* 105: 1287–9.

Singh, A. (1995) 'Asian Capitalism and Financial Crisis', in J. Grieve Smith and J. Michie (eds), *Global Instability and World Economic Governance*, London: Routledge.

Singh, A. (2003) 'Income Inequality in Advanced Economies: A Critical Examination of the Trade and Technology Theories and an Alternative Perspective', in J. Ghosh and C. Chandrasekhar (eds), *Work and Well-Being in the Age of Finance*, New Delhi: Tulika Books.

Smith, A. and A. Wood (2005) 'Factor Intensity Similarity and Reduction of Dimensionality in Heckscher-Ohlin Models', unpublished paper.

Trefler, D. (1995) 'The Case of the Missing Trade and Other Mysteries', *American Economic Review* 85: 1029–46.

Vanek, J. (1968) 'The Factor Proportions Theory: The *N*-Factor Case', *Kyklos* 21: 749–56.

Williamson, J. (1997) 'Globalization and Inequality, Past and Present', *World Bank Research Observer* 12: 117–35.

Wood, A. (1994a) *North-South Trade, Employment and Inequality: Changing Fortunes in a Skill-Driven World*, Oxford: Clarendon Press.

Wood, A. (1994b) 'Give Heckscher and Ohlin a Chance!', *Weltwirtschaftliches Archiv* 130: 20–49.

Wood, A. (1997) 'Openness and Wage Inequality in Developing Countries: The Latin American Challenge to East Asian Conventional Wisdom', *World Bank Economic Review* 11: 33–57.

Wood, A. (1998) 'Globalisation and the Rise in Labour Market Inequalities', *Economic Journal* 108: 1463–82.

Wood, A. (2002) 'Globalisation and Wage Inequalities: A Synthesis of Three Theories', *Weltwirtschaftliches Archiv* 138: 54–82.

Wood, A. (2003) 'Could Africa be like America?', in B. Pleskovic and N. Stern (eds), *Annual Bank Conference on Development Economics 2003*, Washington, DC: World Bank.

Wood, A. (2008a) 'Openness is a Matter of Degree: How Trade Costs Reduce Demand Elasticities', working paper 169, Queen Elizabeth House, Oxford University.

Wood, A. (2008b) 'Heckscher-Ohlin-Samuelson Remixed', working paper 170, Queen Elizabeth House, Oxford University.

Wood, A. and K. Berge (1997) 'Exporting Manufactures: Human Resources, Natural Resources, and Trade Policy', *Journal of Development Studies* 34: 35–59.

Wood, A. and J. Mayer (2001) 'Africa's Export Structure in a Comparative Perspective', *Cambridge Journal of Economics* 25: 369–94.

# 10
# Growth Rates, Economic Structure, Energy Use and Sources of Demand*

*Codrina Rada von Arnim and Lance Taylor*

## Introduction

At the conference celebrating Ajit, almost every speaker talked about his approach to economic research: immerse yourself in the data and the 'facts', with due heed for their errors and incompleteness; examine them from all angles and think hard; draw out their theoretical and policy implications.

We can scarcely claim to match Ajit in generating deep insights, but we have tried to follow in his footsteps in investigating the growth and development performance of non-industrialized countries in the latter part of the twentieth century, in particular a 'great divergence' of their growth rates of per capita GDP since around 1980. The goal is to explore the factors underlying observed patterns of growth, and trace out plausible lines of causation for their diversity. We have attempted to organize the data in such a way as to highlight salient relationships, or the lack thereof, among key economic variables.

To keep the discussion within bounds, the data are organized in terms of 12 regional groups, including 57 developing and transition countries: the rapidly growing East Asian economies (or the 'Tigers'), South East Asia, China, South Asia, semi-industrialized 'Latin America' (including South Africa and Turkey with economic structures similar to their counterparts in the western hemisphere), the Andean countries, Central America and the Caribbean, Central and Eastern Europe, Russia and Ukraine representing the former USSR, 'representative' and 'other'

*Research supported by the United Nations Department of Economic and Social Affairs. Encouragement and thoughtful inputs from José Antonio Ocampo are gratefully acknowledged.

countries in sub-Saharan Africa,[1] and the Middle East. The nations in each group are listed in the Appendix.

### Divergence in the twentieth century

To set the discussion Figure 10.1[2] shows GDP and sectoral per capita output growth rates by region in constant 1990 US dollars.[3] We identify three cohorts of regions and countries that had similar patterns of growth.

There was sustained growth in the Tigers, China, South East Asia and South Asia (dominated by India) at very respectable rates. Relative to the other regions, South Asia had less robust expansion and South East Asia did not bounce back as strongly from the 1997 crisis as did the Tigers. These regions 'diverged upwardly' from the rest of the developing world.

The second, late recovery group includes semi-industrialized Latin America, Central America and the Caribbean, and Central and Eastern Europe. All the regions showed somewhat faster growth late in the century, although formerly socialist Europe is in an ambiguous situation.

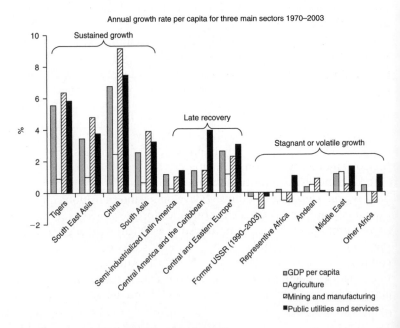

*Figure 10.1*   Sectoral growth rates 1970–2003
*Source*: World Bank, World Development Indicators 2005 database.
*Data for Mining and manufacturing output for Czechoslovakia is not available prior to 1980.

Over the period 1970–2003 it grew slightly faster in per capita terms than South Asia (2.7 per cent vs 2.6 per cent per year) but because of the transition shock around 1990 it seems more appropriate to call its case one of 'late recovery'.

Finally, the two African regions with Other Africa dominated by Nigeria, the Andean group, the Middle East, and Russia and Ukraine were either stagnant throughout the period or experienced volatile economic expansion. Data from recent years show that Representative Africa and Russia and Ukraine began to grow again. If growth continues they should shift into the late recovery group.

## Identifying structural change

Sustained growth in successful regions was associated with changes in economic structure in several dimensions. With a few exceptions, the slow growers did not generate such changes. Growth over years and decades in per capita output requires economic transformation characterized by higher productivity and increasing returns to scale. The evidence supports this point of view. Recognizing the structural shifts that occurred in the regions with consistent growth can help chart future directions that other developing economies may be able to take. Needless to say, any economy is a unique entity with its own characteristics that require its own policies. But stylized facts show that there are dynamic movements of key macrovariables that show up in connection with sustained output growth across different economic systems. We analyse these movements from several angles, in terms of formalized decomposition exercises and more informal analysis of data on energy use, human capital accumulation and foreign direct investment (FDI).[4]

One decomposition breaks down labour productivity growth between agricultural, industrial and service sectors. Overall productivity growth comes out as an average of own-rates of growth, weighted by output shares, for all sectors along with 'reallocation effects' which are positive for sectors with relatively low average productivity in which employment falls or for high-productivity sectors in which employment rises.[5]

A second exercise focuses on growth rates of the economy-wide employment to population ratio which is decomposed into an average of growth rates of the ratio by sectors weighted by employment shares. At both the national and sectoral levels, the ratio of employment to total population will rise if the growth rate of output per capita exceeds growth of labour productivity.[6] An economy can be considered to be performing well if it has both sustained productivity growth and a stable or rising employment–population ratio.

Third, we examine the association between capital stock and output growth. We also contrast growth rates of labour and capital productivity and ask how they feed into widely used but fundamentally misleading calculations of 'total factor productivity growth' (TFPG). A simple accounting identity states that the growth rate of labour productivity is equal to the sum of the growth rates of capital productivity and the capital/labour ratio. The formula helps explain the 'Asian' pattern of falling capital productivity over time. A similar identity applies to the growth rates of labour and energy productivity. The details are presented below.

Finally, we look at net borrowing flows – incomes minus expenditures – over time for the government, the private and the rest of the world 'institutional sectors', normalized by GDP.[7] As an accounting identity, borrowings must sum to zero: (private investment – saving) + (public spending – taxes) + (exports – imports) = 0, with a positive entry indicating that a sector is a net contributor to effective demand.

Changing sectoral roles in this equation can be important aspects of the growth process. Mutually offsetting co-movements of government and foreign net borrowing occurred sporadically at most. In other words, the widely accepted 'twin deficits' view of macro adjustment does not seem to apply. Nor do the data suggest that 'consumption-smoothing' behaviour – an important feature of mainstream Ricardian equivalence growth theory – is empirically relevant. Macroeconomic flexibility, on the other hand, may be very important. Strong fluctuations in private and foreign net borrowing did not derail growth in the upwardly diverging Tigers and, to a lesser extent, South East Asia.

## Output growth patterns

The contrast in Figure 10.1 between Asia and Eastern Europe and the other regions is striking. The Asian regions (even South Asia) had very high growth rates in industry. Service sector growth was strong in Central and Eastern Europe and, to a lesser extent, in Latin America and Central America and the Caribbean.

Figures 10.2 and 10.3 present scatter plots of per capita GDP growth in the agriculture and industry sectors vs the percentage changes in their respective sectoral shares (again 1970–2003). The rapidly growing Asian countries identified in Figure 10.1 showed substantial shifts in shares in the classic movement from primary toward secondary and tertiary sectors.

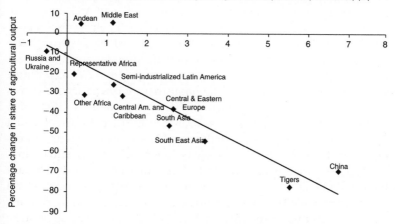

*Source*: World Bank, World Development Indicators 2005 database.
*Figure 10.2* Growth performance and structural change in agriculture

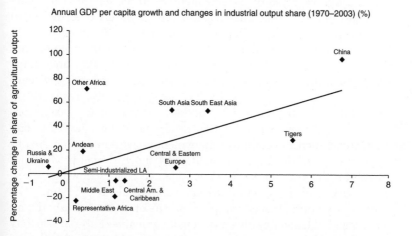

*Source*: World Bank, World Development Indicators 2005 database.
*Figure 10.3* Growth performance and structural change in industry

Figure 10.2, for the agricultural share, shows a negatively sloped regression line for the whole 12-region sample. But contrast the results for the five fast-growing regions with those for the others. While the former show a clear relationship between faster output growth and a decreasing share, the lagging seven regions generate a random scatter – a result that will repeat itself for several other indicators of structural change. Among the rapid growers, China's agricultural share fell by an astonishing 34 percentage points over the period. In South and South East Asia, agriculture saw its output share decline 19 and 17 percentage points, respectively. The rising agricultural shares in the Andean and Middle Eastern regions are anomalous as is the decrease accompanied by negative growth in Russia and Ukraine.

Similar observations apply to the industrial sector and service sectors with clear associations emerging for the rapid growers and ill-defined data clouds for the other regions. Growth is associated with structural change and the absence of growth is not. The growing regions had rising industrial shares, as can be observed in Figure 10.3 (less so in Central and Eastern Europe, which prior to 1970 had already been pushed toward industrial specialization). Four slow growers suffered long-term deindustrialization, while the industrial share in Russia and Ukraine scarcely budged. Big shifts in industrial shares in the Middle East and Other Africa (with Nigeria as the largest economy included) were driven by developments in the petroleum sector.

The fast growers had predictable increases in the service sector share as well (details not shown here). The Tiger region service share rose to 64 per cent by 2003, and supported strong job creation, as is reported below. There was no apparent relationship for the lagging regions.

## Labour productivity growth

Historically, labour productivity increases have been the major contributing factor to growth in real GDP per capita. At the same time, faster productivity increases cut into employment growth unless they are offset by rising effective demand. Figure 10.4 shows overall productivity growth for the period 1991–2003/04. The five rapidly growing regions had productivity growth rates exceeding – some greatly exceeding – the rich country norm of 2 per cent per year. The others fell well short, and the former USSR had negative productivity growth.

In terms of phasing over time, more detailed results (not presented here) show that Russia/Ukraine suffered an enormous productivity collapse (−9.7 per cent per year) in 1991–95, but then recovered to 5.6 per cent (1999–2003). Central and Eastern Europe showed a similar though far less violent pattern. The Tiger region rapidly recovered its productivity growth rate of 4–5 per cent per year after the 1997 Asian crisis. South East Asia also had 4–5 per cent annual productivity growth prior to 1997, but rates tailed off thereafter. The other regions had growth rate fluctuations over time but no clear trends.

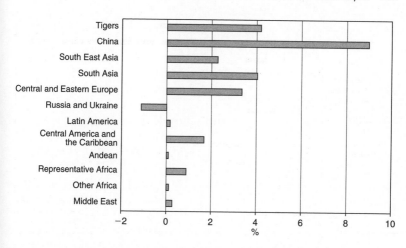

*Source*: International Labour Office GET database, for employment; World Bank, World Development Indicators 2005 database, for output.

*Figure 10.4* Overall labour productivity growth, 1991–2003/4

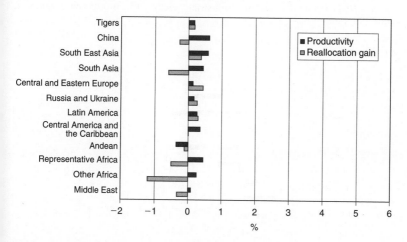

*Source*: International Labour Office, GET database, for employment; World Bank, World Development Indicators 2005 database, for output.

*Figure 10.5* Contribution of agriculture sector to productivity growth, 1991–2003/4

Figures 10.5 through to 10.7 summarize direct and reallocation contributions by sector to overall productivity increases. Agriculture in Figure 10.5 evidently did not play a crucial role in the process. In several countries agriculture's reallocation effects were negative. The meaning is

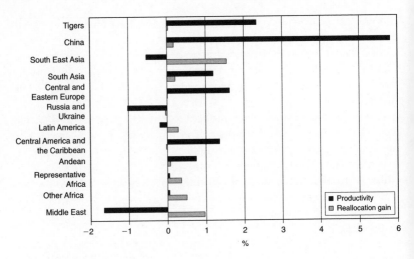

*Source*: International Labour Office, GET database, for employment; World Bank, World Development Indicators 2005 database, for output.

*Figure 10.6* Contribution of industrial sector to productivity growth, 1991–2003/4

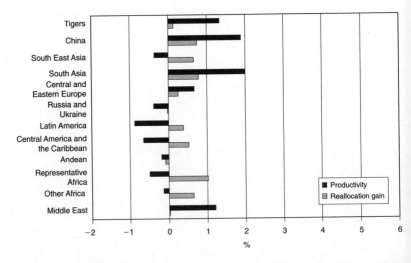

*Source*: International Labour Office, GET database, for employment and World Bank, World Development Indicators 2005 database, for output.

*Figure 10.7* Contribution of service sector to productivity growth, 1991–2003/4

that this sector, with its relatively low average productivity, had positive employment growth. This finding is not surprising in regions such as China, South Asia and Africa where agriculture's share in total employment is significant, but the result is slightly discordant in the Middle East. More disquieting is the sector's poor productivity performance in Africa.

The industrial sector's own productivity growth made a substantial contribution to the total in four of the rapidly growing regions (Figure 10.6) and there was a strong reallocation contribution in South East Asia, the outlier. The direct contribution of nearly 6 per cent per year in China is striking. Industry made a visible contribution in the two poorer western hemisphere regions but detracted from overall performance in Russia and Ukraine and the Middle East, with the latter gaining from reallocation.

Services in Figure 10.7 also added to the total in the rapid growers: as with industry, a negative direct but positive reallocation contribution in South East Asia. Elsewhere, the direct contribution from services was typically negative with modest positive contributions from reallocation. This distinction among regions has implications for job creation, as discussed below.

Finally, from an alternative dataset we were able to do decompositions for the period 1980–2000 for the four Asian regions (1986 as the starting

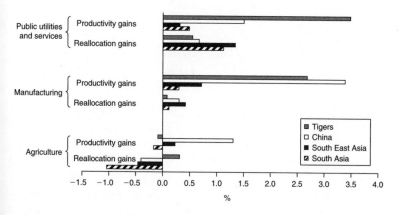

*Source*: Employment data are from the International Centre for the Study of East Asian Development, http://www.icsead.or.jp. Data for sectoral output are from UN National Accounts database.

*Figure 10.8* Productivity decomposition for selected Asian regions, 1980(6)–2000

year for South Asia). The results are in Figure 10.8. The same general pattern holds as in Figures 10.5 through to 10.7, with services playing a more important role in the Tigers.

The bottom line on productivity growth is that the two non-agricultural sectors made solid contributions to the total in the fast-growing regions, even as their overall importance in the economy rose. Elsewhere the results were a mixed bag, with no clear patterns emerging. Insofar as it is measured by average labour productivity growth, technological advance was evident in the growing regions and absent or, at best, sporadically present in other corners of the world.

## Employment growth patterns

Figure 10.9 summarizes results regarding shifts in sectoral employment to population ratios in terms of their contributions to changes in the economy-wide ratio. Regional growth rates of the overall ratio hovered around zero, with more positive than negative values. As noted above, at both the sectoral and national levels, the ratio(s) will grow when the growth rate of output per capita exceeds labour productivity growth. The ratio(s) will also tend to rise when population growth is negative, as was the case in Eastern Europe and the former Soviet Union.

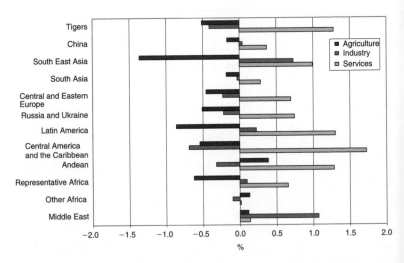

*Source*: International Labour Office, GET database, for employment and World Bank, World Development Indicators 2005 database, for output.

*Figure 10.9*  Sectoral shifts in employment/population ratios, 1991–2003/4

The most striking outcome in Figure 10.9 is the apparent similarity of all 12 regions in the sense that services showed a rising employment to output ratio everywhere, rather strongly, except in Other Africa, the Middle East and (to an extent) South Asia. The details, however, differed between fast- and slow-growing regions.

For the rapid growers, the positive contribution of services to employment growth shows that output per capita grew faster than the sector's rising productivity levels that underlie its positive contributions to growth overall (darker bars in Figure 10.7). Positive reallocation gains were due to the fact that services have relatively high average productivity. In the slower growing regions, direct contributions of services to economy-wide productivity were weak but rising demand still created jobs. Productivity did not increase rapidly within the sector but, via reallocation effects, the shifts in employment toward it (reflected in Figure 10.9) added to overall productivity growth.

Relative to total population, agriculture was a source of employable labour in nine regions, very strongly in South East Asia, and a sink only in the Middle East, Other Africa and (especially) in the Andean region. Only in the Middle East and South East Asia was the industrial sector a strong provider of jobs (a fact explaining South East Asian industry's strong reallocation contribution to overall productivity growth in Figure 10.6). Consistent with Figures 10.1 and 10.6, industry's rate of productivity growth tended to exceed its growth in demand per capita. An old structuralist observation in development economics is that the industrial sector is the main motor for productivity increases but not for job creation.

## Capital productivity and total factor productivity growth (TFPG)

The next topic is the role of capital accumulation in growth – a hearty perennial in mainstream economics. Following standard procedures (and blithely ignoring the Cambridge controversies), we computed 'capital stock' growth rates for the regions by cumulating real gross fixed capital formation over time from a postulated initial level of the stock (capital–output ratio of 2.5) with a depreciation rate of 0.05. After a decade or two such estimates of the capital growth rate should be insensitive to the parameters because capital stock growth tends to converge to investment growth over time.[8]

Figure 10.10 compares growth rates of output and the capital stock. In contrast to most other indicators discussed herein, there is a clear

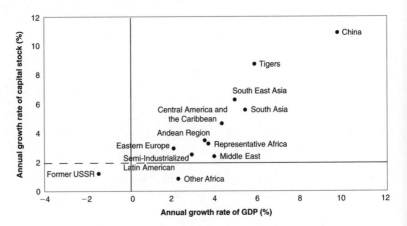

*Figure 10.10*   Output and capital stock growth rates, 1990–2004

positive association between the two growth rates across all regions – the usual empirical result. This relationship is usually thought to emerge from the supply side, as discussed immediately below, but it also could be attributed to demand. In a simple demand-driven growth model, if investment increases at a certain rate then output and (as just indicated) the capital stock will ultimately grow at that rate as well. The fact that the slope of the putative relationship between the two growth rates in Figure 10.10 is close to one argues more for demand- than supply-side causality. In the latter, the slope would lie below 45 degrees, with a less than one-for-one partial impact of faster capital growth on output growth.[9]

Also note that the capital growth rate exceeded output growth in the Tigers, China, South East Asia and the former USSR. These regions had falling capital productivity. Such an outcome can be expected in the rapidly growing Asian regions where industrial restructuring took place towards capital-intensive industries. Nevertheless these findings can also be said to be the outcome of accounting requirements. As noted above, the difference between labour and capital productivity growth rates must be equal to the difference between capital and labour growth rates as a 'theorem of accounting'. If capital grows faster than labour, then labour productivity has to grow faster than capital productivity.[10] If the capital to labour ratio rises very rapidly, then capital productivity growth may even have to be negative. This outcome is sometimes said to characterize an 'Asian' pattern of growth, or a 'Marx bias' in technical progress. It can also result from negative labour force growth as in the former USSR and Eastern Europe.

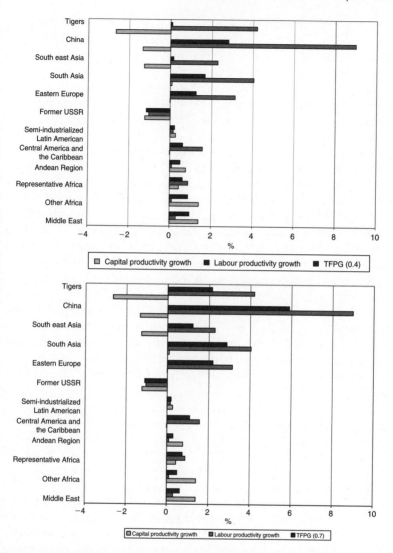

*Sources*: GFCF and GDP data comes from World Development Indicators 2005 database; employment data is from International Labour Office, GET database.
*Figure 10.11* Capital and labour productivity growth rates and TFPG, 1991–2004

Capital and labour productivity growth rates are plotted in Figure 10.11. Again note the contrast between regions. The rapid growers all had negative or nearly zero capital productivity growth rates and rising labour productivity which could have resulted from better technology 'embodied' in new capital goods. Detailed data show that China's capital productivity fell more rapidly over time. The former USSR lost on both fronts and the rest had small, mostly positive, growth of both indicators.

Instead of asking whether capital stock growth impacts directly on labour productivity (a question we could not directly address with our dataset), much of the academic literature focuses on TFPG or the 'residual'. TFPG turns out to be a weighted average of labour and capital productivity growth rates, with the weights being the labour and non-labour income shares of value added at factor cost. The question then becomes: what is the labour share? In developing countries, the share of remunerated labour income in GDP is likely to be less than 40 per cent. Most economically active people are not paid wages but rather toil within unincorporated proprietorships such as urban petty commerce, as labourers on peasant farms, etc. The market value of their work must be imputed in one way or another, with all the calculations being extremely dubious.

Figure 10.11 shows estimates of TFPG for labour shares of 0.4 (realistic?) and 0.7 (the standard number), respectively. Either way, because of their negative capital productivity growth, TFPG in the rapidly growing regions fell well short of labour productivity growth. For the lower labour share, TFPG in the Tigers and South East Asia was close to zero. Such findings are often used to portray the failings of the 'Asian model', but mostly they reflect an accounting identity and the arbitrary nature of the TFPG indicator.

## Energy productivity growth and energy/labour ratios

There is an old idea, perhaps dating to the nineteenth century 'energetics' movement (Mirowski, 1989; Martinez-Alier with Schlüpmann, 1991), that the crucial factor behind rising labour productivity and per capita income is increasing use of energy. One can make this a bit more precise by comparing growth rates of labour productivity, energy productivity and the energy/labour ratio. As noted above, the latter two growth rates must sum to the first as an algebraic identity.

For our 12 regional groups and the rich countries in the OECD, Figure 10.12 presents two scatter diagrams of growth rates of labour productivity and the energy/labour ratio, for the periods 1970–90 and 1990–2004. The energy sources included are fossil fuels plus minor contributions from 'solids' such as wood, peat, etc.

As with the growth rate of capital stock, there appears to be a robust relationship between increasing energy use per worker and labour

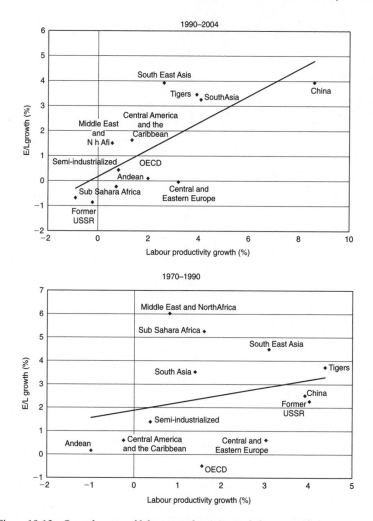

*Figure 10.12* Growth rates of labour productivity and the energy/labour ratio

productivity growth, with a steeper slope and a better fit in the latter period. Similar results show up when growth rates are compared at the individual country level. The slope of the relationship in the latter period is around 0.6, implying a substantial contribution of more energy use to higher labour productivity.

Table 10.1 presents the data in numerical form for the regions and selected countries. The units are terajoules of energy per worker per

*Table 10.1* Growth of energy productivity, labour productivity and the energy/labour ratio

| | Selected OECD | Central and Eastern Europe | USSR | Tigers | South East Asia | China | South Asia | Semi-Industrialized countries | Central America and the Caribbean | Andean | Middle East | Sub-Saharan Africa |
|---|---|---|---|---|---|---|---|---|---|---|---|---|
| **1970–1990** | | | | | | | | | | | | |
| Growth rate energy productivity | 1.9% | 2.3% | −0.4% | 0.3% | 1.4% | 1.3% | 2.0% | −1.2% | −1.0% | −1.4% | −4.9% | −3.1% |
| Growth rate labour productivity | 1.7% | 3.0% | 1.7% | 4.4% | 3.1% | 3.9% | 1.4% | 0.4% | −0.2% | −1.0% | 0.8% | 1.6% |
| Growth rate E/L | −0.3% | 0.8% | 2.1% | 4.0% | 4.5% | 2.6% | 3.5% | 1.6% | 0.8% | 0.4% | 6.0% | 4.9% |
| E/L beginning year (1970) | 0.51 | 0.21 | 0.26 | 0.08 | 0.01 | 0.02 | 0.01 | 0.09 | 0.04 | 0.04 | 0.05 | 0.01 |
| E/L end year (1990) | 0.48 | 0.25 | 0.39 | 0.18 | 0.03 | 0.04 | 0.02 | 0.13 | 0.05 | 0.05 | 0.16 | 0.01 |
| **1990–2004** | | | | | | | | | | | | |
| Growth rate energy productivity | 1.8% | 3.2% | 4.4% | 0.4% | 1.2% | 4.4% | 0.6% | 0.3% | −0.3% | 0.8% | −0.9% | −0.3% |
| Growth rate labour productivity | 2.0% | 3.2% | 4.3% | 3.9% | 2.6% | 8.6% | 4.1% | 0.8% | 1.3% | 0.7% | 0.6% | −0.9% |
| Growth rate E/L | 0.1% | 0.0% | −0.2% | 3.5% | 3.9% | 4.0% | 3.2% | 0.5% | 1.6% | 0.0% | 1.5% | −0.6% |
| E/L beginning year (1990) | 0.48 | 0.24 | 0.39 | 0.18 | 0.03 | 0.04 | 0.02 | 0.13 | 0.05 | 0.05 | 0.16 | 0.01 |
| E/L end year (2004) | 0.49 | 0.25 | 0.38 | 0.29 | 0.05 | 0.07 | 0.04 | 0.14 | 0.07 | 0.05 | 0.20 | 0.01 |

year.[11] There is a wide range of energy/labour ratios – from 0.01 (77 gallons of gasoline) in sub-Saharan Africa to 0.67 (5,150 gallons) in Saudi Arabia in 2004. By way of comparison, the ratio is 0.58 in the US and less than 0.3 in Western European countries, the Tigers and Japan.

In the context of global warming, the numbers are not reassuring. For example, at China's growth rate of the energy/labour ratio of 4 per cent per year, it would take the economy around 22 years to attain Sweden's 'moderate' ratio of 0.16, with energy productivity rising 4 per cent per year more slowly than labour productivity. As its per capita income rises and possibilities for appropriating more advanced technologies and taking advantage of surplus labour recede, China's labour productivity growth rate will almost certainly decline, perhaps creating even greater reliance on energy.

Rough calculations by climate experts (e.g. Socolow and Pacala, 2006) suggest that developing countries might have to reduce their fossil fuel energy/labour ratios by 1 per cent per year to hold greenhouse gas emissions in check. A handful of countries are in this range, but they are stagnant with negligible or negative labour productivity growth.

The key policy question is whether in the near future rich country energy/labour ratios can be reduced (or energy productivity increased relative to labour productivity) substantially by technological innovation and social rearrangements. In the recent period, there has been no significant downward trend in the ratios in the industrialized world. But if such innovations do work out, then perhaps they can be passed to developing economies before the momentum of their population growth overwhelms all possibilities for combating global warming. Given the environmental constraints and considering that only 16 per cent of the world's population lives in rich countries, and almost all population growth is in the poor ones, realistic prospects for successful economic performance and poverty alleviation may not be very bright.

## Human capital (education)

Mixed results reappear with regard to accumulation of human capital, which we measure by average years of schooling. The output growth rates summarized in Figure 10.1 have no clear connection at the regional and country level with more education because all regions raised their levels, some quite substantially. In 2000, the highest attained levels of education by far were in the Tigers, Eastern Europe and the core of the former USSR with 9–10 average years of schooling and skilled workers making up about two-thirds of the labour force. The lowest were in Africa

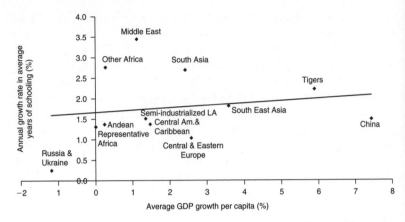

*Sources*: Data on education is from Barro and Lee (2000), http://www.cid.harvard.edu/ciddata/ciddata.html; data on growth rates of GDP per capita is from UN National Accounts.

*Figure 10.13*   Economic growth and educational improvements, 1970–2000

with slightly more than three average years of schooling. Other Africa's numbers were somewhat better than in the representative region.

How about relationships between growth in education and output? Figure 10.13 presents a scatter plot of GDP growth per capita vs growth in average years of schooling. The regression line shows a putative positive relationship between output expansion and educational growth, but it really only holds for the fast-growing regions, and not that strongly for Central and Eastern Europe and South Asia. As in Figures 10.2 and 10.3, and in contrast to the picture for physical capital accumulation in Figure 10.10 and energy use in Figure 10.12, the slow-growing regions inhabit an amorphous data cloud. They did no worse at accumulating human capital than the others, but they saw scant returns in growth. Education is a public good that should be supported for many reasons, but over the medium run its contribution to more rapid real income growth appears to be weak. More human capital may be a necessary or an enabling condition for sustained output growth, but it is clearly not sufficient.

## Foreign direct investment

Foreign direct investment is often touted as a potential source of technologically upgraded physical capital and managerial know-how more generally. But it is not obvious what level of FDI is 'significant'. As a share of GDP, for example, how large does it have to be or how rapidly should it grow to generate important repercussions on output growth?

FDI also tends to fluctuate over time. As a share of GDP between 1970 and 2001, it went from 1.6 per cent to 3 per cent (1997) to 3.1 per cent (2004) in the Tigers. Somewhat similar patterns appeared in South East Asia and China. FDI/GDP in South Asia peaked at 0.9 per cent in 1997, fell back, and then up to 0.8 per cent in 2004. Aside from South Asia, the rapidly growing economies received some inflows, with China absorbing a very substantial share of the worldwide total. Eastern Europe resembled Eastern Asia in seeing the FDI share of GDP rise from 0.4 per cent in 1990 to 4.8 per cent in 2000 and 4 per cent in 2004. Russia received relatively little FDI: it peaked at 1.7 per cent of GDP in 1999. Central America and the Caribbean had strong fluctuations – nearly 4 per cent in the 1970s down to 0.4 per cent in 1982, back to above 4 per cent in the 1990s with the assembly/tourism boom, and then some decline. Latin America saw 2 per cent toward the end of the period. Some members of the slow-growing group of economies did little worse than the fast-growers in garnering FDI, without a lot of apparent pay-off. The Andes were up to 5.5 per cent in 1993 and 3 per cent in 2004, with no positive impact on growth. Africa and the Middle East got negligible quantities of FDI.

Figure 10.14 shows a scatter of per capita growth rates vs shares of FDI in GDP. A positively sloped relationship shows up for Asia, as usual. The remaining regions demonstrate their usual blob of data points. A relatively large FDI inflow may possibly have a slightly stronger association than rising education with growth, but the relationship is still very weak.

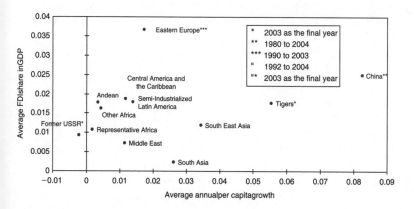

*Figure 10.14*  Economic growth and foreign direct investment
*Source*: UNCTAD Handbook of Statistics, 2005.

## Open economies and their patterns of net borrowing

Next we take up interactions between demand and supply. The focus is on the balance of payments, often the fulcrum for both short- and long-term limitations on growth in developing economies. There are at least three incompatible contemporary doctrines regarding how open macroeconomies operate. Twin deficits (TD) and Ricardian equivalence (RE) dogmata are widely spread in mainstream literature, while development and heterodox economists often favour a structural gap (SG) explanation of external balance.

In development macroeconomics, the twin deficits hypothesis traces back at least to the IMF economist Jacques Polak's (1957) blueprint for the 'financial programming' exercises that to this day are the linchpin of the Fund's stabilization packages worldwide. The recipe for action is to cut the fiscal deficit, which is supposed to improve the economy's external position. Polak was drawing on a long tradition of monetarist analysis of the balance of payments. In one variant, unless the private sector chooses to increase its saving – or, more precisely, reduce its net borrowing as discussed below – then a higher fiscal deficit must be paid for by domestic money creation. Aggregate demand consequently goes up. Under tacit assumptions that all resources are fully employed and the domestic price level is tied to foreign prices by arbitrage in foreign trade (PPP applies), the higher demand has to spill over into a bigger trade deficit.

Ricardian equivalence (Barro, 1974) emerges from dynamic optimal savings models postulating that all resources are fully employed and that households smooth their consumption (or, more generally, expenditure) over time. It plays a far more central role in contemporary mainstream macroeconomics than Polak's somewhat dated monetarism.[12] Along the lines of Say's Law, RE broadly asserts that a change in fiscal net borrowing will be offset by an equal shift in private net lending. In an open economy context, any one country's external position then has to be determined by intertemporal trade-offs between consumption and saving with all countries in the world producing the same good. Traditional counter-cyclical fiscal policy cannot possibly play a role.

However, TD and RE stories are not compatible because they assign different roles to private and foreign net borrowing. Under TD, private borrowing is 'neutral' in that it does not respond to shifts in the foreign or fiscal positions. Under RE, the current account is neutral with regard to fiscal shifts while private and government borrowing dance the trade-offs.

Finally, causality can also be interpreted as running the other way – from the foreign to the fiscal and/or private sector financial gap. In other words, the economy is externally constrained. The external position is 'structural' and will persist in the face of plausible domestic policy changes, i.e. within 'reasonable' ranges of real exchange rate values and the level of economic activity, the trade deficit – or surplus, say for China or Germany – will not change by very much. It need not be close to zero because of lacking or excess competitiveness of domestic producing sectors.

SG analysis resembles full employment RE in that its binding external gap imposes a supply constraint on the system. Particularly in a developing country context, the question becomes, how does effective demand adjust to meet the commodity supply permitted by available imports? To hold demand stable, any shift in the private or public sector net borrowing position has to be reflected into an offsetting change in the other domestic gap, as under RE. Mechanisms that can make this happen are sketched below. If private net borrowing is neutral, then fiscal deficit will reflect a shift in the external gap: TD with causality reversed. It becomes interesting to see what patterns emerge from the data.

Several borrowing styles can be identified. In the Asian regions in Figure 10.15, the fiscal role was rather passive, with major adjustments taking place between private and foreign net borrowing. The private and foreign co-movements were relatively large, with swings up and down exceeding 10 per cent of GDP in the Tigers and South East Asia. Big reductions in external deficits were forced from abroad in the 1997 crisis, but upswings tended to be associated with falling private saving and rising import propensities. Maintaining very high per capita income growth over a 25-year period with the macroeconomy subject to such extreme fluctuations is a feat perhaps unprecedented historically.

Figure 10.16 shows the history for two regions with persistently high levels of government net borrowing – rapidly growing South Asia and economically stagnant middle income Latin America. South Asia's private net lending share resembles China's, except that the private surplus financed a fiscal deficit while China's external account was in surplus. The large fiscal deficit (reflecting the situation in India) did not create an equally large external gap because along SG lines hard currency was not available (until very recently) to pay for expanded imports. The private sector was the only possible source of finance for the government's net borrowing.

Except for the latter part of the recessionary 'lost decade' of the 1980s, Latin America appeared to have a more or less structural external deficit.

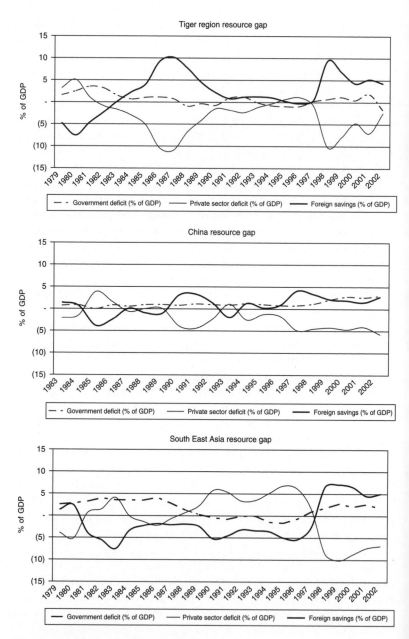

*Source*: United Nations Common Database.
*Figure 10.15* Resource gaps by institutional sectors in the Tigers, China and South East Asia

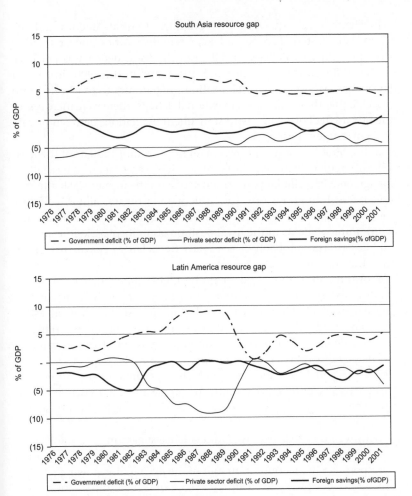

*Source*: United Nations Common Database.
*Figure 10.16* Resource gaps by institutional sectors in South Asia and semi-industrialized Latin America

Note the wide offsetting swings in the government and private borrowing flows along East Asian lines, unfortunately associated with a long period of economic stagnation as opposed to the other region's rapid growth. A massive dose of fiscal austerity in the late 1980s, courtesy of the IMF, had a very modest impact on the external deficit but was met by increased private borrowing, in a pattern that later partially reversed.

In Figure 10.17, the Andean economies, Central America and the Caribbean, Eastern Europe and Representative Africa appear to have structural external deficits. In all cases the fiscal deficit was cut back (in the 1980s in Latin America and Africa, and in the 1990s in Eastern Europe) as IMF-sponsored stabilization programmes were wheeled into place. Rather than reductions in external deficits, there were increases in the private net borrowing, with subsequent oscillations between private and government positions.

In the Middle East (not shown here) from around 1980 until the mid-1990s, a trend reduction in the fiscal deficit was accompanied by a falling foreign deficit. A similar pattern showed up in the former-USSR after the mid-1990s. In both regions, the 'structural' factor was almost certainly the external position, with the fiscal accounts accommodating. In other words improvements in the fiscal position, as in Russia/Ukraine and the Middle East, were probably driven by a better balance of payments, rather than the opposite.

Crowding-out of private demand by higher public demand under a binding external constraint that holds output roughly constant is a familiar story. Harking back to Polak's monetarist stance, if prices are not stabilized by PPP then they may begin to rise in response to higher effective demand. Inflation tax and forced saving mechanisms can kick in, reducing real demand by the private sector (Taylor, 2004). In Figures 10.15 and 10.16, such processes also appeared to work in reverse. Austerity relaxed the squeeze on the private sector, and its demand went up by enough to keep output close to the limit imposed by a structural external gap.

With regard to RE, there is scant evidence suggesting the presence of consumption-smoothing in the sense of rising private sector net lending in response to higher output. In four of the five rapidly growing regions, private net borrowing went up as a share of GDP and net lending fell during periods of sustained, rapid growth. The exception is China after the mid-1980s, but there it is at least plausible to argue that the rising external surplus drove the observed rise in private net lending rather than the reverse.

## Policy implications

A major policy shift occurred worldwide beginning in the 1970s and 1980s – a move on the part of most countries to deregulate or liberalize their external current and capital accounts along with domestic

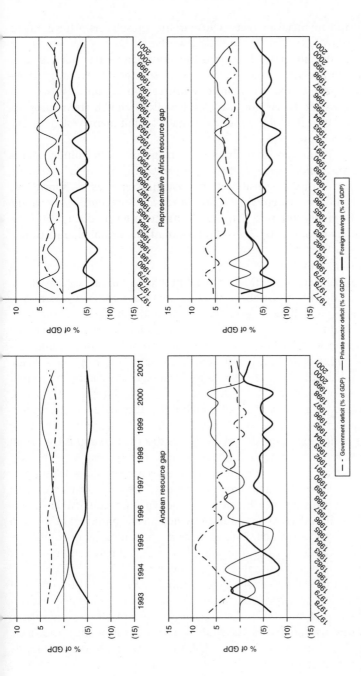

*Source* United Nations Common Database.
*Figure 10.17* Resource gaps by institutional sectors in Central and Eastern Europe, Central America and the Caribbean, the Andean region and Representative Africa

labour and financial markets. Our empirical results help trace out its implications.

Figure 10.1 illustrates how growth performances deteriorated after 1980 in many parts of the world. Clear success cases at the country level – various Tigers, China, Vietnam in South East Asia, and more recently India – are scarcely paragons of neo-liberalism. Some Eastern European policy-makers think of themselves in that way, but many vestiges of the old order remain.

Moreover, the fact that structural change in several dimensions – output and labour share shifts accompanied by sustained productivity growth with strong reallocation effects in some cases – showed up strongly in the fast-growing economies, and sporadically elsewhere, carry an implicit message that intelligent sector-level policies can facilitate the development process. To an extent, structural change can be planned.

In macroterms, austerity was supposed to lead to improvement in external balances along IMF financial programming lines. The decompositions described just above show clearly that was not the common outcome. Even falling government deficits and rising external surpluses in the Middle East and Russia are better explained from the external than domestic side. More typical were co-movements of private and government or, less frequently, private and foreign borrowing flows. These patterns have to be examined in terms of the specific macrobehaviour of each economy concerned.

Macroeconomic flexibility, although difficult to define and probably even harder to attain, also appears to be important. Witness the wide swings in net borrowing flows between 1980 and 2000 in the Tigers and South East Asia. Through it all, they continued to grow.

Stated goals of the liberalization package were to enhance labour productivity and employment growth. Outside the consistently expanding economies, this did not happen. Productivity movements across sectors differed in detail across slow-growing and stagnant regions but did not add up to very much. Employment to population ratios rose in the Andean and Middle Eastern regions.[13] Elsewhere, liberalization did not help create jobs – industrial jobs in particular.

Privatization and financial deregulation were followed by financial crises in many countries, sometimes more than once. They help explain the erratic performances in Latin America, Eastern Europe and Russia. As noted above, South East Asia did not recover as strongly as the Tigers from the 1997 crisis. China and India to a large extent evaded its impacts by maintaining capital controls.

Finally, the supply-side emphasis of the new policy package – austerity supposedly leading to higher saving and investment rates, an emphasis on human capital accumulation, and opening economies to foreign direct investment – did not seem to bear fruit outside the rapidly growing regions. There was a clear association between capital stock growth and output growth across all regions, but here the supply-side interpretation is not compelling. The results in Figure 10.10 can just as well be explained by rapid capital stock growth contributing to labour productivity growth and driving output growth from the side of demand with savings adjusting endogenously, rather than by higher savings leading to more capital which fed into output via some sort of aggregate production function.

A supply-side interpretation is more appropriate for the changes in (fossil fuel) energy/labour ratios presented in Figure 10.12 and Table 10.1. The key policy question that arises is whether in the near future rich-country energy/labour ratios can be reduced (or energy productivity increased relative to labour productivity) substantially by technological innovation and social rearrangements. If such innovations work out, then perhaps they can be passed to developing economies before the momentum of their population growth overwhelms all possibilities for combating global warming.

Results across the regions differed. Fast-growing regions were less zealous about applying the liberalization philosophy, and performed better. Elsewhere, there was enough variety to suggest that specific aspects of each region and its economies were important in shaping outcomes. Structure matters. The policy analysis challenge is to figure out just how and why.

## Appendix: countries in the regional groups

**Representative Africa:** Ghana, Kenya, Uganda and Tanzania.
**Other Africa:** Cameroon, Ethiopia, Ivory Coast, Mozambique, Nigeria, Zimbabwe.
**Central America and the Caribbean:** Costa Rica, Dominican Republic, El Salvador, Guatemala, Jamaica.
**Andean Region:** Bolivia, Ecuador, Peru.
**Semi-industrialized Latin America (with Turkey and South Africa as additions):** Argentina, Brazil, Chile, Colombia, Mexico, Venezuela, Turkey, South Africa.
**South Asia:** Bangladesh, India, Pakistan, Sri Lanka.
**China.**

**South East Asia:** Indonesia, Philippines, Thailand, Vietnam.
**Tigers:** Korea, Malaysia, Singapore, Taiwan.
**Middle East:** Algeria, Egypt, Morocco, Tunisia, Iran, Iraq, Jordan, Saudi Arabia, Syria, Yemen.
**Former-USSR:** Russian Federation, Ukraine.
**Eastern Europe:** Bulgaria, Czech Republic, Hungary, Poland, Romania, Slovakia.

## Notes

1. The representative group is made up of four countries often discussed in the development literature, and the others are included essentially on grounds of data availability.
2. Figures 10.1–11 and 10.13–17 have appeared in our DESA Working Paper No. 34, United Nations, September 2006, entitled 'Developing and Transition Economies in the Late 20th Century: Diverging Growth Rates, Economic structures and Sources of Demand'.
3. It is customary to make international income comparisons in terms of purchasing power parity (or PPP). However, by over-valuing the cost of labour, PPP estimates distort the macroeconomic relationships that are at the heart of our analysis. When it comes to policy formation, it is far more useful to think about macrorelationships in traditional 'real' terms.
4. See United Nations (2006) for the algebra of the decompositions.
5. The approach follows Syrquin (1986).
6. The original insight is Pasinetti's (1981). The assertion about growth rates in the text holds true if labour force participation rates are stable.
7. The approach followed here is a variant on a demand decomposition proposed by Godley and Cripps (1983).
8. A caveat: our capital stock series for the former-USSR and Eastern Europe begin in 1990, which means that the estimated growth rates are less reliable than those for other regions where the base year was 1970.
9. That is, the 45-degree slope would not fit a neoclassical aggregate production function. It could be 'explained' by a constant capital-output ratio, but that in turn is inconsistent with the 'Asian' pattern of falling capital productivity discussed immediately below.
10. This sort of 'decreasing returns' to more capital is built into many mainstream and heterodox growth models, which mostly serve to rationalize the accounting identity described in the text.
11. One terajoule is roughly equivalent to 7,700 gallons of gasoline or 32 tons of coal.
12. Although, as we will see below, Polak *sans* PPP can help explain recent interactions between public and private sector deficits in several developing regions.
13. A rise of the ratio in Russia/Ukraine can be discounted because of negative population growth.

# References

Barro, Robert J. (1974) 'Are Government Bonds Net Wealth?', *Journal of Political Economy* 82: 1095–117.

Barro, Robert J. and Jong-Wha Lee (2000) 'International Data on Educational Attainment: Updates and Implications', CID working paper 42, available at http://www.cid.harvard.edu/cidwp/042.htm.

Godley, Wynne and T. Francis Cripps (1983) *Macroeconomics*, London: Fontana.

Martinez-Alier, Juan with Klaus Schlüpmann (1991) *Ecological Economics: Energy, Environment, and Society*, Oxford: Basil Blackwell.

Mirowski, Philip (1989) *More Heat than Light*, Cambridge: Cambridge University Press.

Pasinetti, Luigi L. (1981) *Structural Change and Economic Growth*, Cambridge: Cambridge University Press.

Polak, J. J. (1957) 'Monetary Analysis of Income Formation and Payments Problems', International Monetary Fund Staff Papers 6: 1–50.

Socolow, Robert H. and Stephen W. Pacala (2006) 'A Plan to Keep Carbon in Check', *Scientific American* 295 (3): 50–7.

Syrquin, Moshe (1986) 'Productivity Growth and Factor Reallocation', in H. B. Chenery, S. Robinson and M. Syrquin (eds), *Industrialization and Growth*, New York: Oxford University Press.

Taylor, Lance (2004) *Reconstructing Macroeconomics*, Cambridge, MA: Harvard University Press.

United Nations (2006) *World Economic and Social Survey*, New York: United Nations.

# 11
# Macro Adjustment Policies and Horizontal Inequalities

*Arnim Langer and Frances Stewart*

## Introduction

Among his impressive range of significant writings, Ajit Singh has contributed to the critical literature on the impact of neo-liberal 'adjustment' policies on economic development and distribution, focusing especially on capital account liberalization (for example, Singh, 2007). Yet while there has been a considerable amount of analysis on the impact of structural adjustment policies on poverty and inequality among individuals (or what we define here as vertical inequality – VI),[1] there has been almost none into the impact of structural adjustment on inequality between culturally defined groups, or horizontal inequality (HI). In this chapter we will investigate this issue.

HIs encompass multiple dimensions – political, social, economic and cultural status. All of these dimensions are important in terms of causing grievances and mobilizing people politically, sometimes leading to violent conflict. In this chapter, however, we are concerned only with the socio-economic dimension: that is, group inequalities in a vector of social inputs and human development achievements (such as access to education and health services, nutrition rates, literacy rates, life expectancy, infant mortality rates, and so on), and a vector of economic inputs and achievements, including access to a variety of assets, to employment of different types, and the consequent consumption and incomes.

Although relatively neglected in economic analysis, socio-economic HIs are important from a number of perspectives: they can have adverse effects on the well-being of members of the deprived groups, they can impede efficiency, they may make it very difficult to eradicate poverty, they lead to unfair and exclusionary societies, and they raise the risk of violent conflict (Stewart, 2001, 2008).

Because of their clear political significance, in some heterogeneous societies (notably Malaysia, South Africa, Northern Ireland, Fiji) a variety of policies have been adopted to attempt to reduce HIs – for example, through affirmative action of various kinds (giving preferences to particular groups in employment, education and asset ownership), through the careful allocation of public expenditure and the use of the legal system to eliminate discrimination. While these policies can achieve much, their impact can be severely reduced or even offset if macroeconomic policies simultaneously work to increase HIs. Conversely, if macropolicies support a reduction of HIs, the effectiveness of the other policies will be greatly increased (and HIs may fall even without any explicit affirmative action).

Hence it is important to analyse the impact of structural adjustment policies on HIs – which is the aim of this chapter. We will discuss the meaning of HIs and why they are important, and identify the macro-policies to be analysed. Then we will analyse how one might *expect* these policies to affect HIs, before drawing on empirical evidence. Finally, we will conclude with some discussion of the type of analysis needed in designing macropolicies in heterogeneous societies, and policy prescriptions suggested by our analysis.

## Defining group inequalities – why they are important

First, it is necessary to consider the type of groups under consideration. This chapter is concerned with group distinctions that are widely recognized by people in a particular society as of social and political significance. In practice, important group distinctions often arise from differences in religion (for example, from differences between major religions, such as Islam and Christianity, and groupings within them, such as Shia and Sunni, Catholic and Protestant). In some societies ethnic distinctions are important (for example, Ewes and Akans in Ghana; Igbo, Hausa-Fulani and Yoruba in Nigeria). In some societies – such as India and Nepal – caste forms a major basis of social distinction and discrimination. Sometimes geographical distinctions are important (often accompanied by some ethnic or religious differences), such as in the case of East Timor or Eritrea. And in other societies, what we call 'race' seems to be the significant differentiating group characteristic, such as in Malaysia or Brazil.

Socially significant group identities arise partly from individuals' *own* perceptions of membership of and identity with a particular group and partly from the perceptions of *those outside the group* about others. An important question – long debated by anthropologists[2] – then is why and when some differences are perceived as being socially significant, and others are not, both by group members themselves and by others. Here we will not enter that debate, but note that group distinctions are formed and *re*formed historically; that leaders, educators and the media, among others, are important influences over how significant group distinctions evolve; that groups often have uncertain boundaries, and are fluid with new groups emerging and old ones ceasing to be important. Yet despite the way boundaries evolve, at any one time group distinctions are an important way that people see themselves, and interact, and consequently are relevant to the well-being of individuals and the health of society. Moreover, as ideology has become less important as a source of identity and political mobilization, ethnic and religious distinctions seem to have become more important, as indicated by the increasing proportion of violent conflicts that are presented and labelled as 'ethnic' (Stewart and Brown, 2008: 424).

While the determinants of group well-being and prospects go well beyond their social and economic situation and include political and cultural status dimensions, this chapter is concerned only with socio-economic aspects. There are multiple elements within the broad socio-economic category which may be important to people, as noted in the introduction. Most of these elements are significant in themselves and are also instrumental for achieving others. For example, education is wanted in itself (as an important basic human right) and also as a means to enhance incomes, and similarly access to land represents status and security and also generates incomes.

While certain socio-economic outcomes are relevant across all societies – notably incomes, health and nutrition – what is needed to achieve these outcomes can vary across societies, and therefore also the particular inequalities which are of most significance. For example, access to primary education may be an important source of inequality in very poor societies, but in more developed countries where there is universal primary education, access at higher educational levels is more significant. Equally, access to and ownership of land is of huge importance where agriculture accounts for a considerable proportion of output and employment, but becomes less important as development proceeds, and access to housing and formal sector jobs becomes more important.

HIs matter because:

- Unequal access to political, economic and social resources, and inequalities of cultural status, can have a serious negative impact on the welfare of members of poorer groups who mind about their relative position and that of their group. This is illustrated by research in the US showing that the psychological health of blacks in the US is adversely affected by the position of the group to which they belong (see, for example, Broman, 1997; Brown *et al.*, 1999). The position of the group, as a factor determining individual welfare, has been modelled theoretically by Akerlof and Kranton (2000).
- Severe horizontal inequalities may reduce the growth potential of society, because they mean that some people do not have access to education or jobs on the basis of their potential merit or efficiency but are discriminated against because of the group they belong to. As deprived groups get improved access to education and jobs, the potential of the economy can be realized more fully. This was exemplified by the rapid growth experienced in Malaysia as policies enabled the majority Malay population to participate in economic transformation (Faaland *et al.*, 2003).
- Horizontal inequalities can prove a major handicap to the elimination of poverty because it is difficult to reach members of deprived groups effectively with programmes of assistance. This is especially so because deprived groups face multiple disadvantages and discrimination and these need to be confronted together. This has been a serious problem, for example, in tackling poverty in the Andean countries (Hall and Patrinos, 2006).
- Sharp group inequalities make violent group mobilization and ethnic conflicts more likely, by providing powerful grievances which leaders can use to mobilize people, by calling on cultural markers (often common ethnicity or religion) and pointing to group exploitation. Evidence across countries has found a significant relationship between HIs and the onset of violent conflict (see, for example, Østby, 2006). Other statistical cross-country work supporting this relationship includes Gurr's successive studies of relative deprivation and conflict (Gurr, 1970, 1993; Gurr and Moore, 1997), and Barrows's investigation of sub-Saharan African countries in the 1960s (Barrows, 1976). Within country studies present a similar picture (see, for example, Mancini, 2005 on Indonesia; Murshed and Gates, 2005 on Nepal) showing that the location of conflict within the country is related to the extent of group inequality. Of course, not all countries with high

HIs experience conflict – it is a matter of increased likelihood of greater incidence of conflict as HIs increase.

Hence the extent of socio-economic HIs is an important issue in any heterogeneous society and should be a concern for policy, especially in economies which are vulnerable, from a conflict perspective, for other reasons. Research has shown that countries with low per capita incomes and those that have recently experienced conflict are particularly prone to conflict (Auvinen and Nafziger, 1999), so it is especially important to consider the impact of macropolicies on HIs in low-income and post-conflict economies.

## What macro or structural adjustment policies?

Four types of policy make up International Monetary Fund (IMF)/World Bank adjustment and stabilization policies:

1. (Dis)absorption policies;
2. Switching policies;
3. Capital account liberalization and financial reforms;
4. Other efficiency promoting policies.

We shall focus just on the first two. The effect of capital account liberalization – which Ajit Singh[3] has so powerfully analysed both for general implications and for VI, although not for HI – clearly has important potential implications for HIs, although it has limited relevance for the poorest countries. This is an issue which we shall reserve for future analysis. The fourth category consists of a large range of policies, which mainly do not qualify as macropolicies.

Disabsorption policies are those policies that reduce total expenditure in the economy, releasing resources for exports and/or reducing imports and inflationary pressures. Policies include raising taxation and other sources of revenue, reducing public expenditure, and imposing monetary restrictions (reduced money supply, raised interest rates) which lead to a cutback in private expenditure. Real devaluation of the exchange rate also has a disabsorption effect, by reducing real domestic incomes.

Switching policies are policies which aim to encourage resources to move into the tradable sector, encouraging resources to move into the export sector and into the production of import substitutes, hence improving the balance of trade. Policies include exchange rate depreciation and reduced taxes of exports. Reductions in tariffs and import quotas, which typically form part of the adjustment policy package, can, however, offset the impact of devaluation in promoting import substitution. Generally, the combination of devaluation and tariff reforms reduces the overall disincentive to import and changes the relative prices of particular imports, the details varying across cases.

Such policies were highly visible in the 1980s, with disabsorption policies dominating. For example from 1980–84, all 93 IMF agreements included limits on credit expansion, 92 per cent included restraints on public expenditure, 83 per cent reduced public sector deficits, while just half the agreements involved exchange rate reforms, and a similar proportion involved trade liberalization (IMF, 1986). Since the early 2000s, poor countries' policy-making has been dominated by Poverty Reduction Strategy Papers (PRSPs), while middle income countries have done much to accumulate their own resources, or to borrow from the private sector, and have aimed to avoid the ministrations of the IMF. Nonetheless, despite these changes, the disabsorption and switching policies remain an essential aspect of policy-making in poor countries, as shown by analysis of the macro-aspects of the PRSPs (Stewart and Wang, 2005). Moreover, control over absorption has become an important policy tool of the middle income countries in their efforts to avoid needing the assistance of the IFIs, and exchange rate depreciation has become an important tool to avoid a recurrence of financial crises like those in East Asia and Mexico in the 1990s.

## How would one expect these policies to affect HIs?

The likely distributional impact of the two sets of policies depends on two factors. First, the precise design of policies. For example, whether taxes are raised or public expenditure reduced in the case of disabsorption policies; the type of tax and expenditure, and whether they are increased/reduced; and similarly for the nature of the exchange rate and trade policy reforms in the case of switching policies. Second, the impact depends on how the different salient groups are positioned in the economy.

Suppose there are just two groups, a richer group, $R$, and a poorer group, $P$, with HIs being measured in summary by the ratio of average per capita incomes of the two, $y^r/y^p$.[4] The two groups will then differ on average as to their consumption as well as income levels. So if the additional taxation is progressive (i.e. bears more heavily on the rich), it will reduce the incomes of $R$ more than $P$ and consequently reduce the HI; but if it is regressive, the reverse will occur. The two groups are also likely to differ as to how they benefit from public expenditure. Social expenditure tends to be distributed progressively and the rest of public expenditure regressively, while the overall distributional impact of public expenditure varies across societies, but on balance seems to be mildly progressive (i.e. slightly favouring the poor) (Van de Walle *et al.*, 1995; Chu *et al.*, 2000; Cornia, 2004). Then public expenditure cuts that are disproportionately concentrated on the social sectors will hurt $P$ relatively to $R$, and conversely if they are concentrated on other sectors, while a 'neutral' across-the-board cut will tend to hurt $P$ more than $R$.

This assumes that the only way the two groups differ is with respect to income levels, but the groups are not defined by their incomes but by some cultural characteristics, which may affect the distributional impact. For example, some groups save more than others, so they will be less affected by consumption taxes as against income taxes; some groups consume less alcohol, so will be less affected by alcohol tax rises; groups differ in the use they make of public services (for example some groups are more likely to attend school for cultural reasons), and thus will be differentially affected by different types of expenditure cuts. Groups are often concentrated in particular regions – for example Muslims in the North of Nigeria, indigenous people in the highlands of Peru. Consequently, any tax increases or expenditure cuts that are not regionally neutral will have implications for group distribution.

In general, a typical aspect of a society with severe HIs is that the distribution of the benefit of public expenditure is unequal across the groups, i.e. $p^p < p^r$, where $p^p$ represents public expenditure benefits per head of group $P$, and $p^r$ represents public expenditure benefits per head of group $R$. While 'neutral' decreases in expenditure (i.e. affecting everyone proportionately to their initial benefits) would leave HIs unchanged, such neutrality cannot be assumed as it is likely that group $R$ will control the budget and may ensure that the cuts fall more than proportionately on $P$.

We have so far considered the two groups as consumers of public goods, but they are also producers. As producers, $R$ can, perhaps, be expected to suffer from cutbacks in public employment more than $P$, but if the cutbacks consist in labour-intensive infrastructural expenditure this might not be the case.

Hence a careful analysis of the characteristics of the different groups and of the design of tax increases or expenditure cuts is necessary to identify the impact on HIs from disabsorption policies. It is therefore difficult to make any *a priori* generalizations, though one can state, fairly confidently, that (a) tax increases are likely to be more beneficial for poor groups than expenditure reductions; (b) however, because an important aspect of HIs is distorted public expenditure against poorer groups, expenditure cuts may actually improve their relative position, assuming that the cuts are not also distorted; (c) progressive tax increases are more beneficial than regressive ones; (d) expenditure cuts focused on social sectors are likely to worsen HIs relative to expenditure cuts that protect social expenditure; (e) cutbacks in public sector employment may hurt $R$ more than $P$, but again where the cuts fall is critical.

Turning to switching policies, we again need to differentiate the impact on groups as producers and groups as consumers. The outcome on groups as producers depends largely on group specialization in production. This is often quite marked as a result of colonial policy and its aftermath and geographic disadvantage. Thus, colonial policy involved a sharp racial division of labour in what is now Malaysia, with the Chinese the trading and entrepreneurial class, the Indians imported to work on plantations and the Malays subsistence farmers (Brown, 1997). Similarly, in many African economies, particular groups were picked out by colonialists for privileged education and for specialization in cash crops – often a specialization associated with advantages of geography, so that southern groups were favoured for education and cash crops in west and east African countries (see, for example, Songsore, 2003 for Ghana; Ghai and Court, 1974 for Kenya). In other economies, settlers took all the best land and the top jobs in the civil services, and where settlers remained in the country, post-independence, as in Latin America and South and Central Africa, this became a major source of HIs (Figueroa *et al.*, 1996). In some economies colonial powers imported indentured or slave labour to work on plantations (for example, Brazil and British Guiana) and build roads or railways (for example, Kenya). Consequently, for these (and other) reasons, $R$ and $P$ tend to be differently inserted into the economy.

Switching policies favour some sectors (tradables) and hurt others (non-tradables). Hence their impact on HIs depends on whether the ethnic division of labour follows this tradable/non-tradable distinction. For some economies it is clear that there is such an overlap, with $P$ being more specialized in non-tradables (subsistence), and $R$ more specialized in tradables. This broadly seems to be the case with respect to cash crops in many African economies. Below we exemplify this in more depth in the case of Ghana. But Ghana is just one example which typifies a swathe of countries across Africa.

However, elsewhere the impact is somewhat different. In economies with plantations and very poorly paid plantation labour, these workers (typically being members of a particular group) are often the poorest, with incomes below the peasant food producers; for example, the Indian plantation workers in Malaysia or Guiana, or the Afro-Brazilians in Brazil. For these economies, switching policies may favour plantations and hurt the somewhat richer peasant farmers. However, these gains are not necessarily passed on to the workers, but may go largely to the plantation owners who belong to the *R* group. A third type of economy is one where there are incipient labour intensive industries, and switching favours this sector. The HI implications depend on which group the new labourers come from. In Malaysia, the poorest group, the *bumiputera*, supplied much of this new labour – assisted by supportive education and employment policies (Faaland *et al.*, 2003).

A fourth type is where comparative advantage lies with skill or capital intensive products (like software services and call centres in India, or aeroplanes in Brazil). In these cases, switching policies will favour producers of these products, who, generally, are likely to be in group *R*. However, in the case of skill-intensive products, this also depends on complementary education and training policies that might be designed to improve capacities and job access of *P*.

There can also be regional and HI consequences from rapid industrialization, where one region of a country benefits much more than others, creating regional and, quite often, ethnic HIs. China is an obvious example. Thailand is another. Although Thailand has seen rapid growth and labour-intensive industrialization over the past 25 years, the three mainly Malay-Muslim provinces have remained at levels well below the national average (see Figure 11.1). While two of the three Muslim-Malay provinces – Yala and Narathiwat – experienced a significant decline in their relative economic standing, each falling by around 20 per cent of relative GDP per capita, the third one, Pattani, did better, but remained nonetheless significantly below the national average (Brown, 2008).

A fifth type of economy is one that specializes in minerals – for example oil. In such economies, the revenue from the resources tends to be disproportionately received by *R*, either directly or indirectly via government redistributionary policies. Where this is the case, any across-the-board depreciation would increase such revenue and tend to worsen HIs. But multiple exchange rates might prevent this effect and could be designed to help particular groups. A further complication is that non-tradables extend beyond subsistence agriculture to import-substituting activity behind heavy protection. Often it is *R* rather than *P* that is concentrated in this sector. If this protection is withdrawn as part of the switching policies, then undoubtedly some *R* will lose. This may apply in any of the four types of economy differentiated above.

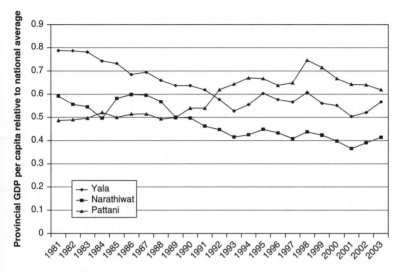

*Figure 11.1* Thailand: relative GDP per capita in three Malay-Muslim dominated provinces, 1981–2003
*Source*: Brown (2008).

Turning to the impact of exchange rate changes and tariff reforms on groups as consumers, the outcome depends on the design of the policies. It appears that tariff and quota reductions tend to favour richer groups, as import tariffs often bear most heavily on luxury consumption, but such reductions may not be universal (although they normally are), though tariffs could be retained on the products consumed by the rich, thereby altering the distributional impact.

It is possible to generalize a bit more about the likely impact of switching policies on groups as producers, compared with disabsorption policies on HIs. First, in economies where there is crop specialization by group, and crops are the main tradables, switching policies are likely to increase HIs. Second, in plantation economies, switching policies may somewhat improve them. Third, in economies in which the policies promote labour intensive industrialization, those with basic education are likely to gain (Wood and Ridau-Cano, 1996), which in the normal case would tend to favour the richer and better educated group(s), but this can be offset by education and employment policies that favour the poorer groups. Fourth, regionally, effective switching policies that promote rapid industrialization are likely to lead to imbalances and accentuate or create regional HIs. Fifth, where the policies dismantle the protection of privileged import-substitution, it is possible that they

*Table 11.1* Summary of expectations of how macropolicy changes are likely to affect HIs

| Type of exports of economy | Primary product agricultural products | Labour-intensive industrial products | Capital or skill intensive industrial products | Minerals (for example oil) |
|---|---|---|---|---|
| Switching policies | Worsen HIs | Depends on labour force skills, complementary policies; may worsen regional HIs | Probably worsen HIs | Worsen HIs |
| Reduced import-substituting protection | Improve HIs | | | |
| Tax rises | Improve HIs, but depends on design | | | |
| Expenditure cuts | Depends on design | | | |

improve HIs. Finally, like disabsorption policies (but to a lesser extent), switching policies can be designed to help or hurt particular groups.

## The example of Ghana

In order to illustrate the impact of adjustment policies on group or horizontal inequalities, in this section we will analyse the adjustment experiences of Ghana, focusing on the evolution of the main socio-economic cleavage. In the Ghanaian case, we therefore analyse how the adjustment polices affected the socio-economic North–South divide.

### Ghana's horizontal inequalities and the adjustment experience

Like several other West African countries (for example, Côte d'Ivoire, Togo, Benin and Nigeria), the sharpest socio-economic or developmental divide in Ghana is between the northern and southern regions, which overlap closely with ethnic differences and is also associated with religious differences. This developmental North–South divide arises from a combination of circumstances and policies (see, e.g., Bening, 1975; Roe and Schneider, 1992; Songsore, 2003):

1. The geographical concentration of most agricultural activities/ resources, particularly tree crops such as cocoa, as well as natural

resources, notably minerals and forest resources, in the southern regions;
2. The British colonial policy of investing more heavily in those regions where exploitable resources, such as gold, diamonds, timber and cocoa, were available or readily produced and cheapest to export;
3. Post-colonial development strategies and investment patterns.


At the time of gaining independence from Britain in 1957, Ghana had one of the most successful economies in Africa, with an average annual real growth rate of well over 5 per cent, substantial foreign reserves and a strong civil service (Mensah *et al.*, 2006). Ghana's successful economic record in the 1950s was based on an open economy with the private sector as the main source of growth (particularly small-scale cocoa farming). But from 1957, Ghana's first prime minister (and later president), Kwame Nkrumah, changed this to a state-led modernization strategy based on import-substituting industrialization. Despite the increasing importance of the public sector, the main source of funding for this industrialization continued to come from the cocoa sector, which provided about 70 per cent of Ghana's export earnings (Dordunoo and Nyanteng, 1997). Although some liberalization efforts were initiated following Nkrumah's removal from power in February 1966, with the ascendancy to power of Colonel Ignatius Kutu Acheampong in 1972, Nkrumah's policies of statism and controls again became the dominant economic strategy.

This state-led approach had disastrous consequences for Ghana's economy, particularly as a result of reduced production of cocoa (partly due to adverse prices) and worsening international terms of trade, and a large external debt such that Ghana was unable to pay for the imports needed to run the industrial sector to capacity. Besides the economic strategy adopted, several exogenous factors were also responsible for the economic crisis, most notably the persistently unfavourable terms of trade for Ghana's main export products, severe droughts in 1978/79 and 1982/83, the repatriation of one million Ghanaians from Nigeria in 1983, and the high international interest rates sparked by the global economic crisis at the end of the 1970s and the subsequent switch to monetarist policies in the advanced countries (Mensah *et al.*, 2006).

Against the backdrop of the economic malaise of the 1970s, Flight-Lieutenant Jerry Rawlings, who took power in a *coup d'état* in December 1981, established a military regime known as the Provisional National Defence Council (PNDC). Although the PNDC regime initially responded to the prevailing economic problems in much the same way as previous governments had, in 1983 it reversed its economic course dramatically and started to implement an extensive economic reform programme – locally known as the Economic Reform Programme (ERP) – with the support of the IMF and the World Bank (Herbst, 1993). Ghana's adjustment policies evolved through four phases: (i) ERP I – the period of economic stabilization and recovery (1983–86); (ii) ERP II – the period of structural adjustment and growth (1987–92); (iii) ERP III – the period of accelerated growth (1993–2000); and (iv) PRSP – the phase from 2001 to date.[5] In what follows, we focus on the first three phases of Ghana's adjustment process.

ERP I (1983–86) consisted of 'a stabilization package designed to reduce inflation and achieve external equilibrium', and 'a programme to promote economic growth and export recovery through a realignment of incentives toward productive activity and the rehabilitation of economic and social infrastructure' (Hutchful, 2002, p. 56). A major component of the programme was the devaluation of Ghana's currency, the cedi, which changed from 2.75 cedis to $1 in 1983 to 160 cedis to $1 in 1986 (Leite *et al.*, 2000). The government also adjusted prices for other goods and services, including the cocoa producer price, retail petroleum prices and utility tariffs. For instance, the producer price of cocoa was increased to 86,000 cedis per tonne for the 1986/87 crop year, which was a 50 per cent increase relative to 1985/86 and a quadrupling relative to 1983/84 (Roe and Schneider, 1992).

In the monetary and fiscal sphere, policies included the introduction of

> strict credit ceilings, increases in interest rates with the objective of reaching positive interest rates, reform of the tax structure to broaden the tax base and at the same time reduce the tax burden on corporations and the cocoa sector, and other measures to increase revenue, shrink the budget deficit (through retrenchment, elimination of subsidies, higher fees for government services, etc.) and reduce the reliance on the banking system.
>
> (Hutchful, 2002, p. 56)

The government also launched an Export Sector Rehabilitation Programme 'designed to rehabilitate the export sectors by relieving supply and input bottlenecks, improving producer incentives, and reforming the State Cocoa Marketing Board (Cocobod)' (ibid.). In the mining sector, new legislation boosted incentives for (foreign) mining corporations, among other things, by reducing mining royalties, granting allowances on capitalization expenditure for field reconnaissance and prospecting, and exempting mining sector machinery from import duties (Mensah *et al.*, 2006).

ERP II (1987–92) inaugurated the adjustment phase and was intended to deepen ongoing reforms (Hutchful, 2002). During this phase, comprehensive reforms were directed towards Ghana's cocoa sector. In particular, in 1988, the government, with support from the World Bank, launched the Cocoa Rehabilitation Programme (CRP). The CRP's two main objectives were to improve incentives for cocoa farmers by further raising the cocoa producer price and to lower the costs of the State Cocoa Marketing Board (Dordunoo and Nyanteng, 1997). Nearly 12,000 of the staff of the State Cocoa Marketing Board were made redundant in 1987 (Leite *et al.*, 2000, p. 26). Moreover, as part of the CRP, 'efforts were also made to improve the living conditions of farmers with rural development projects in feeder roads, healthcare and marketing facilities' (Mensah *et al.*, 2006, p. 111). Other reforms that were launched under ERP II included the introduction of a new Banking Law and new regulations for savings and loans companies; the establishment of the Ghana Stock Exchange Company in November 1990; and the adoption of a new Investment Code (Hutchful, 2002).

Under pressure from concerned citizens and international observers such as Oxfam and UNICEF, the government introduced the Programme of Actions to Mitigate the Social Costs of Adjustment (PAMSCAD) in 1987/88 in order to mitigate the adverse socio-economic impact of the structural adjustment programmes on certain vulnerable groups in society (Mensah *et al.*, 2006). PAMSCAD was targeted at four vulnerable groups: 'first, small farmers and hired labour; second, poor households with limited access to basic social services such as health, education, water, etc.; third, the unemployed and those with meagre earnings, especially urban youth; and finally, households in the northern regions' (Hutchful, 2002, p. 117). As part of PAMSCAD, five types of projects (i.e. community initiative projects; employment generation projects; redeployment projects; projects aimed at providing basic needs and services, including water, sanitation, health, nutrition and shelter; and projects aimed at improving educational infrastructure) were undertaken to improve the socio-economic situation of the four target groups (ibid.).

Under ERP III (1993–2000) growth acceleration became the main objective. 'The Accelerated Growth Strategy (AGS), published in 1993 emphasized sustainable development and poverty-alleviation through private sector development' (Hutchful, 2002, p. 57). In addition, the programme 'stressed the strengthening of inter-sectoral linkages (in particular through agro-industry), poverty reduction through

*Table 11.2*   Ghana's macroeconomic performance, 1983–98 (per cent unless otherwise stated)

|      | Real GDP growth | Real GDP per capita growth | Inflation (CPI) | Export of cocoa (FAO) (metric tons) |
|------|------|------|------|------|
| 1982 | −6.9 | −9.7 | 22.3  | 260,130 |
| 1983 | −4.6 | −7.7 | 123.8 | 166,390 |
| 1984 | 8.6  | 4.9  | 39.7  | 162,070 |
| 1985 | 5.1  | 1.3  | 10.3  | 187,790 |
| 1986 | 5.2  | 1.6  | 24.6  | 211,420 |
| 1987 | 4.8  | 1.3  | 39.8  | 218,850 |
| 1988 | 5.6  | 2.2  | 31.4  | 223,260 |
| 1989 | 5.1  | 1.8  | 25.2  | 265,810 |
| 1990 | 3.3  | 0.2  | 37.3  | 269,730 |
| 1991 | 5.3  | 2.2  | 18.1  | 265,200 |
| 1992 | 3.9  | 1.0  | 10.0  | 243,100 |
| 1993 | 5.0  | 2.1  | 25.0  | 278,380 |
| 1994 | 3.3  | 0.6  | 24.9  | 252,420 |
| 1995 | 4.0  | 1.4  | 74.3  | 253,260 |
| 1996 | 4.6  | 1.9  | 46.6  | 371,990 |
| 1997 | 4.2  | 1.5  | 27.9  | 303,710 |
| 1998 | 4.6  | 1.9  | 19.3  | –       |

*Source*: World Bank, Africa 2000 Database.

labour-intensive and high-productivity activities, enhanced access of the poor to social services, further progress in human resource development (particularly primary education and health), capacity building and public-sector management, and private-sector development' (ibid.).

As shown in Table 11.2, Ghana's economic performance recovered after 1983, and a period of sustained growth followed. Other macroeconomic indicators also improved significantly, although there were some serious fiscal slippages in the run-up to the elections of 1992 and 1996 (Leite *et al.*, 2000). For example, before the 1996 election the mechanism for automatically adjusting retail petroleum prices for changes in the price of imported oil and the exchange rate was suspended, which caused a substantial shortfall in petroleum tax collections (ibid.). While overall GDP growth of 4–5 per cent was maintained in the 1990s, 'both domestic and export production demonstrated significant fluctuations' (Hutchful, 2002, p. 66).

Although Ghana's structural adjustment process contributed to restoring economic growth and macroeconomic stability, different regions benefited in different degrees from the recovery. Table 11.3 shows how some important adjustment policies are likely to have affected the

*Table 11.3* Distributional effects of some adjustment policies on the North–South divide

|  | Northern regions | Southern regions |
| --- | --- | --- |
| **Export Sector Rehabilitation Programme** |  |  |
| Cocoa Reform Programme (CRP) |  |  |
| – Cocoa prices |  | ++ |
| – Removal of subsidies on farm inputs |  | – |
| – Rural development initiatives |  | + |
| Mining sector rehabilitation |  | + |
| Forestry sector rehabilitation |  | + |
| **Employment retrenchment policies** |  |  |
| – State Cocoa Marketing Board |  | – |
| – Other public/civil service |  | – |
| **Price changes as a result of subsidy cuts and** |  |  |
| **tax changes:** |  |  |
| Food | (+) ? | + ? |
| Manufactures | (+) ? | + ? |
| Gasoline | (–) | – |
| Tobacco | (–) | – |
| Alcohol | (–) | – |
| Education | (–) | – |
| Hospital | (–) | – |
| **PAMSCAD** | (+) | (+) |

*Notes*: 'The symbols in this table express the nature of the effects of adjustment as negative and positive. The symbols are doubled where the effects have been relatively strong; they are put within brackets where they have been relatively weak. Blanks indicate that there have been no or negligible effects' (Roe and Schneider, 1992, p. 140).
*Source*: Authors devised, based on approach of Roe and Schneider (1992, p. 140).

North–South divide. In line with the ERP's objective to restore economic growth by rehabilitating Ghana's export economy, most external funding went to the Greater Accra region (where the capital is located) and the cocoa, timber and mineral industries in the western, eastern, Ashanti and Brong Ahafo regions, all in the southern part of the country. Ghana's northern regions largely failed to benefit from the ERP's economic stimulus (Songsore, 2003).

However, the retrenchment policies which resulted in a large number of lay-offs among the staff of the Cocoa Board and other civil/public service institutions also predominantly affected the southern regions. Price changes as a result of subsidy cuts, fee increases and tax changes, changes in the exchange rate, import quotas, tariffs and other indirect taxation show a diverse picture. The impact of these price changes was generally smaller in the northern regions because fewer people there had

*Table 11.4*  Incidence of poverty by region (per cent)

| Survey and region | Poverty line = ¢900,000 | | Poverty line = ¢700,000 | |
|---|---|---|---|---|
| | Incidence | Share of total poverty | Incidence | Share of total poverty |
| **GLSS3 (1991/92)** | | | | |
| Accra | 22.4 | 3.6 | 11.6 | 2.7 |
| Urban coastal | 28.3 | 4.8 | 14.9 | 3.6 |
| Urban forest | 25.8 | 5.6 | 12.9 | 4.0 |
| Urban savannah | 37.9 | 4.0 | 27.0 | 4.0 |
| Rural coastal | 49.7 | 13.8 | 30.7 | 12.2 |
| Rural forest | 60.8 | 35.4 | 45.1 | 37.4 |
| Rural savannah | 72.1 | 32.8 | 55.9 | 36.2 |
| All Ghana | 50.8 | 100.0 | 35.7 | 100.0 |
| **GLSS4 (1998/99)** | | | | |
| Accra | 4.7 | 0.9 | 2.4 | 0.6 |
| Urban coastal | 26.8 | 5.3 | 17.1 | 5.1 |
| Urban forest | 24.8 | 5.9 | 15.1 | 5.2 |
| Urban savannah | 42.2 | 4.4 | 29.7 | 4.5 |
| Rural coastal | 46.3 | 16.1 | 30.1 | 15.1 |
| Rural forest | 41.4 | 31.6 | 24.4 | 26.9 |
| Rural savannah | 70.5 | 35.6 | 58.2 | 42.6 |
| All Ghana | 42.6 | 100.0 | 29.4 | 100.0 |

*Note*: GLSS = Ghana Living Standards Survey.
*Source*: Leite *et al.* (2000, p. 10).

access to these goods and services before the adjustment process was initiated. While the projects that were undertaken as part of PAMSCAD generally had a positive impact on the situation in both the northern and southern regions, due to a serious funding shortfall the overall impact was rather limited. Out of an overall pledge to commit $84 to support PAMSCAD by the international community donors in February 1988, by the end of July 1990 only about $15 million in donor financing had been received (Leite *et al.*, 2000). Consequently, overall, the adjustment policies appeared to have benefited the northern regions considerably less than the southern regions.

This assessment is confirmed by the regional evolution of poverty in the 1990s, shown in Table 11.4. While there was an overall decline in poverty at the national level, this reduction in poverty was not evenly distributed. Indeed, while the Accra region and the rural forest regions (i.e. where most of the cocoa plantations and mining and timber industries are located) saw a sharp decline in poverty, in the northern or savannah regions, in contrast, the incidence of poverty increased in the 1990s, except in the rural savannah regions. Moreover, not only was the decline in poverty (measured as the number of people living on less than the 900,000 cedis) in the rural savannah regions very small, and consequently the incidence of poverty remained very high in northern rural areas at more than 70 per cent, but also extreme poverty (measured as the number of people living on less than 700,000 cedis) actually increased in the rural savannah regions.[6] Therefore, according to this socio-economic indicator, Ghana's North–South divide clearly deteriorated under this phase of structural adjustment.

In general, Ghana's stabilization and adjustment policies did not take horizontal inequalities into account explicitly, though the poverty reduction strategies followed from 2001 do emphasize the need to reduce regional disparities. As shown, the design of the policies on balance helped the already privileged regions and did little for the most deprived region – the North – thereby exacerbating this aspect of horizontal inequalities in Ghana, which was also adversely affected by conflict in the North. Compensatory policies, such as PAMSCAD, did something to offset the impact of the programmes, but they were on too small a scale to prevent a widening of HIs in Ghana.

## Some implications for policy

First, as we have shown, macropolicies can have a major impact on HIs, which may go either way. Cuts in public expenditure can offset policies intended to improve the position of deprived groups, while switching policies can reduce income earning opportunities in such a way as to undermine other affirmative action. But conversely, it is possible that macropolicies can involve expenditure increases which benefit deprived groups, and switching policies may offer income earning opportunities to such groups, while reductions in public sector employment and import protection can hurt richer groups particularly. However, in the one case we have explored in this chapter, Ghana, poverty actually rose among some deprived regions (and groups) at a time when growth was positive and poverty was falling nationally. It is therefore important to consider the impact on HIs in designing macropolicies.

Second, the design of policies can greatly affect their impact on HIs. With disabsorption policies in particular, they can be designed in such a way as to improve HIs – through the balance of tax increases to expenditure reductions, and through the design of tax increases and where the expenditure reductions fall. Where HIs are not an explicit consideration, the impact is likely to be harmful, simply because the budget tends to be under the control of the more privileged groups. A conscious – and possibly politically difficult – policy is needed to ensure that the disabsorption policies do not worsen HIs (and preferably improve them). Design of policies is also relevant to switching policies. Differential exchange rates may be used to help particular groups. And dismantling of import protection can be designed in ways that hurt the richer groups most. Again this is generally not a consideration, and reduced tariffs often permit imports of luxury goods at low prices.

Third, complementary policies can help to make the macropolicies contribute to reducing HIs. In particular, education and training of the poorer groups will enable them to exploit the opportunities offered by a more open trading regime. Similarly, anti-discriminatory employment policies will permit the poorer groups to participate in the gains from international trade. Moreover, compensatory policies can be introduced to offset some adverse effects. Again such complementary or compensatory policies do not normally form part of the adjustment policy packages. Indeed, in the efficiency promoting part of the package, formal direct affirmative action comes under attack.

## Notes

1. See, for example, Bourguignon *et al.* (1992), Stewart (1995), Singh (2000), Agénor (2004).
2. See Banks (1996) and Ukiwo (2005) for that debate.
3. See Singh (2007) for the latest of many powerful critiques of liberalization policies.
4. This is a simplified way of measuring HIs; we might use a measure that also incorporates some weighting for different parts of the income distribution of the two groups (see, Mancini *et al.*, 2008).
5. This overview draws on Hutchful (2002) and Dordunoo and Nyanteng (1997) who both identify three phases in the evolution of Ghana's adjustment policies (although with somewhat different time periods); we have added the fourth one (i.e. the PRSP phase).
6. The poverty line is anchored on caloric requirements and is therefore a nutrition-based poverty line. 'It focuses on the expenditure needed to meet the nutritional requirements of household members and was set at ¢700,000 per adult per year for the 1998/99 survey year. Persons whose total expenditure falls below this level are considered extremely poor. An upper line was also established which incorporates both essential food and non-food needs and set at ¢900,000 per adult per year' (Leite *et al.*, 2000, p. 9).

## References

Agénor, P.-R. (2004) 'Macroeconomic Adjustment and the Poor: Analytical Issues and Cross-Country Evidence', *Journal of Economic Surveys* 18: 351–408.

Akerlof, G. A. and R. E. Kranton (2000) 'Economics and Identity', *Quarterly Journal of Economics* cxv (3): 715–53.

Auvinen, J. and E. W. Nafziger (1999) 'The Sources of Humanitarian Emergencies', *Journal of Conflict Resolution* 43: 267–90.

Banks, M. (1996) *Ethnicity: Anthropological Constructions*, London: Routledge.

Barrows, W. L. (1976) 'Ethnic Diversity and Political Instability in Black Africa', *Comparative Political Studies* 9 (2): 139–70.

Bening, R. B. (1975) 'Colonial Development Policy in Northern Ghana, 1989–1950', *Bulletin of the Ghana Geographical Association* 17: 65–79.

Bourguignon, F., J. de Melo and C. Morrison (1992) 'Poverty and Income Distribution during Adjustment: Issues and Evidence from the OECD Project', *World Development* 19 (11): 1485–508.

Broman, C. (1997) 'Race-related Factors and Life Satisfaction among African Americans', *Journal of Black Psychology* 23 (1): 36–49.

Brown, G. K. (2008) 'Horizontal Inequalities and Separatism in Southeast Asia: A Comparative Perspective', in F. Stewart (ed.), *Horizontal Inequalities and Conflict: Understanding Group Violence in Multiethnic Societies*, London: Palgrave.

Brown, I. (1997) *Economic Change in South-East Asia, c. 1830–1980*, Kuala Lumpur: Oxford University Press.

Brown, T. N., D. R. Williams, J. S. Jackson, H. Neighbours, S. Sellers, T. Myriam, and K. Brown (1999) 'Being Black and Feeling Blue: Mental Health Consequences of Racial Discrimination', *Race and Society* 2 (2): 117–31.

Chu, K.-Y., H. R. Davoodi, S. Gupta and World Institute for Development Economics Research (2000) *Income Distribution and Tax, and Government Social Spending Policies in Developing Countries*, Helsinki: World Institute for Development Economics Research of the United Nations University.

Cornia, G. A. (2004) *Inequality, Growth, and Poverty in an Era of Liberalization and Globalization*, Oxford: Oxford University Press.

Dordunoo, C. K. and V. K. Nyanteng (1997) 'Overview of Ghanaian Economic Development', in V. K. Nyanteng (ed.), *Policies and Options for Ghanaian Economic Development*, Accra: Institute of Statistical, Social and Economic Research, University of Ghana.

Faaland, J., J. Parkinson and R. Saniman (2003) *Growth and Ethnic Inequality – Malaysia's New Economic Policy*, Kuala Lumpur: Utusan Publications.

Figueroa, A., Altamirano, T. and Sulmont, D. (1996) 'Social exclusion and equality in Peru,' Research series No. 104, Geneva: International Institute of Labour Studies.

Ghai, D. and D. Court (1974) *Education, Society and Development: New Perspectives from Kenya*, Nairobi: Oxford University Press.

Gurr, T. R. (1970) *Why Men Rebel*, Princeton, NJ: Princeton University Press.

Gurr, T. R. (1993) *Minorities at Risk: A Global View of Ethnopolitical Conflicts*, Washington, DC: Institute of Peace Press.

Gurr, T. R. and W. H. Moore (1997) 'Ethnopolitical Rebellion: A Cross-sectional Analysis of the 1980s with Risk Assessments for the 1990s', *American Journal of Political Science* 41 (4): 1079–103.

Hall, G. and H. A. Patrinos (eds) (2006) *Indigenous Peoples, Poverty and Human Development in Latin America*, Basingstoke: Palgrave Macmillan.

Herbst, J. (1993) *The Politics of Reform in Ghana, 1982–1991*, Berkeley, CA: University of California Press.

Hutchful, E. (2002) *Ghana's Adjustment Experience: The Paradox of Reform*, Geneva and Oxford: UNRISD and James Currey.

IMF (1986) 'Fund-Supported Programs, Fiscal Policy and Income Distribution', Washington, DC: IMF.

Leite, S. P., A. Pellechio, L. Zanforlin, G. Begashaw, S. Fabrizio and J. Harnack (2000) 'Ghana: Economic Development in a Democratic Environment', IMF occasional papers 1999, Washington: IMF.

Mancini, L. (2005) 'Horizontal Inequalities and Communal Violence: Evidence from Indonesian Districts', CRISE working paper 22, Oxford: Centre for Research on Inequality, Human Security and Ethnicity, University of Oxford.

Mancini, L., F. Stewart and G. Brown (2008) 'Approaches to the Measurement of Horizontal Inequalities', in F. Stewart (ed.), *Horizontal Inequalities and Conflict: Understanding Group Violence in Multiethnic Societies*, London: Palgrave.

Mensah, J., R. Oppong-Koranteng and K. Frempah-Yeboah (2006) 'Understanding Economic Reforms: the Case of Ghana', in J. Mensah (ed.), *Understanding Economic Reforms in Africa: A Tale of Seven Nations*, Basingstoke: Palgrave Macmillan.

Murshed, M. S. and S. Gates (2005) 'Spatial-horizontal Inequality and the Maoist Insurgency in Nepal', *Review of Development Economics* 9 (1): 121–34.

Østby, G. (2006) 'Horizontal Inequalities, Political Environment and Civil Conflict: Evidence from 55 Developing Countries', CRISE working paper 28, Oxford: Centre for Research on Inequality, Human Security and Ethnicity, University of Oxford.

Roe, A. and H. Schneider (1992) *Adjustment and Equity in Ghana*, Paris: Development Centre of the Organisation for Economic Co-Operation and Development (OECD).

Singh, A. (2000) 'Global Economic Trends and Social Development', occasional paper 9, Geneva: United Nations Research Institute for Social Development.

Singh, A. (2007) 'Capital Account Liberalization, Free Long-term Capital Flows, Financial Crises and Economic Development', in A. Shaikh (ed.), *Globalization and the Myths of Free Trade*, London: Routledge.

Songsore, J. (2003) *Regional Development in Ghana: The Theory and the Reality*, Accra: Woeli.

Stewart, F. (1995) *Adjustment and Poverty: Options and Choices*, London: Routledge.

Stewart, F. (2001) 'Horizontal Inequalities: A Neglected Dimension of Development', WIDER Annual Lectures 5, Helsinki: WIDER.

Stewart, F. (ed.) (2008) *Horizontal Inequalities and Conflict: Understanding Group Violence in Multiethnic Societies*, London: Palgrave Macmillan.

Stewart, F. and G. Brown (2008) 'The Economics of War: Causes and Consequences', in A. Dutt and J. Roe (eds), *International Handbook of Development Economics 2*, London: Edward Elgar.

Stewart, F. and M. Wang (2005) 'Poverty Reduction Strategy Papers within the Human Rights Perspective', in P. Alston and M. Robinson (eds), *Human Rights and Development*, Oxford: Oxford University Press.

Ukiwo, U. (2005) 'The Study of Ethnicity in Nigeria', *Oxford Development Studies* 33 (1): 7–24.

Van de Walle, D., K. Nead and World Bank (1995) *Public Spending and the Poor: Theory and Evidence*, Baltimore, MD: Johns Hopkins University Press.

Wood, A. and C. Ridao-Cano (1996) 'Skills, Trade and International Inequality', IDS working paper 47, Sussex: IDS.

# Appendix: Ajit Singh Publications

Modern Business Enterprise, Corporate Organization, Finance and Governance in Advanced Economies and in Emerging Markets; The Theory of the Firm, Takeovers and the Stock Market; The Financial System and the Real Economy

Marris, R. L. and A. Singh (1966) 'A Measure of a Firm's Average Share Price', *Journal of the Royal Statistical Society*, Series A (General), 129, Part I.

Singh, A. and G. Whittington (1968) *Growth, Profitability and Valuation*, Cambridge: Cambridge University Press.

Singh, A. (1971) *Takeovers: Their Relevance to the Stock Market and the Theory of the Firm*, Cambridge: Cambridge University Press.

Singh, A. (1975) 'Takeovers, Economic Natural Selection and the Theory of the Firm: Evidence from the Post-War UK Experience', *Economic Journal*, 85 (339), September. (Republished in an Italian translation in *Problemi di Teoria Dell'Impresa*; and in L. Wagner (ed.), *Readings in Applied Microeconomics*, Oxford: Oxford University Press: 1981; and in G. Marchildon (ed.), *Mergers and Acquisitions*, London: Edward Elgar: 207–25, 1992.

Singh, A. and G. Whittington (1975) 'The Size and Growth of Firms', *Review of Economic Studies*, XLII (1), January. (Republished in an Italian translation in A. H. Cardani and U. Pedol (eds), *Problemi di Teoria Dell'Impressa*, Etas Libri, 1980).

Singh, A. (1976) 'Review of Douglas Kuehn, *Takeovers and the Theory of the Firm*', *Journal of Economic Literature*, 14 (2) (June).

Cosh, A., A. Hughes and A. Singh (1980) 'The Causes and Effects of Mergers in the UK: An Empirical Investigation for the late 1960s at the Microeconomic Level', in *The Determinants and Effects of Mergers: An International Comparison*, Cambridge, Mass: Oelgeschlager, Gunn & Hain.

Hughes, A., D. Mueller and A. Singh (1980) 'Hypotheses about Mergers', in *The Determinants and Effects of Mergers: An International Comparison*, Cambridge, Mass: Oelgeschlager, Gunn & Hain.

Hughes, A., D. Mueller and A. Singh (1980) 'Competition Policy in the 1980s: The Implications of the International Merger Wave', in *The Determinants and Effects of Mergers: An International Comparison*, Cambridge, Mass: Oelgeschlager, Gunn & Hain.

Hughes, A. and A. Singh (1980) 'Mergers, Concentration and Competition in Advanced Capitalist Economies: An International Perspective', in *The Determinants and Effects of Mergers: An International Comparison*, Cambridge, Mass.: Oelgeschlager, Gunn & Hain.

Cosh, A. D., A. Hughes, K. Lee and A. Singh (1989) 'Institutional Investment and the Market for Corporate Control', *International Journal of Industrial Organisation*, March.

Cosh, A. D., A. Hughes and A. Singh (1990) 'Takeovers, Short-termism and Finance-industry Relations in the UK Economy: Analytical and Policy issues', in *Takeovers and Short-termism in the UK*, London, Industrial Policy Paper No. 3, Institute of Public Policy Research.

Hughes, A. and A. Singh (1990) 'Takeovers and the Stock Market', *Contributions to Political Economy*, 6, 1987. (Republished in J. Eatwell, M. Milgate, and P. Newman (eds), *Financial Markets*, London/New York: Macmillan.)

Singh, A. (1990) 'The Institution of a Stock Market in a Socialist Economy: Notes on the Chinese Economic Reform Programme', in Dong Fureng and Peter Nolan (eds), *The Chinese Economy and its Future: Achievements and Problems of Post-Mao Reforms*, Cambridge: Polity Press.

Cosh, A. D., A. Hughes and A. Singh (1992) 'Openness, Financial Innovation and the Changing Structure of the UK and the Global Capital Markets', in Juliet Schor and Tariq Banuri (eds), *Financial Openness and National Autonomy*, Oxford: Clarendon Press.

Singh, A. (1992) 'Corporate Takeovers', in *The New Palgrave Dictionary of Money and Finance*, edited by John Eatwell, Murray Milgate and Peter Newman, London/New York: Macmillan.

Singh, A. and J. Hamid (1992) *Corporate Financial Structures in Developing Countries*, IFC Technical Paper No. 1, World Bank, Washington, DC (xii + 147 pp.). This monograph was among the first studies of its kind.

Singh, A. (1993) 'Regulation of Mergers: A New Agenda', in Roger Sugden (ed.), *Industrial Economic Regulation: A Framework and an Exploration*, London: Routledge.

Singh, A. (1993) 'The Stock Market and Economic Development: Should Developing Countries Encourage Stock Markets?', *UNCTAD Review*, 4.

Singh, A. (1993) 'Normative Relative alle Fusioni Negli USA e nel Regno Unito: Una Nuova Agenda', *Economia e Politica Industriale*, 77.

Amsden, A. and A. Singh (1994) 'The Optimal Degree of Competition and Dynamic Efficiency in Japan and Korea', *European Economic Review*, 38 (3/4): 940–51.

Amsden, A. and A. Singh, (1994) 'Concurrence Dirigée et Efficacité Dynamique en Asie; Japon; Koree du Sud; Taiwan', *Revue du Tiers-Monde*, 139, July–September: 643–57.

Singh, A. (1994) 'Takeover delle Imprese: Una Rassegna', *Economia e Politica Industriale*, 82.

Singh, A. (1994) 'How do Large Corporations in Developing Countries Finance their Growth?', in Richard O'Brien (ed.), *The AMEX Bank Prize Essays: Finance and the International Economy*, New York: Oxford University Press.

Singh, A. (1995) 'The Stock Market, Economic Efficiency and Industrial Development', in P. Arestis and V. Chick (eds), *Finance, Development and Structural Change: Post-Keynesian Perspectives*, London: Edward Elgar.

Singh, A. (1995) *Corporate Financial Patterns in Industrialising Economies: A Comparative International Study*, IFC Technical Paper No. 2, World Bank, Washington, DC (ISBN 0-8213-3231-7).

Cosh, A. D., A. Hughes, K. Lee and A. Singh (1996) 'Takeovers, Institutional Investment and the Persistence of Profits', ESRC Centre for Business Research, University of Cambridge, Working Paper No. 30, March. Subsequently published in Ian Begg and S. G. B. Henry (eds), *Applied Economics and Public Policy*, Cambridge, Cambridge University Press, 1998: 107–44.

Singh, A. (1996) 'Emerging Markets, Industrialisation and Development', in S. Sen, *Financial Fragility, Debt and Economic Reforms*, London/New York: Macmillan.

Singh, A. (1996) 'Pension Reform, the Stock Market, Capital Formation and Economic Growth: A Critical Commentary on the World Bank's Proposals', *International Social Security Review*, 49 (3): 21–44.

Singh, A. (1996) 'The Stock Market, the Financing of Corporate Growth and Indian Industrial Development', *Journal of International Finance*, 4 (2) (Fall): 1–17.

Singh, A. (1996) 'Profits, Savings, Investment and Fast Economic Growth: A Perspective on Asian Catch-up and Implications for Latin America', Department of Applied Economics, University of Cambridge, Discussion Paper in Finance and Accounting, No. AF33.

Singh, A. (1996) 'Investment, Savings and Economic Growth in East Asia', *International Capital Markets*, 16 (4) (December): 9–13.

Singh, A. (1997) 'Financial Liberalisation, the Stock Market and Economic Development', *Economic Journal*, May: 771–82. Subsequently republished in Portuguese in *Nova Economia*, (2000) 8 (1) (July) 1998; also republished in H. Dixon (ed.), *Controversies in Macro-Economics: Growth Trade and Policy*, Oxford: Blackwell: 206–18.

Singh, A. (1997) 'Portfolio Equity Flows and Stock Markets in Financial Liberalisation', *Development*, 40, (3): 22–9.

Whittington, G., V. Saporta, and A. Singh (1997) *The Effects of Hyper-Inflation on Accounting Ratios: Financing of Corporate Growth in Industrialising Economies*, IFC Technical Paper No. 3, World Bank, Washington, DC.

Singh, A. (1998) 'Savings, Investment and the Corporation in the East Asian Miracle', UNCTAD, Geneva, Study No. 9. Subsequently published in the *Journal of Development Studies*, 34 (6): 112–37. Subsequently republished in Y. Akyuz and R. Kozul-Wright (eds), *East Asian Development*, London: Frank Cass.

Singh, A. (1998) 'Liberalisation, the Stock Market and the Market for Corporate Control: A Bridge too far for the Indian Economy?', in I. J. Ahulwalia and I. M. D. Little (eds), *India's Economic Reform and Development*, New Delhi: Oxford University Press: 169–96. Also republished in Sima Motamen-Samadian and Celso Garrido (eds), *Emerging Markets: Past and Present Experiences, and Future Prospects*, London: Macmillan.

Singh, A. and B. Weisse (1998) 'Emerging Stock Markets, Portfolio Capital Flows and Long-term Economic Growth: Micro and Macroeconomic Perspectives', *World Development*, 26 (4) (April): 607–22.

Glen, J., A. Singh, and R. Matthias (1999) 'How Intensive Is Competition in Emerging Markets? An Analysis of Corporate Rates of Return from Nine Emerging Markets', International Monetary Fund Working Paper, No. WP/99/32, Washington, DC.

Singh, A. (1999) 'Should Africa Promote Stock Market Capitalism?', *Journal of International Development*, 11 (3): 343–67.

Singh, A. and R. Dhumale (1999) 'Competition Policy, Development and Developing Countries', Working Paper 7, South Centre, Geneva. Republished in P. Arestis, M. C. Baddeley and J. S. L. McCombie (eds), *What Global Economic Crisis?*, Basingstoke: Palgrave.

Glen, J., K. Lee and A. Singh (2000) 'Competition, Corporate Governance and Financing of Corporate Growth in Emerging Markets', Department of Applied Economics, Cambridge, Discussion Papers in Accounting and Finance, No. AF46.

Singh, A. (2000) 'The Anglo-Saxon Market for Corporate Control, the Financial System and International Competitiveness', Department of Applied Economics, Discussion Paper in Finance and Accounting, No. AF16, 1995. A revised version of this paper was published in C. Howes and A. Singh (eds), *Competitiveness Matters*, Ann Arbor, Mich.: University of Michigan Press.

Singh, A., A. Singh and B. Weisse (2000) 'Information Technology, Venture Capital and the Stock Market', Department of Applied Economics, Cambridge, Discussion Papers in Accounting and Finance, No. AF47.

Singh, A. and J. A. Zammit (2000) 'International Capital Flows: Identifying the Gender Dimension', *World Development*, 28 (7): 1249–68.

Glen, J., K. Lee and A. Singh (2001) 'Persistence of Profitability and Competition in Emerging Markets', *Economics Letters*, 72: 247–53.

Glen, J., K. Lee and A. Singh (2001) 'Intensity of Competition in Emerging Markets and in Advanced Economies', *Viertejahrsheft zur Wirtschaftsforschung*, 2: 70.

Singh, A. (2001) 'Financial Liberalisation and Globalisation: Implications for Industrial and Industrialising Economies', in K. S. Jomo and S. Nagraj (eds), *Globalisation versus Development*, Basingstoke: Macmillan.

Singh, A. and B. Weisse (2001) 'Mergers and Acquisitions', in Jonathan Michie (ed.), *Reader's Guide to the Social Sciences*, vol. 2, London: Fitzroy Dearborn.

Glen, J., K. Lee and A. Singh (2002) 'Corporate Profitability and the Dynamics of Competition in Emerging Markets: A Time Series Analysis', Working Paper No. 248, Working Paper Series, Centre for Business Research, University of Cambridge. A revised version published in *Economic Journal*, 113 (November) 2003: F465–F484.

Singh, A. (2002) 'Competition and Competition Policy in Emerging Markets: International and Developmental Dimensions', Working Paper No. 246, Working Paper Series, Centre for Business Research, University of Cambridge (2002). Also available in the G-24 Discussion Paper Series, No.18, UNCTAD, and Center for International Development, Harvard University, September.

Singh, A. (2002) 'Corporate Governance, the Big Business Groups and the G-7 Reform Agenda: A Critical Analysis', *Seoul Journal of Economics*, 15, (2): 103–48.

Singh, A. (2002) 'Competition, Corporate Governance and Selection in Emerging Markets', Working Paper (247, Working Paper Series, Centre for Business Research, University of Cambridge. A revised version of this paper published in *Economic Journal*, 113 (November) 2003): F443–F464.

Glen, J. and A. Singh (2003) 'Capital Structure, Rates of Return and Financing Corporate Growth: Comparing Developed and Emerging Markets', Working Paper No. 265, Centre for Business Research, University of Cambridge. A revised version published in Robert E. Litan, Michael Pomerleano, V. Sundararajan (eds), *Future of Domestic Capital Markets*, Washington, DC: Brookings Press, (2003): 373–416.

Singh, Ajit., Alaka Singh and Bruce Weisse (2003) 'Corporate Governance, Competition, the New International Financial Architecture and Large Corporations in Emerging Markets', Working Paper No. 250, Working Paper Series, Centre for Business Research, University of Cambridge, 2002. A revised version published subsequently in UNCTAD (ed.), *Management of Capital Flows*, Geneva: UNCTAD: 1–70.

Singh, A. (2003) 'Corporate Governance, Corporate Finance and Stock Markets in Emerging Countries', Working Paper No. 258, Working Paper Series, Centre for Business Research, University of Cambridge. A revised version published in *Journal of Corporate Law Studies*, 3, Part 1 (April): 41–72.

Singh, A. (2003) 'The New International Financial Architecture, Corporate Governance and Competition in Emerging Markets: New Issues for Developing Economies', in Ha-Joon Chang (ed.), *Rethinking Development Economics*, London: Anthem Press: 377–403.

Glen, J. and A. Singh (2004) 'Comparing Capital Structures and Rates of Return in Developed and Emerging Markets', *Emerging Markets Review*, 5 (2): 161–92.

Glen, J. and A. Singh (2004) 'Corporate Governance, Competition and Finance: Re-thinking Lessons from the Asian Crisis', CBR Working Paper No. 288, June. Subsequently published in *Eastern Economic Journal*, 31(2) (Spring) 2005: 219–42. The paper won an honourable mention in the Otto Eckstein competition for the best article in the journal for the two years 2004–2006.

Singh, A. (2004) 'Corporate Social Responsibility': A Developmental Perspective', *Oil, Gas and Energy Law Journal* (Special Issue on Business and Human Rights). Available at: www.gasandoil.com/ogel

Singh, A. (2004) *Multilateral Competition Policy and Economic Development. A Developing Country Perspective on the European Community Proposals*, UNCTAD Series, on Issues in Competition Law and Policy, United Nations, New York and Geneva (UNCTAD/DITC/CLP/2003/10).

Singh, A. and R. Dhumale R. (2004) 'Competition Policy, Development and Developing Countries', in P. Arestis, M. Baddeley and J. McCombie (eds), *What Global Economic Crisis?*, Paperback edn, Basingstoke: Palgrave Macmillan: 122–45.

Singh, A., J. Glen, A. Zammit, R. De Hoyos, Alaka Singh and B. Weisse (2005) 'Shareholder Value Maximisation, Stock Market and New Technology: Should the US Corporate Model Be the Universal Standard?', *Asia–Europe Papers*, Discussion Paper No.1, July. Also published as CBR Working paper No. 315. Subsequently published in *International Review of Applied Economics*, 19 (4) (October) 2005: 419–37.

Singh, A. (2006) 'Stock Market and Economic Development', in David Alexander Clark (ed.), *The Elgar Companion to Development Studies*, Cheltenham: Edward Elgar: 584–90.

Singh, A. and A. Zammit (2006) 'Corporate Governance, Crony Capitalism and Economic Crises: Should the US Business Model Replace the Asian Way of Doing Business?', Working Paper No. 329, June, Working Paper Series, Cambridge Centre for Business Research, Cambridge. Subsequently published in *Corporate Governance: An International Review*, July 2006.

Singh, A. (2007) 'Economic Crisis and the Asian Way of Doing Business', *Business Economist*, 38 (2): 9–21. This paper was short-listed for the Rybczynski Prize.

Fagernas, S., P. Sarkar and A. Singh (2007) 'The Legal Protection of Investors and Stock Market Development', Working Paper, 343, 2007, Working Paper Series, Cambridge Centre for Business Research, Cambridge. Forthcoming in Gugler, K. and B. Yurtoglu (eds), *The Economics of Corporate Governance and Mergers: Essays in Honour of Dennis Mueller*, London: Edward Elgar.

Armour, J., S. Deakin, P. Sarkar, M. Siems and A. Singh (2007) 'Shareholder Protection and Stock Market Development: An Empirical Test of the Legal Origins Hypothesis', Working Paper 358, 2007, Working Paper Series, Cambridge Centre for Business Research, Cambridge. Also available as ECGI – Law Working Paper No. 108/2008.

In relation to the contributions above, my long-term research programme has been to investigate the workings of the financial markets and examine their implications for the real economy. I have focused increasingly during the last ten years or more on emerging markets. The current themes of the research programme are (a) issues of stock market, corporate control and corporate governance, including those related to the financial crisis in East Asia; (b) analyses of micro- as well as macroeconomic aspects of foreign capital flows into these economies. I am carrying out research projects on these subjects at the Cambridge Endowment for Research in Finance (CERF) at the Judge Business School, Cambridge, in collaboration with colleagues from the IFC (World Bank) and Universities of Leicester, Birmingham and Vienna. The research programme has been consolidated and extended to include work on law and finance at the Centre for Business Research (CBR) in Cambridge. The latter project is being carried out in collaboration with Professor Simon Deakin of the Law Faculty, Cambridge, and Professor John Armour of the Law Faculty at Oxford. The project is funded to the tune of £200,000 by the ESRC. The project has also been awarded additional funding of £30,000 by the Newton Trust.

I am also carrying out other research under the auspices of the Centre for Business Research, Cambridge, investigating questions relating to the state of competition in product and capital markets in the UK and other industrial countries.

## Deindustrialization and Long-term Structural Changes in the United Kingdom and other Advanced Economies; North–South Competition and Issues of Employment and Unemployment in the North and the South; Liberalization and Globalization of Financial and Product Markets

Singh, A. (1977) 'UK Industry and the World Economy: A Case of De-Industrialisation?', *Cambridge Journal of Economics*, 1 (2). Also published in A. P. Jacquemin and H. W. de Jong (eds), *Welfare Aspects of Industrial Markets*, Nijenrode Studies in Economics, vol. 2, The Hague, 1977. Also republished in C. H. Feinstein (ed.), *The Managed Economy: Essays in British Economic Policy and Performance since 1930*, Economic History Society, Oxford: Clarendon Press, 1983.

Singh, A. (1979) 'North Sea Oil and the Reconstruction of UK Industry', in F. Blackaby (ed.), *De-industrialisation*, National Institute of Economic and Social Research, Economic Policy Paper No. 2, London: Heinemann.

Singh, A. (1980) 'De-industrialisation in the UK and Investment Planning', in W. Hafkamp and G. Reuten (eds), *Investment and Unemployment: Perspectives on Policy and Planning*, Brussels/Alphen aan de Rijn: Samson.

Singh, A. (1980) 'Industrial Policy and the Economics of Disequilibrium: A Reply to Professors de Jong and Van der Zwan', in W. Hafkamp and G. Reuten (eds), *Investment and Unemployment: Perspectives on Policy and Planning*, Brussels/ Alphen aan de Rijn: Samson.

Singh, A. (1981) 'Third World Industrialisation and the Structure of the World Economy', in D. Currie, D. Peel and W. Peters (eds), *Microeconomic Analysis: Essays in Microeconomics and Economic Development*, London: Croom Helm.

Singh, A. (1981) 'Uncertainty, Multiple Objectives and Optimal Regulation: The Regulation of the Petroleum Industry in Norway', Comment on Mr Ekbo's paper in T. Barker, and V. Brailovsky (eds), *Oil or Industry?*, London: Academic Press.

Singh, A. (1982) 'Structural Changes in the UK Economy: A Long-Term Structural Analysis of the UK's Trade with Less Developed Countries and its impact on the UK Economy', Vienna : UNIDO.

Singh, A. (1984) 'Long-Term Structural Disequilibrium of the UK Economy: Employment, Trade and Import Controls', in R. Parboni (ed.), *L'Europa Nella Crisi Economica Mondiale*, Milan: Franco Agnelli. Also published in G. Sjostedt and B. Sunderlius (eds), *Free Trade – Managed Trade? Perspectives on a Realistic International Trade Order*, London: Swedish Institute of International Affairs/ Westview Press 1986.

Singh, A. (1985) 'The World Trading and Payments System, Economic Growth and Structural Change', *Economic and Political Weekly*, XX (1) (January).

Singh, A. (1987) 'Manufacturing and De-industrialisation', *The New Palgrave: A Dictionary of Economics*, London: Macmillan.

Singh, A. (1989) 'Third World Competition and De-Industrialisation in Advanced Countries', *Cambridge Journal of Economics* (March) 1989. Republished in T. Lawson, J. G. Palma and J. Sender (eds), *Kaldor's Political Economy*, London: Academic Press.

Glyn, A., A. Hughes, A. Lipietz and A. Singh (1990) 'The Rise and Fall of the Golden Age: A Historical Analysis of Post-War Capitalism in the Developed Market Economies', in S. Marglin and J. Schor (eds), *The Golden Age of Capitalism: Re-interpreting the Post-War Experience*, Oxford: Clarendon Press.

Singh, A. (1990) 'Global Rules and a New Golden Age: Southern Competition, Labour Standards and Industrial Development in the North and the South', in *Labour Standards, Development and the Global Economy*, US Department of Labor, Washington, DC.

Singh, A. (1991) 'International Competitiveness and Industrial Policy', in Irfan Ul Haque (ed.), *International Competitiveness*, DC: EDI Seminar Series, World Bank, Washington.

Singh, A. (1991) 'Labour Markets and Structural Adjustments: A Global View', in Guy Standing and Victor Tokman (eds), *Towards Social Adjustment: Labour Market Issues in Structural Adjustment*, Geneva: ILO.

Singh, A. (1992) 'Industrial Policy in the South: Alternative Perspectives for the 1990s', in Keith Cowling and Roger Sugden (eds), *Current Issues in Industrial Strategy*, Manchester: Manchester University Press.

Singh, A. (1992) 'Comment: The Political Economy of Growth', in J. Michie (ed.), *The Economic Legacy 1979–1992*, London: Academic Press.

Chang, H. and A. Singh (1993) 'Public Enterprises in Developing Countries and Economic Efficiency: Analytical, Empirical and Policy Issues', *UNCTAD Review*, No. 4.

Singh, A. (1994) 'Global Economic Changes, Skills and International Competitiveness', *International Labour Review*, 133 (2): 167–83.

Singh, A. (1994) 'Growing Independently of the World Economy: Asian Economic Development Since 1980', *UNCTAD Review*, September 1994: 91–106.

Singh, A. (1994) 'Industrial Policy in Europe: Implications for Developing Countries', in P. Bianchi, K. Cowling and R. Sugden (eds), *Europe's Economic Challenge*, London: Routledge: 60–78.

Howes, C. and A. Singh (1995) 'Long-term Trends in the World Economy: The Gender Dimension', *World Development*, 23 (11) (November): 1895–911.

Singh, A. (1995) 'Institutional Requirements for Full Employment in Advanced Economies', *International Labour Review*, 135 (4–5) (December).

Singh, A. (1995) 'Review of Adrian Wood', *North–South Trade Employment and Inequality*, *Economic Journal*, 105 (432) (September): 1287–9.

Singh, A. and J. A. Zammit (1995) 'Employment and Unemployment: North and South', in J. Grieve-Smith and J. Michie (eds), *Managing the Global Economy*, Oxford: Oxford University Press: 93–110.

Singh, A. (1996) 'Expanding Employment in the Global Economy: The High Road or the Low Road', in P. Arestis, G. Palma and M. Sawyer (eds), *Essays in Honour of Geoff Harcourt*, London: Edward Elgar.

Singh, A. (1996) 'Supporting the South's Industrial Revolution After the Cold War: Developing Countries and the Emerging New International Economic Order', in D. Bourantonis and M. Evriviades (eds), *A United Nations for the Twenty-first Century: Peace, Security and Development*, The Hague: Kluwer Law International: 287–306.

Singh, A. (1996) 'The World Economy Under the Market Supremacy Model and Third World Industrialisation', Malcolm Adiseshiah Memorial Lecture, 1995 Annual Meeting of the Indian Economic Association, published in the *Indian Economic Journal*, 44 (1) (July–September).

Singh, A. (1996) 'The Post-Uruguay Round World Trading System, Industrialisation, Trade and Development', in *Expansion of Trading Opportunities to the Year 2000 for Asia-Pacific Developing Countries*, Geneva: United Nations.

Chang, H.-J. and A. Singh (1997) 'Can Large Firms be run Efficiently Without Being Bureaucratic? Some Critical Comments on Bureaucrats in Business', *Journal of International Development*, 9 (6): 865–75.

Singh, A. (1997) 'Liberalisation and Globalisation: An Unhealthy Euphoria', in Jonathan Michie and John Grieve-Smith (eds), *Employment and Economic Performance*, Oxford: Oxford University Press.

Singh, A. (1997) 'Catching Up With the West: A Perspective on Asian Economic Development and Lessons for Latin America', in Louis Emmerij (ed.), *Economic and Social Development into the XXI Century*, Washington, DC: Inter-American Development Bank.

Singh, A. (1998) *Financial Crisis in East Asia: The End of the Asian Model?*, ILO Discussion Paper No. 24, Geneva, November.

Singh, A. and J.A. Zammit (1998) 'Foreign Direct Investment: Towards Co-operative Institutional Arrangements between the North and the South?', in J. Michie and J. Smith (eds), *Globalisation, Growth and Governance*, Oxford: Oxford University Press: 30–49.

Chang, H.- J. and A. Singh, (1999) 'Lessons from the Asian Crisis', *South Letter*, 1 and 2 (33): 5–8.

Howes, C. and A. Singh (1999) 'National Competitiveness, Dynamics of Adjustment and Long Term Economic Growth: Conceptual, Empirical and Policy Issues', DAE Discussion Papers in Finance and Accounting, No. AF43, University of Cambridge.

Singh, A. (1999) 'Asian Capitalism and the Financial Crisis', in Jonathan Michie and John Grieve-Smith (eds), *Global Instability and World Economic Governance*, London: Routledge. Also published in John Eatwell and Lance Taylor (eds), *International Capital Market: Systems in Transitions*, Oxford: Oxford University Press, 2002.

Singh, A. (1999) 'Asian Crisis: What Really Happened in Asia?', *Economic Bulletin*, National Institute for Economic Policy, 1 (1): 13–16.

Singh, A. (1999) 'Global Unemployment, Long-run Economic Growth and Labour Market Rigidities: A Commentary', Special contribution in B. Dibroy (ed.), *Perspectives on Globalization and Employment*, Office of Development Studies Discussion Paper Series, UNDP: 50–69.

Singh, A. and B. Weisse (1999) 'The Asian Model: A Crisis Foretold?', *International Social Science Journal*, 160: 203–15.

Howes, C. and A. Singh (2000a) (eds) *Competitiveness Matters: Industry and Economic Performance in the US*, Ann Arbor, Mich.: University of Michigan Press.

Howes, C. and A. Singh (2000b) 'Competitiveness Matters: An Introduction', in Howes and Singh (2000a): 1–30.

Singh, A. (2000) Foreword to Michael Kitson and Jonathan Michie, *The Political Economy of Competitiveness*, London: Routledge.

Singh, A. and A. Zammit (2000) *The Global Labour Standards Controversy: Critical Issues for Developing Countries*, South Centre, Geneva, ISBN 929162 0130; ISSN 1607-5323.

Singh, A. (2001) 'Income Inequality in Advanced Economies: A Critical Examination of the Trade and Technology Theories and an Alternative Perspective', Working Paper No. 219, Centre for Business Research, University of Cambridge. Subsequently published in Jayati Ghosh and C. P. Chandrasekhar (eds), *Work and Well-Being in the Age of Finance*, New Delhi: Tulika Books (2003): 349–63.

Singh, A. and B. Weisse (2001) 'Deindustrialisation', in Jonathan Michie (ed.), *Reader's Guide to the Social Sciences*, vol. 1, London: Fitzroy Dearborn.

Singh, A. and B. Weisse (2001) 'Asian Model of Capitalism', in Jonathan Michie (ed.), *Reader's Guide to the Social Sciences*, vol. 1, London: Fitzroy Dearborn.

Singh, A. and J. A. Zammit (2003) 'Globalisation, Labour Standards and Economic Development', Working Paper No. 257, Centre for Business Research, University of Cambridge. Subsequently published in revised form in Jonathan Michie (ed.), *The Handbook of Globalisation*, Cheltenham: Edward Elgar, 2003: 191–215.

Singh, A. (2003) 'Capital Account Liberalisation, Free Long-term Capital Flows, Financial Crises and Economic Development', Centre for Business Research Working Paper No. 245, University of Cambridge, December. Subsequently published in a revised form in the *Eastern Economic Journal*, 29 (2) (Spring) 2003: 191–216. Also published in P. Arestis, M. Baddeley and J McCombie (eds), *Globalisation, Regionalism and Economic Activity*, Cheltenham: Edward Elgar, 2003: 15–46.

Singh, A. and J. A. Zammit (2003) 'Labour Standards and the "Race to the Bottom": Re-thinking Globalization and Workers' Rights from Developmental and Solidaristic Perspectives', Centre for Business Research Working Paper No. 279,

University of Cambridge, March. A revised version subsequently published in the *Oxford Review of Economic Policy*, 20 (1), (Spring) 2004: 85–104.

Singh, A. (2004) 'Introductory Note to the Prebsich Report', *Recalling UNCTAD I at UNCTAD XI*, South Centre, Geneva, June.

Singh, A. (2004) 'Corporate Profitability and Competition in Emerging Markets', in M. Luthra (ed.), *Tapping UK's Diversity to Connect With Emerging Markets with Special Reference to India and China. A Consultation Day Seminar Report on the White Paper – Globalisation, A Force for Good*, London: UK Department of Trade and Investment.

Singh, A. and R. Dhumale (2004) 'Globalisation, Technology, and Income Inequality: A Critical Analysis', in C. A. Cornea (ed.), *Inequality, Growth, and Poverty in an Era of Liberalization and Globalisation*, UNU-WIDER Studies in Development Economics, Oxford: UNU-WIDER and UNDP/Oxford University Press: 145–65.

Dasgupta, S. and A. Singh (2005) 'Will Services Be the New Engine of Indian Economic Growth?', Working Paper No. 310, Centre for Business Research, University of Cambridge, September. Subsequently published in *Development and Change*, 36 (6): 1035–57.

Singh, A. (2005) 'IED, Globalizacion y Desarrollo Economio: Hacia la Reforma de las Reglas del Juego Nacionales e Internacionales', in *Ekonomiaz*, Eusko Jaurlaritza Gobierno Vasco, (55): 14–39.

Singh, A. (2005) 'Special and Differential Treatment: The Multilateral Trading System and Economic Development in the Twenty-first Century', in Kevin P. Gallagher (ed.), *Putting Development First*, London: Zed Books: 233–63.

Singh, A. (2005) 'Globalisation and the Regulation of FDI: New Proposals from the European Community and Japan', *Contributions to Political Economy*, 24: 99–121.

Singh, A. (2005) 'FDI, Globalisation and Economic Development: Towards Reforming National and International Rules of the Game', Centre for Business Research Working Paper No. 304, University of Cambridge, March.

Dasgupta, Sukti and Ajit Singh (2006) 'Manufacturing, Services and Premature De-Industrialisation in Developing Countries: a Kaldorian Empirical Analysis', Working Paper No. 327, Centre for Business Research, University of Cambridge, June. Subsequently republished in George Mavrotas and Anthony Shorrocks (eds), *Advancing Development: Core Themes in Global Economics*, Palgrave Macmillan in association with the United Nations University-World Institute for Development Economics Research (UNU-WIDER): 435–56.

Fagernas, S. and A. Singh (2006) 'Globalisation, Instability and Economic Insecurity', Working Paper No. 328, Centre for Business Research, University of Cambridge, June.

Singh, A. (2006) 'William Brian Reddaway 1913–2002 Memorial', *Proceedings of the British Academy*, 138, London: British Academy: 285–306.

Singh, A. (2007) 'Capital Account Liberalization, Free Long-Term Capital Flows, Financial Crises and Economic Development' in Anwar Shaikh (ed.), *Globalization and the Myths of Free Trade*, Oxford: Routledge: 259–87.

Singh, A. (2007) 'Legacy – Lal Jayawardena: Crafting Development Policy', in George Mavrotas and Anthony Shorrocks (eds), *Advancing Development: Core Themes in Global Economics*, Palgrave Macmillan in association with the United Nations University-World Institute for Development Economics Research (UNU-WIDER): xxxv–xxxviii.

Singh, A. (2007) 'Does Integration of India and China with the World Economy Harm the US Workers? A Commentary on the Freeman Thesis', *Indian Journal of Labour Economics*, 50 (3) (July–September): 457–66.

Singh, Ajit (Forthcoming) 'The Past, Present and Future of Industrial Policy in India: Adapting to the Changing Domestic and International Environment' in M. Cimoli, G. Dosi and J. Stiglitz (eds), *Policies and Development*, Oxford University Press. Forthcoming.

## Industrialization, Economic Development and Economic Policy in Emerging Markets

Paine, S. H. and A. Singh (1973) 'The Shanghai Diesel Engine Factory', *Cambridge Review*, 94, June.

Singh, A. (1973) 'Die Politische Ökonomie der Sozialistischen Entwicklung in China seit 1948', lecture delivered in 1972 at the University of Heidelberg and subsequently published in P. Hennicke (ed.), *Probleme des Sozialismus und der Uebergangsgesellschaften*, Frankfurt am Main. Published in English in *Economic and Political Weekly*, VIII (47).

Singh, A. (1975) *An Essay on the Political Economy of Chinese Development*, Thames Papers in Political Economy, London.

Singh, A. (1979) 'The "Basic Needs" Approach to Development and the New International Economic Order: The Significance of Third World Industrialisation', *World Development*, 7, June.

Eatwell, J. L. and A. Singh (1981) 'Is the Mexican Economy Overheated? Some Issues of Short- and Medium-Term Economic Policy', *Economia Mexicana*, Analisis y Perspectivas, No. 3, Centro de Investigacion y Docensia Economicas, AC (CIDE), Mexico.

Eatwell, J. L. and A. Singh (1981) 'Is the Mexican Economy Overheated? A Further Note on Imports and Capacity Utilisation', *Economia Mexicana*, Analisis y Perspectivas, No. 3, Centro de Investigacion y Docensia Economicas, AC (CIDE), Mexico.

Singh, A. (1981) 'Mexican Economy at the Crossroads: Policy Options in a Semi-Industrial Oil Exporting Country', a Commentary on Mr Brailovsky's paper', in T. Barker and V. Brailovsky (eds), *Oil or Industry?*, London: Academic Press.

Singh, A. (1982) 'Industrialisation in Africa: A Structuralist View', in M. Fransman (ed.), *Industry and Accumulation in Africa*, London: Heinemann.

Singh, A. (1982) 'Foreign Aid for Structural Change: Industrial Development Policy Issues in Lesotho', in M. Fransman (ed.), *Industry and Accumulation in Africa*, London: Heinemann.

Singh, A. (1982) 'The Present Crisis of the Mexican Economy From a Mexican Perspective', *South*, October.

Singh, A. (1982) 'Basic Needs and Industrialisation', in ILO, *Basic Needs in Danger: A Basic Needs Oriented Development Strategy for Tanzania*, Addis Ababa: ILO.

Singh, A. (1983) 'Ante Un Mundo En Desequilibrio, El Neoliberalismo No Podra Dar Recomendaciones Adecuadas: Quienes las Sigan Marcharan Por Mal Comino', in Sohel Riffka (ed.), *Los Modelos de la Crisis*, Ecuador: Ildis: 141–50.

Singh, A. (1984) 'The Present Crisis of the Tanzanian Economy: Notes on the Economics and Politics of Devaluation', *African Development*, IX (2). Also published in JASPA/ILO, *The Challenge of Employment and Basic Needs in Africa*, Nairobi: Oxford University Press 1986.

Singh, A. (1984) 'Deceleration in World Economic Growth and Industrial Development in the Third World: UNCTAD Twenty Years on', *Bulletin of the Institute of Development Studies*, University of Sussex, 15 (3) (July).

Singh, A. (1984) 'The Interrupted Industrial Revolution of the Third World: Prospects and Policies for Resumption', *Industry and Development*, 12. Also published in G. Sjostedt and B. Sunderlius (eds), *Free Trade – Managed Trade? Perspectives on a Realistic International Trade Order*, London: Swedish Institute of International Affairs/Westview Press, 1986.

Singh, A. (1985) 'The Continuing Crisis of the Tanzanian Economy: The Political Economy of Alternative Policy Options', *African Development*, X (1/2).

Singh, A. (1986) 'Crisis and Recovery in the Mexican Economy: The Role of the Capital Goods Sector', in M. Fransman (ed.), *Machinery and Economic Development*, London: Macmillan.

Singh, A. (1986) 'Tanzania and the IMF: The Analytics of Alternative Adjustment Programmes', *Development and Change*, 17 (3) (July): 425–54.

Singh, A. (1986) 'The Great Continental Divide: The Asian and Latin American Countries in the World Economic Crisis', *Labour and Society*, 1 (3) (September).

Singh, A. (1986) 'The IMF–World Bank Policy Programme in Africa: A Commentary', in P. Lawrence (ed.), *The World Recession and the Food Crisis in Africa*, London: James Currey/Review of African Political Economy.

Singh, A. (1986) 'The World Economic Crisis, Stabilisation and Structural Adjustment: An Overview', *Labour and Society*, 1 (3) (September).

Singh, A. (1987) 'Exogenous Shocks and De-Industrialisation in Africa: Prospects and Strategies for Re-Industrialisation', in RISNODEC, *African Economic Crisis*, New Delhi.

Singh, A. (1988) 'Employment and Output in a Semi-Industrial Economy: Modelling Alternative Policy Options in Mexico', in M. Hopkins (ed.), *Employment Forecasting*, London: Pinter.

Singh, A. (1988) 'Industrial Policy in Developing Countries: The Foreign Exchange Cost of Exports', *Industry and Development*, 23.

Singh, A. (1988) 'La Révolution Industrielle Inachevée du Tiers Monde', *Revue Tiers-Monde*, XXIX (115) (July–September).

Singh, A. and J. Ghosh (1988) 'Import Liberalisation and the New Industrial Strategy: An Analysis of their Impact on Output and Employment in the Indian Economy', *Economic and Political Weekly*, XXIII (45, 46 and 47), Special edition.

Singh, A. and H. Tabatabai, (1990) 'Facing the Crisis: Third World Agriculture in the 1980s', *International Labour Review*, 129 (4).

Hughes, A. and A. Singh (1991) 'The World Economic Slow-Down and the Asian and Latin American Economies: A Comparative Analysis of Economic Structure, Policy and Performance', in T. Banuri (ed.), *Economic Liberalisation: No Panacea*, Oxford: Clarendon Press.

Singh, A. (1991) 'The Role of the Government in Indian Industrial Development', in Irfan Ul Haque (ed.), *International Competitiveness: Interaction of the Public and the Private Sectors*, EDI Seminar Series, Washington, DC: World Bank.

Singh, A. (1992) 'Urbanisation, Poverty and Employment: The Large Metropolis in the Third World', *Contributions to Political Economy*, 11.

Singh, A. (1992) 'The Actual Crisis of Economic Development in the 1980s: An Alternative Perspective for the Future', in A. Dutt and K. Jameson (eds), *New Directions in Development Economics*, London: Edward Elgar.

Singh, A. and H. Tabatabai (1992) 'Agriculture and Economic Development in the 1990s: A New Analytical and Policy Agenda', *International Labour Review*, 131.

Singh, A. (1993) 'Asian Economic Success and Latin American Failure in the 1980s: New Analyses and Future Policy Implications', *International Review of Applied Economics*, 7 (3).

Singh, A. (1993) ' "Close" vs. "Strategic" Integration with the World Economy and "Market-Friendly Approach to Development" vs. an "Industrial Policy"', University of Duisburg, *INEF Report*, 4.

Singh, A. and H. Tabatabai (eds) (1993) *Economic Crisis and Third World Agriculture*, Cambridge: Cambridge University Press.

Singh, A. and H. Tabatabai (1993) 'Third World Agriculture in a Crisis Environment: Analytical and Policy Issues', in *Economic Crisis and Third World Agriculture*, Cambridge: Cambridge University Press.

Singh, A. and H. Tabatabai (1993) 'The World Economic Crisis and Third World Agriculture in the 1980s', in *Economic Crisis and Third World Agriculture*, Cambridge: Cambridge University Press.

Dutt, A., K. Kim and A. Singh (eds) (1994) *The State, Markets and Development*, London: Edward Elgar.

Dutt, A., K. Kim and A. Singh (1994) 'The State, Markets and Development: An Introduction', in A. Dutt, K. Kim and A. Singh (eds), *The State, Markets and Development*, London: Edward Elgar: 3–21.

Singh, A. (1994) 'State Intervention and the Market-Friendly Approach to Development: A Critical Analysis of the World Bank Theses', in A. Dutt, K. Kim and A. Singh (eds), *The State, Markets and Development*, London: Edward Elgar, London: 38–61.

Singh, A. (1994) 'Openness and Market-Friendly Approach to Development: Learning the Right Lessons from Development Experience', *World Development*, 22 (12) (December): 1811–23.

Singh, A. (1994) 'The Present State of Industry in the Third World: Prospects and Policies for the Future', in G. K. Chadha (ed.), *Sectoral Issues in the Indian Economy: Policy and Perspectives*, New Delhi: Har-Anand Publications.

Singh, A. (1994) 'From the Plan to the Market: Controlled Reform in China' (in French), *Revue Tiers-Monde*, XXXV, (139) (July–September): 659–84.

Singh, A. (1995) 'The State and Industrialisation in India: Successes and Failures and Lessons for the Future', in H. Chang and R. E. Rowthorn (eds), *The Role of the State in Economic Change*, Oxford: Clarendon Press: 170–86.

Singh, A. (1995) 'Asia y America Latina Comparidos: Divergencias Economicas en los años '80', *Dessarollo Economico, Revista de Ciencias Sociales*, 34 (136) (January–March): 513–32.

Singh, A. (1995) *How Did East Asia Grow so Fast? Slow Progress Towards an Analytical Consensus*, UNCTAD Discussion Paper No. 97, Geneva, February. Republished as an Occasional Paper by RIS Publications in Delhi, 1995.

Singh, A. (1995) 'Competitive Markets and Economic Development,' *International Papers in Political Economy*, 2 (1): 1–40. Republished in P. Arestis and M. Sawyer (eds), *Political Economy of Economic Policy*, London: Macmillan, 1998.

Singh, A. (1995) 'The Causes of Fast Economic Growth in East Asia', *UNCTAD Review*, Geneva): 91–127.

Singh, A. (1996) 'The Plan, the Market and Evolutionary Economic Reform in China', in Abu Abdullah and Azizur, Rahman Khan (eds), *State, Market and Development: Essays in Honour of Rehman Sobhan*, Dhaka University Press. Republished in Spanish as 'El Plan, el Mercado, y la Transicion Gradual en China', in *Revista de Estudios Asiaticos*, 3, July–December 1996.

Singh, A. (1999) 'Growth, Its Sources and Consequences', in G. Thompson (ed.), *Economic Dynamism in the Pacific Region: The Growth of Integration and Competitiveness*, London/New York: Routledge/Open University: 55–82.

Singh, A. (1999) 'Review article on M. Aoki, H.-K. Kim and M. Okuno-Fujiwara' (eds), *The Role of Government in East Asian Economic Development*, *Journal of Development Economics*, 59: 565–72.

Singh, A. (2000) *Global Economic Trends and Social Development*, Occasional Paper 9, United Nations Research Institute for Social Development, Geneva, June. ISBN: 92-9085-030-2.

Singh, A. (2000) 'Contribution to Free Trade and the "Starving Child" Defence: A Symposium', *Nation*, 24 April.

Singh, A. and R. Dhumale (2000) 'Competition Policy, Development and Developing Countries, *South Letter*, 2 (36): 13–15.

Singh, A. (2001) 'What Role South–South Cooperation: A 50-year Overview', *South Letter*, 1 and 2 (37): 5–10.

Singh, A. (2002) 'Aid, Conditionality and Development', *Development and Change*, 33 (2): 295–305. Subsequently published in J. P. Pronk *et al.* (eds), *Catalysing Development? A Debate on Aid*, Oxford: Blackwell: 77–88.

Singh, A. (2003) 'South–South Co-operation: A Historical Perspective', in *South Centre High Level Policy Forum*, Geneva: South Centre: 95–112, ISBN 92 9162 023 8.

Singh, A. (2004) 'Standing on the Crossroads: The Indian Economy in the 21st Century', *Annual Report*, Bank of Luxembourg: 21–7.

Singh, A. (2005) 'Lal Jayawardena: Crafting Development Policy', *Development and Change*, 36 (6): 1219–23.

Singh, A. (2006) 'Foreword', in 'Independent Social Scientists' Alliance of Turkey', *On Economic and Social Life in Turkey in 2005*: 1–2.

Singh, A. (2007) 'Globalization and Industrial Revolutions in India and China: Implications for Advanced and Developing Economies and for National and International Policies', Working Paper 81, Policy Integration Department, International Labour Organisation, March 2007.

# Epilogue

To call Ajit a warrior is to court banality: virtually everything in life is a battle of some sort, requiring strategy and force, from penetrating Dunkirk's beaches to pinning a baby's diaper. Keynes elevated the conversation a notch by referring to the struggle over ideas in the marketplace, not the battle for slaves or land on blood-soaked terrain. Still, some of the best ideas, when original, receive almost nothing in the marketplace (such as the Internet) while some of the worst (breast implants) turn out to be treasure troves for their designers.

Ajit is a hero because he fought valiantly not against hostile ideas but against a whole ideology about economic development, a much more lethal phenomenon to beat than a mere notion. Whether by chance or by choice, Ajit fought along the same lines as the Vietcong, whom he, like many in his generation, greatly admired:

> During the spring of 1954, the Vietminh surrounded the elite of French forces and cut it off from reinforcement by land. Crucial to Giap's plans were the 105-mm howitzers of equal or larger bore than much of the French artillery, that the Chinese had captured from Chiang Kai-shek forces and handed over to Giap. The guns had to be broken down into many parts, then carried through jungle paths and over newly built steep mountain trails on bicycles, by tens of thousands of foot soldiers and peasant porters. The French were ambushed and overcome by sheer force. With white flags flying, they surrendered at Dien Bien Phu. (George McT. Kahin, *Intervention: How America Became Involved in Vietnam*)

What is most striking about Giap's understanding of war is how the key instrument of fighting, guns, is 'broken down into many parts' and then carried to where it is most needed through a highly social process of cooperation and coordination. These have become the strengths of the developing world in conquering global markets. When Japan was building its silk and textile industries, it defeated China and Lancashire, respectively, by breaking down every stage in the production process so as to subject it to intense scrutiny and improvement. When Japan entered the global automobile industry, its cars were first known for their poor quality, then for their superb engineering. Every step in the production process was isolated from the cover-up of inventory and subject to intense experimentation. In the case of Ajit, whether his subject was economic development or the theory of the firm, every step of the way, every argument and every charge, was carefully and meticulously fine-tuned and tested for battles to come.

But if Giap disassembled guns, and Japan disassembled production stages, what did Ajit disaggregate in honing his artillery against the ideologues whose power began to soar after the Third-World debt crises of the 1980s? Each piece in the puzzle that Ajit sought to solve was information, facts and knowledge. Ajit was a genius in taking a fact, kneading it, and then using it to discredit a mountain of words and a moribund theory. Ajit fought theory against theory, but his theories were tightly supported with facts. Following in the footsteps of his mentors, especially Brian Reddaway, he loved facts about India and decolonization, which he learned in the Punjab; facts about social conflict, which he learned at Howard University; methods of assessing facts, which he learned from Dale Jorgensen at Berkeley; and facts about how the world worked and was changing, which he kept abreast of from his collaborations with NGOs in the South and his own voracious research up North.

Now, in 2008, there is an eerie silence before the storm, as the world economy threatens to implode from financial instability, bringing the emerging economies down with it. Where is Ajit in all this? Where is the warrior? At the commanding heights, he continues to be a pioneer in the field of finance and the firm in the developing world, introducing firm-specific numbers that are so sorely absent in many other economists' work on the growth of Third-World enterprise.

There is, thus, nothing banal in the metaphor of the warrior when it comes to Ajit Singh, especially in light of his own personal battle against Parkinson's disease, with which he was diagnosed at a very young age. He has conquered and he has won: the Golden Age that he celebrated (1950–80) remains the acme of economic development, the Dark Age that he criticized (1980–2000) is the nadir, while the commodity boom of the last few years (that he disparaged) is teetering.

We thank Ajit deeply for all he has given us, as a friend and as a great intellect, and we wish him well in the coming years.

ALICE AMSDEN
*MIT*

# Index

Key: **bold** = extended discussion; f = figure; n = note; t = table.

241